"If you haven't quite got the hang of 'adul... ...
often funny financial advice. You'll be inspired by how she successfully
sidestepped student loan debt, negotiated a 40 percent (*yes, 40 percent!*)
raise, and managed to tackle a host of thorny money situations in her relationship, her friendships, and even with her parents and bosses. Best of all,
Erin reveals how you can do all this too. *Broke Millennial* is not your typical personal finance book. This is the wisdom I wish I had before I made a
financial mess of things in my twenties and early thirties!"

—Lynnette Khalfani-Cox,
cofounder of AskTheMoneyCoach.com and
New York Times bestselling author of
Zero Debt: The Ultimate Guide to Financial Freedom

"*Broke Millennial* takes the typical preaching out of money lessons and
replaces it with humor, empathy, and a fun, pick-your-financial-path twist,
for successfully navigating all the financial questions you'll face in the real
world."

—Farnoosh Torabi,
financial expert and host of the award-winning podcast *So Money*

"This is the ultimate millennial guidebook on personal finance. Erin
Lowry takes you on a journey from basic money concepts to retirement
fundamentals, and from salary negotiation to home ownership. She also
does a great job of reducing jargon and sharing knowledge that is practical
and actionable. If there is a book you must read to get your financial life
together, I highly recommend *Broke Millennial*."

—Jason Vitug,
bestselling author of *You Only Live Once:
The Roadmap to Financial Wellness and a Purposeful Life*

"*Broke Millennial* is my go-to personal finance book when I am working
with millennials. It's filled with practical step-by-step instructions and
guides that any twenty- or thirty-something can easily use to change their
financial situation."

—Lauren Greutman, frugal living expert at LaurenGreutman.com

"Lowry brings into sharp focus what's going to matter money-wise to young adults starting out in the world at a time when the odds seem stacked against them. *Broke Millennial* is rich with specific advice to guide readers on the path to financial wellness. Millennials who may be over-spending because of #FOMO need to read this book—stat!"

—Bobbi Rebell,
author of *How to Be a Financial Grownup:*
Proven Advice from High Achievers on How to
Live Your Dreams and Have Financial Freedom

"Thinking about money, especially when you don't have much, can be painful. But Erin Lowry shows that you don't need to be a mathematical genius to get on the right track. She makes it easy for people to build a financially healthy plan for life. Spend some time with this book and your financial decisions and confidence will improve, no doubt."

—Nick Clements, cofounder of MagnifyMoney.com

BROKE
MILLENNIAL

BROKE
MILLENNIAL

Stop Scraping By
and Get Your Financial
Life Together

Erin Lowry

A TarcherPerigee Book

tarcherperigee

An imprint of Penguin Random House LLC
375 Hudson Street
New York, New York 10014

Most TarcherPerigee books are available at special quantity discounts for bulk purchase for
sales promotions, premiums, fund-raising, and educational needs. Special books or book
excerpts also can be created to fit specific needs. For details, write: SpecialMarkets@
penguinrandomhouse.com.

Library of Congress Cataloging-in-Publication Data
Names: Lowry, Erin, author.
Title: Broke millennial : stop scraping by and get your financial life
    together / Erin Lowry.
Description: First edition. | New York : TarcherPerigee, 2017.
Identifiers: LCCN 2016055468 (print) | LCCN 2017008897 (ebook) | ISBN
    9780143130406 (paperback) | ISBN 9781524704056 (ebook) /
Subjects: LCSH: Finance, Personal. | BISAC: BUSINESS & ECONOMICS / Personal
    Finance / Money Management. | BUSINESS & ECONOMICS / Personal Finance /
    Budgeting. | SELF-HELP / Personal Growth / Success.
Classification: LCC HG179 .L696 2017 (print) | LCC HG179 (ebook) | DDC
    332.024—dc23
LC record available at https://lccn.loc.gov/2016055468

Printed in the United States of America
10   9   8   7   6   5   4   3   2

Book design by Katy Riegel

THIS BOOK IS DEDICATED TO . . .

. . . my dad, for playing his self-proclaimed role of villain so graciously and laying all the groundwork for my financial education.

. . . my mom, for teaching me how to ask for the order.

. . . Cailin, for showing me why it's important to never give up on your childhood dreams.

. . . Peach, for knowing the best way to keep me awake on a road trip is to ask about the difference between a traditional and Roth IRA and being happy to listen to the answer.

Contents

Chapter 1

Money Isn't the Worst! Seriously.

IN THE SUMMER OF 1996, a glazed Krispy Kreme donut changed my life. Well, okay, not just one donut: five dozen Krispy Kreme donuts.

It all began on a humid morning in North Carolina when my mom decided to engage in one of the most dangerous and cutthroat suburban activities: hosting a yard sale.

As my sister and I watched her spend the week leading up to it preparing to sell off our unused goods to flocks of women wearing elastic-band sweatpants and scrunchies (this was the nineties, after all), an idea began to germinate in my seven-year-old mind. If people were willing to hand over their hard-earned cash for a used *Abs of Steel* video at 7:30 in the morning, wouldn't they be likely to fork some over to buy donuts from two adorable children?

Suddenly, visions of Toys"R"Us store aisles—and, more specifically, a Nerf Super Soaker I'd been coveting—started to dance in my head.

I pitched the idea to my parents. After a little deliberation, my dad offered to be my backer and stake the capital required to fund my enterprise—as well as drive the car to pick up the donuts. (Again, I was seven.)

My four-year-old sister, Cailin (no, this is not a typo—that's her real name), and I set up shop using our Fisher-Price picnic table as our storefront. I strapped a teal fanny pack around my waist to hold my earnings, donned my purple baseball cap, and we were open for business.

Cailin and I spent the morning of the yard sale calling out to haggard-looking shoppers, neighbors walking their dogs, and gaggles of neon-track-suited moms. We implored them to purchase a glazed Krispy Kreme donut for the inflated price of 50 cents. And slowly but surely, the combination of my sister's doe-like eyes and my enthusiastic sales pitch won them over.

Handing over those donuts to die-hard garage sale enthusiasts and kind neighbors felt like grueling work during an early morning of summer vacation. Finally, with the last donut sold, I peeked into my fanny pack knowing the Super Soaker was mine. Feeling the weight of all those quarters, I imagined I could even buy two Super Soakers and be the ultimate warrior of water fights at the pool.

Then everything went horribly wrong.

My dad strolled over and asked to see the earnings. After having been subjected to seven years of his tyrannical "candy tax" at Halloween (he claimed first dibs on our loot because he chaperoned the trick-or-treating, which set me up nicely to understand taxes in my first real-world paycheck), I clutched the fanny pack to my chest, refusing to show him.

My dad took the fanny pack, dumped our earnings on our picnic table, and carefully counted out the coins. He then proceeded to give me my first lesson in economics.

"You have thirty dollars here," he said.

"Yes," I confidently replied. "I am going to Toys"R"Us."

He looked at me and smiled in that all-knowing way parents do, which left me with a sense of foreboding brewing in the pit of my stomach.

"Well, it cost me eight dollars to buy the donuts you sold," he said while he picked up eight dollars in quarters.* "Then you had Cailin help you sell them, so you need to pay her." He handed my four-year-old sister six dollars. "So, after expenses, your net profit was sixteen dollars." He smiled while pushing the remaining piles of quarters toward me.

I had never felt so cheated in my life.

RATHER THAN CONVINCING ME that my dad was out to swindle us, the Krispy Kreme experience instead has become the cornerstone of my personal finance education. What my dad's lesson started was a long tradition of my parents teaching us essential lessons about money through the use of real-life examples, which are still fresh in my mind 20 years later.

Even if you feel that taking a child's hard-earned donut money is cruel—

---

* In retrospect, I think we got a family discount on the up-front cost of those donuts because, even adjusting for inflation, there's no way several dozen donuts cost only $8.

which, in retrospect, I no longer do, and I could very likely do the same one day to any future kids I may have (hey, apples don't fall far from trees)—these financial lessons served me well when I eventually struck out on my own. For example, they enabled me to get off parental welfare only three weeks after college and muster the confidence to move to New York, knowing I would survive there as an independent early-twentysomething. And even when I wasn't making much, my parents' lessons instilled in me a sense of empowerment over the issue of money rather than ulcer-inducing anxiety.

I quickly learned many of my fellow twentysomethings (and even thirtysomethings) don't have that feeling of empowerment.

SITTING OVER SOBER-UP CUPS OF COFFEE in the wee hours of a New York City morning, my friend Lizzie began to complain about her job working as an assistant to two high-powered executives at a major network—a job she hated with a passion, but it was a steady paycheck and provided insurance.

"Okay, so why don't you quit?" I asked. "The whole point of moving to New York was to try your hand at acting anyway, right?"

Lizzie nodded.

"Well, you're twenty-three with no student loans, no debt, no kids, no husband—doesn't this seem like the right time to be working crappy waitressing jobs and nannying some Upper East Side brats in the name of pursuing your art?" I pressed.

"I don't know—money just really stresses me out!" she burst out. "I just don't pay attention to it and then hope I have enough at the end of the month."

Her terrified response startled me. If a smart, savvy young professional like Lizzie, who came from a family of comfortable means and carried no student loan debt, couldn't handle her relatively simple finances without freaking out, what did that mean for everyone else our age?

Wondering if Lizzie's experience was a common problem with my peers, I started asking around. Without fail, everyone responded with some version of Lizzie's protest: Money was stressful, confusing, scary, and not to be discussed. No one wanted to touch the subject, even while wearing a hazmat suit. But not only was this fear keeping my friends from trying to understand how money worked; it was also preventing them from taking risks to get ahead in their careers and even perpetuating the deadly cycle of living from paycheck to paycheck with no plan for the future.

As I thought about this, I wondered, *Why don't I feel the same way? Am I missing something?*

Then it dawned on me that growing up with parents who constantly used real-life moments to teach me about money (and deprived me of *two* Super Soakers) had prepared me to handle my financial affairs, and my fellow millennials hadn't benefited from such preparation. But after seeing what money fears were doing to Lizzie and others, I needed to find a way to help other millennials experience what I had. So I decided to do what any slightly bored-at-work millennial would do: I started a blog about it.

BrokeMillennial.com launched as a place where I could take stories from my own life experiences and use them to talk about money as a way to take the anxiety and confusion out of personal finance. It became my mission to prove that if I, a journalism and theater double major with a deep-rooted hatred for math, could become financially literate, then so could anyone else. While my parents were responsible for laying the groundwork for my financial literacy, I've always been intrigued by how money worked as well. Despite my aforementioned loathing of mathematics, numbers that were attached to dollar signs seemed to make sense to me. While I never focused on finance in college, I started reading books about personal finance basics like budgeting styles and credit scores and then moved on to studying economics and investing. These topics would find their way onto the blog as I continued to use a storytelling style to demystify basic financial concepts. Over time, I've cultivated and built strong financial skills and a deep knowledge of all money matters.

All of this occurred in the midst of trying to figure out my own financial life and dealing with common millennial scenarios, like not knowing how to negotiate properly for a raise, or working three jobs to make ends meet (I ate a lot of leftovers from a certain well-known mermaid-logo-using coffee chain), or trying to figure out how to set up a 401(k), or learning to stand up for myself in awkward financial situations with friends, or trying to handle moving home after college, an unfortunate reality many young professionals are forced to take these days. Not only have I survived all of these very real and important twentysomething life experiences, but I started sharing some of them on the blog, and now I'm laying my thoughts out for you in this book.

As the site began to gain a following—first by just friends and family, then a few hundred readers, and eventually thousands—my writing and thoughts on personal finance also started to catch the attention of the media. Since then, I've become a go-to expert on millennial personal finance, which has landed me on *CBS Sunday Morning* and gotten me quoted and interviewed in outlets including *The Wall Street Journal, USA Today, Marketplace, NBC News, New York* magazine's Web site The Cut, Mashable, and Refinery29, as well as a contributor position with *Forbes.*

Broke Millennial also led me to a new job at a FinTech start-up focused on comparing financial products for users. Under the guidance of the co-founders, who had illustrious careers in banking and a combined 30 years of experience between them, I began to learn the ins and outs of how banks make money and develop their financial products, and the common tricks and traps of dealing with financial institutions. Eventually, I even progressed to taking Certified Financial Planner courses to officially authenticate my knowledge on the subject of all things personal finance.

After writing the blog for four years and consulting both friends and complete strangers about basic personal finance topics, it's clear to me how much anxiety about money still exists, especially for young people like you, and this needs to be fixed *now.* Failure to do so means you may not be able to afford the kids (or pets) you want to have, there will be no money for your 30-before-30 or 40-before-40 lists, or you'll do those things in lieu of saving wisely, and then you'll have to work until you kick the bucket because you chose to do your whole bucket list first. This may sound dramatic, but the point is that a lack of basic financial education sets you up to be sucked into the stressful black hole of the paycheck-to-paycheck cycle.

The good news is that you can break free of that (or avoid it entirely), and I'll show you how. Despite what Wall Street and some media outlets want you to believe, money isn't complicated, and it doesn't require complex formulas. Financial empowerment does, however, require taking actionable steps toward improving your situation, and I'm here to help you figure out those steps.

I HATE BORING FINANCIAL STUFF, SO WHY SHOULDN'T I PUT THIS BOOK DOWN RIGHT NOW?

First of all, this book isn't a boring lecture on money. (The world doesn't need another one of those.) It's more like a financial roadmap that covers various paths you can take to go from flat broke to financial badass and gives you the tools and information to get there. Whether you read it chronologically or flip through at random (it makes great bathroom reading material, believe it or not), each chapter will give you actionable advice on how to improve and further strengthen your relationship with money.

The first few chapters lay the foundation for you to embark on your journey toward building a healthy financial life. I'll help you determine what your approach is toward money and what psychological blocks or pitfalls may surround it for you, as well as show you how to assess your financial know-how and improve it. Then we'll tackle a host of topics ranging from budgeting to credit cards, paying down debt, and managing student loans. Many of the chapters address sticky situations millennials specifically face, such as negotiating your salary, navigating those awkward times when friendships and finances collide (like what to do when you can't afford to split the dinner bill evenly with your pals), and getting financially naked with your partner. You'll even learn a bit about investing, buying a house, and saving for retirement—and yes, all of those are possible, regardless of how much (or how little) you earn right now.

Though each chapter features stories of my own triumphs and failures in money matters, it's not just me guiding you through this book. You'll also hear from plenty of other millennials who figured out how to manage money successfully through their own missteps and industry, and financial experts offer lots of tips and tricks that will turn any financially clueless reader into a financially confident one.

You can take your sweet, sweet time with this book. Read a chapter at random when you need to spend some quality time in the Whiz Palace or flip to the retirement chapter when you start a new job and have no clue how to handle a 401(k). Maybe you just want to read about someone else screwing up and then figuring out how to make it right. There will be some financial jargon and charts and stats in this book, but it's mostly a safe space for you to learn about money with more than a dash of humor. By the end, you're going to feel confident instead of terrorized each time you balance your budget. Like I said, managing your money can be enjoyable . . . and even, dare I say, fun.

Before you start the adventure, and even if you eventually jump around and read chapters out of sequence, I encourage you to first digest chapters 2 and 3 to help you establish your money mental blocks and financial baseline. Okay, Broke Millennial, let's *get your financial life together.* #GYFLT

Chapter 2

Is Money a Tinder Date or Marriage Material?

DO YOU THINK OF YOUR PAYCHECK as a Tinder date or marriage material? In other words, when it comes to money, do you treat your finances as a hit-it-and-forget-it situation, or are you developing a long-lasting relationship?

Like Tinder and other online dating apps, money offers one big advantage for anyone who masters it:

MONEY GIVES YOU CHOICES

Money can allow you to quit a job to be your own boss or step it up from sleeping in your childhood bed and moving into an apartment of your own. Money helps you travel the world, upgrade to eating organic food, indulge your desire to brew your own craft beer, or snag the latest Apple product (just taking a guess on your tech preferences). Money gives you the opportunity to help others in need. And with proper management and planning, it lets you retire eventually so you don't have to continue exchanging your time and energy for a paycheck until your last breath. Sorry, too dark? Putting in the effort to understand both how money works and how you relate to money can ensure that you set your future self up for a life of leisure instead of feeling forced to remain in the workforce to keep paying the bills.

Now you may be thinking, *That's all great, but how do I get more money so that, using the newest iPhone, I can Instagram a picture of myself sipping my own craft brew made with organic barley and hops from an exotic location?* That's why you want to take a more long-term view—to look at money like it's marriage material, not a random Tinder date. The good news is that the first step in getting a grasp on your financial situation doesn't involve any math. Managing money isn't complicated and doesn't require complex formulas. It does, however, require taking actionable steps to set yourself up for the life you daydream about. In order to successfully turn your financial life around (or just get started), you first need to identify what your money hang-ups are and why they're there.

The way you handle money is primarily driven by your mental attitude toward it, which is shaped by a number of things, such as your relationship to future thinking, how your parents related to money, and your financial fears. That's why it's important to determine what factors are influencing your relationship with money so you can get on the road to financial empowerment.

IT'S UNDERSTANDING MONEY—NOT JUST HAVING IT— THAT EQUALS EMPOWERMENT

You, right now, have a choice: you can either let money control and define your life or you can control it. Most of us would pick the latter option, but unless you take charge of your finances, money will call the shots. In order to put yourself on the road to financial success, you must be willing to take the time to understand your relationship with money and, in turn, control its impact on your life.

Before we go any further, here are some basic principles to follow in order to take command of your finances:

→ Have a grasp on your cash flow (a fancy way of saying "Create a budget").
→ Spend less than you earn (aka live below your means).
→ Remember that a credit history is important, but you don't need to go into debt to build one.
→ Student loans and other debts can be manageable once you learn how to effectively pay them off.
→ Know how to pick good financial products so you aren't paying senseless fees for something you could get done cheaper or for free.
→ Learn why compound interest is awesome.
→ Find out why investing isn't gambling and you need to start putting some money in the market by at least saving for retirement.
→ Understanding why money freaks you out.

We'll explore in depth how to do each of these in the rest of the book.

HOW YOU THINK ABOUT THE FUTURE IMPACTS
YOUR SPENDING TODAY

You might've never given retirement a moment of thought except to either think, *Ha, that's not likely to happen for me* or *Hmm, this company offers a 401(k)? I'll deal with this later.* Or you may also be completely fanatical about saving, saving, saving, even to the detriment of your present self, in order to be prepared for the future.

Like it or not, your ability to think about the future—or lack thereof—completely impacts your financial situation today.[1]

There are three common groupings millennials tend to fall into with regard to their relationships toward both money and the future: Team YOLOFOMO, Team Guarded Optimist, and Team Dreaming About Retirement. Which one do you belong to, and how is that impacting your financial decisions? Read on to find out.

TEAM YOLOFOMO

"Drinks are on me!" "I've only got $150 left in my bank account, but hell yeah, I can take that trip." "Nah, I don't have a 401(k) set up. I'll worry about that in the future." "Shit, I just got another overdraft charge. No worries—I can put this on my card."

Any of those sound familiar? You know where I'm going.

Being part of Team YOLOFOMO definitely means your social media profiles are #blessed, #killinit, and #livingthedream, while your finances are probably a little more #brokemillennial.

Sure, experiences are valuable, and duh YOLO, and double-duh you have FOMO—but this lifestyle choice also means you'll be #WorkingUntil YouDie.

Since that sounds like about as much fun as trying to handle a cross-country road trip with just a map and no GPS, why don't you try figuring out how to be #livingthedream but still #GYFLT by flipping to these chapters:

→ Chapter 3: Do You Have a Gold Star in Personal Finance?
→ Chapter 4: Dealing with the Dreaded B-Word
→ Chapter 6: Credit Reports and Scores: The Report Card for Life
→ Chapter 7: Wait, I *Shouldn't* Just Pay the Minimum Due on My Credit Card?

TEAM GUARDED OPTIMIST

"Don't worry, I'll totally be earning $120,000 by the time I'm thirty-five." "I'm not saving as much as I'd like, but it's no biggie; I can catch up later when I'm making bank."

Do you have a potentially delusional vision of where you and your salary will be in five to ten years? It's okay, we all secretly do. Being an optimist is a trademark of our generation, and not necessarily a bad thing. But to avoid any nasty surprises down the road, it's important to work on being proactive about the reality of your finances today, just in case your idealized vision of the future never quite materializes the way you plan. Chapters you should flip to:

TEAM DREAMING ABOUT RETIREMENT

"I should probably increase my 401(k) contribution from 15 percent to 18 percent." "No, I can't go out with you guys. It's not that I can't afford it; I just don't want to spend money in case something happens later on." "Man, I need to get a side hustle so I can just save it all for later."

Yeah, these people exist. I know because I'm one of them. But this is not a "we're the best" category either. Being hyper-focused on the future is financially beneficial in that it can lead to well-funded 401(k)s, hefty emergency savings, and probably some additional investments, but you may need a dash of Team YOLOFOMO in your life. Pardon the cliché, but we all need some balance, and here comes a second cliché: you can't take the money with you when you die. Trust me, I'm not advocating you pull a 180 and become a big spender, but be sure to take the time and even spend a little money to make memories today instead of waiting until your twilight years. Pulling a Scrooge McDuck at 60 and having tons of money to dive into sounds great in theory, but it's also okay to live a little in the present. Just budget it in with a fun fund! Chapters you should flip to:

→ Chapter 11: I Can't Afford to Split This Dinner Bill Evenly!
→ Chapter 12: Getting Financially Naked with Your Partner
→ Chapter 14: How to Negotiate Salary (or Anything Else) by Learning to Ask for What You Want
→ Chapter 15: Investing: No, It Isn't Gambling!
→ Chapter 16: Retirement: Can It Ever Happen for Me?
→ Chapter 18: But My Broker Said I *Can* Afford This Much House

DO YOUR MENTAL HOMEWORK BEFORE TAKING CONTROL OF YOUR MONEY

Before flipping to the chapters that will help you get on the path toward financial empowerment, you should take a few minutes to address your psychological roadblocks about money. We all have some sort of hang-ups around money, even your friends who seem so financially fit. Failing to address your money roadblocks first will make it difficult to effectively make a change in your financial behaviors. It's not unlike why people need to unearth their reasons for overeating or compulsive shopping or drinking. There's almost always a more deeply rooted issue. Trying to change how you spend or save money without understanding why it's difficult in the first place probably means you'll slip up, get frustrated, and go back to spending without thinking.

Many of these chapters offer a variety of ways to handle financial situations (i.e., best ways to budget, best ways to pay down debt, best ways to start investing). You can't effectively choose the best path until you know your own relationship to money and your roadblocks. So let's work together to uncover where some of your financial pain points may be.

Your Family History May Be Causing Roadblocks

Your relationship to money started way before you got your first credit card or signed for your first student loan. It began forming around the time you started to realize how those around you, most likely your parents, related to money.

Were finances spoken about in hushed voices when you were growing up? Did your parents have open conversations with you about their budgets? Did your childhood friends say it was rude to ask if they got an allowance? Did your parents struggle to make ends meet? Did your family's wealth make you uncomfortable around your peers, or, on the flip side, did you ever feel ashamed for not having as nice a house or clothing or toys as one of your friends?

None of these questions is a condemnation of how you were raised. Your parents likely did the best they could for you and your family with the information available to them and their own psychological relationship with money.

However, knowing where some of your money anxieties and misunderstandings stem from can help you in your own pursuit of financial empowerment.

"I bet your mom still has her First Communion money," one of my uncles said to me in jest when I was in my early twenties. Before that comment, I'd never really given my parents' level of frugality much thought because the financial behaviors you grow up around seem perfectly normal. My parents weren't big spenders on material goods. They notoriously moved their favorite couch (which was older than me) around the world with us instead of ever indulging in the purchase of new living room furniture. My mom didn't have a closet full of designer labels, and my dad didn't own all the latest tech gadgets. Much to the delight of me and my sister, Cailin, my parents did choose to indulge in one area: travel. So early on in our lives, Cailin and I both started to value experiences and memories over possessions.

There is not a single moment in my life when I can remember hearing my parents argue about money. They seemed completely in sync about how and when money should be spent, because they were united in a mentality of living below their means and saving for the future. Almost a decade after I left the house for college, I learned my dad actually managed to save 80 percent of his salary during our family's time living overseas, thanks to the perks of his company subsidizing housing costs and picking up the tab for international school tuition.

I tell you this because my parents, knowingly or not, gave me a blueprint—or a money mind-set, if you will—for how to handle finances that said: "Money isn't stressful as long as you don't spend too much."

However, I too still have hang-ups about money based largely on this mentality. It's difficult for me to spend. I'll agonize over seemingly insignificant purchases. It's hard for me to outsource chores that would save me time and therefore enable me to increase my earning potential. And I spent a bulk of my early twenties saying, "I can't afford to do [fill in millennial indulgence here]" when I certainly could have but just didn't want to spend the money for whatever reason at the time. And you'll find that if you tell people you can't go enough times, they'll just stop inviting you to go along on happy hours, day trips, concerts, and the like.

Despite these hang-ups, which I've identified but still struggle to handle, I'm grateful that the money mentality my parents passed down ultimately included a message of financial control and not fear.

This may not be similar to the mentality you inherited, consciously or not. Your family's approach to finances may have looked more like one of the following:

Scenario 1: Mom and Dad constantly argued about money.

Whether it was snide comments about a recent purchase or full-blown yelling matches over the bills, money may have been a source of tension in your household as you were growing up. Watching parents fight over how much is okay to spend, how much needs to be saved, how they're going to pay the bills, and who does and doesn't contribute to the household can lead to you—the child—believing money is nothing but a source of drama.

This mentality could mean you tend to deal with money as sparingly as possible in order to avoid tension either in your own relationships or just in your psyche. It's also possible it sent you toward the other extreme: to become as educated about finances as possible and make sure you always had enough to cover yourself so you'd never feel the stress of that no-money childhood drama.

Scenario 2: You were scolded for asking about money.

"Mom/Dad, how much do you make?"

"That's none of your concern."

It's not uncommon for parents or other adults to scold children for asking about money. Unfortunately, your parents' unwillingness to have a conversation about money can leave you thinking that it's taboo or dirty—similar to the way many families handle conversations about sex. (While parents may not want to share income details with their children for any number of reasons, it's still important to explain to kids how money works.)

So if Mom or Dad handed you a blueprint that says money is a taboo topic, props to you for even opening this book! You could have decided to avoid talking finances at all costs, which will cost you down the road (if it hasn't already).

Scenario 3: You assumed everything was okay, until it wasn't.

Back-to-school gear, going out to eat routinely, a new car every few years, updated technology in the house—these would've been indicators to you that your family had a comfortable amount of money. You could cover the basic needs plus the luxury extras—but not so luxury that you figured a new car with a big ribbon would be in the driveway on your sixteenth birthday. Or maybe you did and that was part of the problem.

You may have grown up with the belief that money was a nonissue in your home, but unbeknownst to you, your parents were living *at or above* their means. One small hiccup—the primary breadwinner getting fired, a family member getting sick, a downturn in the economy, or a divorce—could upend the entire facade of a comfortable existence.

Living *at or above* their means is emphasized because there tend to be two camps when it comes to spending money: those who live below their means and those who live above their means. Those living below are saving, and those living above are carrying debt to afford the luxury cars, McMansions, and private schools. The third group—those living *at* their means—are technically in a paycheck-to-paycheck cycle, possibly without realizing that's the scenario. They may have a tiny bit saved, but not enough to really mitigate a major dilemma, such as a job loss or illness. Living at your means usually signals to children that everything is okay because there's no tension about money until that single event that triggers the spiral down.

Fortunately, it also may not have occurred, but you may now be understanding that your parents lived at their means because they're realizing retirement isn't a possibility. There just isn't enough saved to support them without a steady influx of cash.

Still Unsure About Your Financial Roadblocks?

Answer the following questions to help you figure out which combination of steps will be best for you:

What's my first memory of money? How does that memory make me feel?

_____

_____

_____

How did I get money to spend growing up?

_____

_____

_____

When I did have money to spend, what did I buy?

_____

_____

_____

What are my financial concerns today?

_____

_____

_____

Why do I have these concerns?

_____

_____

_____

How did my parents talk about money when I was a kid?

_____

_____

_____

Was I told that asking about money was rude or inappropriate?

_____

_____

_____

Did my family's financial situation make me uncomfortable around my peers?

_____

_____

_____

Am I taking actionable steps to ensure that my fears don't happen (e.g., am I saving to make sure I can always pay rent even if I lose my job)?

_____

_____

_____

How can I be sure I'm in control of my money? (List at least three aspects about finance you want to work on understanding.)

_____

_____

_____

Now take some time to read over your answers and reflect on what your responses and gut instincts mean about your underlying money mentality.

Are you worried about money running out? Being in debt forever? Needing to help out your family financially? Then your financial mind-set may be one of fear.

Did you ever get to have healthy conversations about finances growing up, or were you instructed that money is a dirty conversation akin to discussing your sexual proclivities in public? If talking money still seems as dirty as handling the currency itself, then you may have a financial mentality of anxiety or naïveté.

Have the ways in which you spent money as a child evolved, or do you have similar tendencies to this day? You might be feeling helpless or electing to stay that way, or perhaps you're practicing extreme frugality, depending on your early behaviors.

Maybe you're experiencing a mix of several factors.

Once you reflect on how you relate to money and understand some of the reasons why, then I want you to take some time to write three financial goals:

1. Short-term goal: What will you do today, tomorrow, next week, this month, to start making actionable changes to reach the three aspects about finance that you want to work on understanding?

_____

_____

_____

2. Medium-term goal: Set a benchmark to hit that's at least a year away. Do you want to get over a fear of investing? Then plan to have knowledgeably invested at least $1,000 by a year from today.

_____

_____

_____

3. Long-term goal: Decide the one big change you hope to see in yourself over the next few years and moving forward. Perhaps it's about creating the financial mentality you hope to pass down to your children or model for your siblings or friends.

_____

_____

_____

Okay, you've done some of the tough work! Are you ready to get started on building your knowledge so money never needs to cause feelings of fear, anxiety, helplessness, or ignorance ever again?

Let's #GYFLT!

Chapter 3

Do You Have a Gold Star in Personal Finance?

NOW THAT YOU'VE taken the time to address your potential roadblocks when it comes to money, it's time to get a better understanding of the pieces that make up your financial puzzle—and how to put that puzzle together.

In this chapter, we're going to walk through some personal finance 101 topics and then use a scorecard to figure out how much you already know (or think you know) about money. Evaluating your results will help you navigate the following chapters so you know where you should improve your knowledge. Be prepared, because there are no participation trophies handed out here.

FINANCIAL BENCHMARKS AND FORMULAS YOU SHOULD KNOW

People are judgmental. Let's just admit that. We scroll through Instagram, Snapchat, and Facebook to see what everyone else is doing and instantly compare our lives to the carefully curated ones our friends have created for themselves online. So it makes sense that we would do the same with our financial situations. In fact, I'd encourage you to compare yourself to the benchmark savings, debt, and investing averages of your peers, because it can be motivational and help you stay on track to actually be able to retire one day. Yes, this is possible—and proven later in this book—so don't you scoff at me!

How Much You Should Have Saved for Retirement

The following table provides benchmark ratios of how much you *should* have saved by certain ages so you can compare against how much you *actually* have saved.[1]

Age	Ratio
25	0.2:1
30	0.6–0.8:1
35	1.6–1.8:1
45	3–4:1
55	8–10:1
65	16–20:1

The left side of the ratio indicates how many times your salary you should have saved by the age in the left-hand column. For example, if you're 25 years old and earning $55,000 a year, then you're expected to have 0.2 of $55,000 (or $11,000) saved for retirement. If you earned the same salary but were 35, then you'd be expected to have 1.6 (or $88,000) to 1.8 (or $99,000) saved for retirement. By age 65, you need to have up to $1,100,000 saved, assuming you can effectively live off $55,000 a year.

Keep in mind that this chart is based on the average needs of people planning to work for 40 years and then retire at 65 and live off their 401(k) and other investments. There are many factors that could make your situation different, including when you plan to retire, how much you forecast spending per year in retirement, if you plan to have children, any existing or anticipated medical conditions that may require more per year in retirement, and expected or received inheritances that may change what you independently need to save. So it's important to use this chart as a guide only.

That said, if you pulled out your calculator app to determine if you're on target and discovered you're beating the expected ratio, feel free to give yourself a gold star. You can also learn more about retirement by flipping to chapter 16.

Emergency Fund Ratio
Retirement isn't the only thing for which you should be saving. The almighty emergency fund is one of the most harped-on pieces of financial advice, and for good reason. An emergency fund is like creating your own insurance policy against disaster by saving up easily accessible money, which means you should put those funds in a basic savings account so you don't have to sell stocks to get at your money. You're not to touch an emer-

gency fund unless it legitimately qualifies as an emergency, and no, Beyoncé dropping a secret album and announcing a pop-up concert nearby does not count as an emergency.

Emergency funds are there to protect you if your boss calls you in for an unexpected meeting and tells you it's time to clear out your desk and be gone within an hour, or if a pipe bursts in your apartment and ruins all your stuff, and then you need to buy new furniture, clothes, etc., because your renter's insurance company is taking their sweet time in reimbursing you.

The emergency fund target is generally agreed upon by personal finance gurus to be three to six months of living expenses—the amount you need to cover your basic needs. The self-employed are wise to set the target even higher, with six to nine months of expenses in an emergency fund of cash and cash equivalents.*

Emergency fund calculation:

$$\frac{\text{Cash \& Cash Equivalents}}{\text{Amount needed to cover basic needs}} = 3 \text{ to } 6 \text{ months of living expenses}$$

For example: Let's say you need $2,000 a month to cover all your living expenses—rent, utilities, cell phone, student loans, groceries, and transportation. You have $4,300 in a savings account. That means you have only 2.15 months covered. You need to save up at least $6,000 to have a bare minimum emergency savings fund of three months.

$$\frac{\$4,300}{\$2,000} = 2.15 \text{ months covered}$$

I can already sense the eye rolling and sarcastic "yeah, rights" at the notion of managing to save several months' worth of living expenses when you're already dealing with student loans and you're still paying off that year when you were a bit too swipe-happy with your credit card because you didn't totally get how it worked.

Despite feeling like monthly debt obligations and the general cost of

---

* Cash equivalents refer to invested money that's easily accessible and converted into cash—for example, money market funds or certificates of deposits (CDs).

living have you drowning, it's still important to have an emergency fund of some sort, even if you have excessive debt. However, it may make more sense for you to prioritize debt repayment over having the full three to six months of living expenses. So your goal should still be to set aside $1,000 to brace yourself in case the unexpected happens. It's always when every dollar of your paycheck is accounted for and you don't have any savings that your car decides to start smoking on the freeway or your dog eats brownie mix or you break your arm and need $1,200 to hit your deductible. Want to learn more about how to build and maintain an emergency fund? Chapter 10 details exactly how to save, even while paying down debt.

Debt-to-Income Ratio

Debt-to-income (DTI) ratio is exactly like it sounds; you're calculating the percentage of debt you owe relative to the amount of money you're earning. DTI is a key factor lenders use to determine whether to give you a loan. It also keeps you in check about how much more debt you can realistically afford to handle before a big scary word like *bankruptcy* needs to be added to your vocabulary. To calculate your DTI, divide your monthly debt payments by your gross monthly income.

Here's how to calculate your DTI:

$$\frac{\text{(Monthly debt payments)}}{\text{(Gross monthly income)}} = \text{DTI}$$

First, a couple of definitions: Your *monthly debt payments* means debt you've taken on such as student loans, car loans, housing payments, or balances on credit cards that you are paying off in monthly installments. Your *gross monthly income* is the amount you earn each month before the money for taxes, health care, retirement plans, and any other deductions are taken out.

The goal here is to get your DTI ratio as low as possible. Swing too far in the other direction and you'll start flirting with bankruptcy. A severely high DTI ratio makes it nearly impossible for you to recalibrate and pay off your debts on your existing salary. Unless you somehow come into significantly more money, you're likely going to be paying all your monthly income to lenders and creditors, with nothing left over to pay for your basic survival needs, like food.

How low should your DTI be exactly? Well, you'll get mixed advice from lenders. For example, Bank of America writes that you should take steps to reduce a DTI above 36 percent,[2] while others, like the Consumer Financial Protection Bureau, cite 43 percent because most qualified mortgage lenders won't come near you if you exceed the 43 percent ratio.[3] Lenders aren't exactly scurrying to share their underwriting rules (nerd speak for the qualifications used to determine if you'll be approved for a loan), but the educated guess can lead us to assume that lenders experienced that people with DTI above 43 percent were less likely to repay their mortgages, so 43 percent became the breaking point in the underwriting algorithm. We can, however, work under the assumption that it's best for you to have a DTI of 40 percent or less.

So What Is Your Net Worth?

Now that you've learned about some of the individual pieces of the total-financial-picture puzzle, it's time to take a bird's-eye view of your finances. Your net worth provides a snapshot of how you're doing overall by calculating everything you have and everything you owe.

Not to be confused with the immeasurable, touchy-feely notion of self-worth, your net worth is one of the easiest financial calculations to perform. Just don't let a negative number shatter your self-worth!

To determine your net worth, subtract your total liabilities from your total assets.

$$(\text{Total Assets}) - (\text{Total Liabilities}) = \text{Net Worth}$$

Total assets include more than just your income, bank accounts, and investments; you also need to add in any valuable property you may own, including jewelry, collectibles (definitely not Beanie Babies but maybe Pokémon cards), and vehicles. *Total liabilities* include anything you owe, like your student loans, auto loans, mortgage, credit card debt, even that pending Venmo charge you owe your roommate for utilities.

Being net worth positive—meaning you have more money saved and invested than amounts you owe—may feel like an impossible feat in your twenties, perhaps even into your thirties. Even if you don't have debts or loans, it can still be really tough to do more than live paycheck to paycheck when you're young. It's okay to be daunted by this! But it's also still important to track your net worth regularly, even if you keep feeling slightly depressed when your number shows up in the red (financial jargon for being in debt). Tracking your net worth is one of the simplest ways to see if you're making progress toward your financial goals and heading in the right direction. It also forces you to confront your spending, debt repayment plan, and savings strategies.

HOW DO YOU STACK UP?

Benchmarks, formulas, and ratios are great, but checklists are even better. Who doesn't love crossing something off a to-do list? Reflecting on your mental homework with psychological roadblocks from chapter 2 and using all the knowledge you just soaked up in this chapter, let's combine it all to see exactly where you measure up. There are even a few curveballs we haven't gotten into yet, but we will explore those in the following chapters. The following checklists serve as a scorecard to figure out if you're a "Participation Trophy" kind of millennial with your money or a "Gold Star" earner. You might even be on top of your finances enough to earn yourself a "You Went Viral" award. Let's just hope you aren't a "Living in Your Parents' Basement Forever" kind of millennial because that would, well, suck. (But there's hope for you guys too!)

Get out your pen and see what you can check off the following lists.

You're Living in Your Parents' Basement Forever

- ❏ You don't have a savings account.
- ❏ Your credit score is below 650.
- ❏ You're employed part-time and making no effort to get a full-time job.
- ❏ Or you just keep quitting full-time jobs because they aren't fulfilling.
- ❏ You're carrying a balance on a credit card (or several) and paying the minimum due when you remember.
- ❏ You probably got this book as a graduation gift and just happened to flip to this page at random and thought this sounded like you.

Where you should head next: You may be itching to flip to a certain chapter, but I recommend we start at the beginning and work our way chronologically through chapters 1 to 7. This strategy will lay out all the foundational work you need to do (which I promise isn't as painful as it sounds) before kicking it up a notch, at which point you become the captain of your own financial journey. I'll see you in chapter 4: "Dealing with the Dreaded B-Word."

You Get a Participation Trophy, But There's Still Work to Do

- ❏ You've taken a stab at creating a budget.
- ❏ You always pay at least the minimum on your credit card and most of the time a little bit above the minimum.
- ❏ You have a 650+ credit score.
- ❏ You pay the minimum on your non-credit-card debts, such as student loans.
- ❏ You probably think about creating a get-out-of-debt plan, but then binge-watch the latest Netflix original series instead.
- ❏ You contribute the 401(k) percentage to get the match on an employer-matched retirement account, but you didn't set that contribution up until you'd worked at the company for a few years, which means a couple thousand got left on the table.
- ❏ You were motivated enough to pick up this book and begin taking some steps toward getting empowered financially (which is a great start!).

Where you should head next: You've got some basics down, and that's great, but we want to get you to be that financially independent millennial that busts all our generation's stereotypes. Start by focusing on chapters 1 to 6 to provide that strong foundation for a budget, working to a 700+ credit score, finding the best financial products for you, and digging out of debt in the fastest (but also most effective) way possible.

You Get a Financial Gold Star!

- ❏ You have a budget.
- ❏ You contribute 2 percent above what's needed to get the match on an employer-matched retirement plan.
- ❏ If an employer-sponsored retirement account—such as a 401(k)—isn't an option, then you're maxing out an IRA.

❏ You've built a 700+ credit score.

❏ You also check in on your credit reports once a year.

❏ You pay off credit cards on time and in full, and you keep the utilization ratio (the amount of total available credit you use) at 30 percent or less.

❏ You created and started an actionable plan to pay down any debt and are sticking to it by paying above the minimum due on all debts.

❏ You have three months of living expenses in an emergency savings fund if you're debt free, OR you have $1,000 set aside if you're prioritizing debt repayment.

Where you should head next: You've already proven that you can be the master of your finances, but you still have more to learn. Are you 100 percent sure you're using the absolute best financial products (flip to chapter 5) or that you know how to ask for that well-deserved raise at work (go to chapter 14)? What about hiring a financial planner (chapter 17) or navigating the awkward waters of talking money with friends (chapter 11) or even your romantic partner (chapter 12)? Pick a chapter on a topic you're less familiar with to start your next money adventure. I'll see you there!

You Went Viral

❏ You have a budget.

❏ You do a monthly net worth update.

❏ You're contributing 10 percent above the amount needed to get the employer match on a retirement plan *and* maxing out a personal IRA.

❏ You have a deadline to be debt free, accompanied by an actionable plan for how to get there.

❏ You're paying double the minimum amount due on your loans each month.

❏ You have a 750+ credit score.

❏ You check your credit reports from all three bureaus each year.

❏ You have at least six months of living expenses in an emergency savings fund if you're debt free, OR you have at least one month of living expenses saved if you're prioritizing the debt payoff.

❑ You pay off credit cards on time and in full, and you keep the utilization ratio (the amount of total available credit you use) in the single digits.

❑ You've started basic investing outside of retirement accounts, in index funds or exchange-traded funds (ETFs).

Where you should head next: You're #crushingit on the basics, which is great, but you probably still have some work to do. Have you considered going to a financial planner, decided to get financially naked with your partner, figured out how to negotiate for a higher salary, or looked into buying a home? How about giving some thought to what retirement is going to look like for you? We've got all that covered for you in chapters 12, 14, 15, 16, 17, and 18.

YOU'VE GOT THE BACKGROUND, LET'S MOVE ON TO THE REAL WORK

It feels like we've gotten to know each other a little bit now. You know more about me, and we've uncovered some of your money roadblocks and learned how to look at the pieces of the puzzle that is your overall financial picture. Now that you know your money scorecard, it's time to dig into the chapters that will help you sort through your money matters. Let's get started!

Chapter 4

Dealing with the Dreaded B-Word

"THANKS, ERIN," my charge's mother said. "We'll see you in two days."

I smiled and prepared for the babysitter two-step: that awkward moment when the parent seems to forget it's time to pay up or asks you for the grand total and you secretly hope cab fare or tip will get thrown your way.

After a long pause, I started to mumble awkwardly, "Umm . . . It's $80."

"Oh, right," she said while reaching into her Fendi purse. "It's after midnight, so here's $20 for a cab."

I mentally high-fived myself while stuffing the wad of cash into my pocket and scurrying out the door to get to the subway. There was no way I'd be spending the extra $20 on cab fare when I could put it into my savings or "fun fund" envelope.

Forty-five minutes later, I arrived home, quietly shuffled to my room, and pulled open one of my dresser drawers. Inside, my four envelopes sat waiting to be funded: one marked *rent*, one marked *savings*, one marked *fun fund*, and the final one marked *money for Anna* (my roommate, whom I need to reimburse for utilities each month).

Fifty percent of my income went to rent, 25 percent to the Anna envelope for utilities, and 25 percent to savings. The tip money (which in my experience New York City babysitters often receive in addition to a base pay) or cab fare often funded my *fun fund* envelope.

This method of budgeting helped me keep track of my income when about 50 percent of it ended up being in cash between babysitting and working as a barista to supplement my day job working for a late-night talk show.

However, the envelope method—while effective—is incredibly dumb when you're actually storing hundreds of dollars in cash in your New York

City apartment. I still feel thankful my apartment was never robbed, because a dresser certainly isn't an incognito hiding spot for your income. There is no FDIC insurance for the cash stolen out of an apartment, which is why my money is now kept safely in a bank.* There also is a 0 percent interest rate for money kept in my dresser. (Learn more about picking the right checking and savings accounts in chapter 5.)

As my career changed and my income turned into the digital currency of direct deposit, I moved away from hoarding hundreds of dollars in my dresser and switched to a new budgeting system, which I affectionately call the No-Budget Budget.

The No-Budget Budget doesn't focus on tracking every penny, nor does it allocate percentages of my income to predetermined categories, other than savings. But it's still a budget because no matter how you feel about the B-word, having a budget puts you in control of your money. At the very least, you need to understand how much you have coming in and how much is going out each month.

PICKING THE RIGHT BUDGETING STYLE

There are myriad ways you can take control over your money, which is why it's imperative you select one that works not only for your financial situation but also for your personality. The hands-on, type-A people among us may prefer the Tracking Every Penny option to get a daily and detailed overview of their financial situations. If you're more laid-back yet money conscious, you may prefer a percentage-based budget to know where to allocate funds without focusing on monitoring each swipe of the credit or debit card.

In this chapter, we'll review different budgeting styles to help you decide which one is right for you or which one to switch to so you feel empowered instead of overwhelmed.

BUDGET 101 OPTIONS

The Cash Diet

No matter how many fellow millennials tell me, "I spend way more when I just have cash in my wallet," study after study has proven you're going to spend more when you're swiping plastic. This is why the Cash Diet budget

---

* Learn more about FDIC insurance in chapter 5.

is ideal for anyone who routinely gets surprised by just how big their credit card bill is this month or gets dinged with overdraft fees.

Putting all your transactions on a credit card makes it simple to forget how much you've spent by the time your bill is due. Paying off your credit card bill once a week is a simple way to offset this issue because then your bank account will accurately reflect how much you have left to spend. You'll learn more about mastering credit cards in chapter 7. Of course, using a debit card also pulls directly out of your bank account, but there are security issues with constantly swiping your debit card thanks to the rise in debit and credit card fraud. So that's not always the best option.

So what's a diligent millennial trying to stick to a budget to do?

Consider rebooting your financial life in the same way you promise yourself to refresh your body every January first. Instead of doing a juice cleanse or throwing yourself into CrossFit, you use the Cash Diet to get back on track.

The Cash Diet is really as simple as it sounds: you pay for everything in cash. Granted, it's the digital age, so I get that not everything can be paid for with actual dollar bills. If you need to buy a plane ticket or pay your bills, you'll probably have to do those online. But everything else must be paid for in cash.

A simple way to start your Cash Diet is to sit down and add up your monthly income and then subtract your fixed bills. These bills may include rent or mortgage, cell phone bill, utilities, transportation costs, student loans, and cable or Hulu or Netflix. You should also subtract the amount you're putting toward your retirement fund and your savings account. (Think having anything to save sounds impossible? Check out chapter 10.)

The amount left after you subtract your fixed expenses and your savings is yours to spend for that month. It may be wise to divide this number by four and have a fixed amount of cash to use each week. Keeping the cash in your wallet allows you to easily eyeball exactly how much you have left to spend, which makes it easy to evaluate your impulse purchases or your craving for that late-night trip to grab the guilty-pleasure snack of choice.

When you're out of cash, you're out of cash. No more spending for the week or month.

A month of using this budgeting system quickly helps you see how easily you're spending on mindless purchases. It provides you an immediate look at what you think you value versus what you actually value because you're spending the money. This reboot will hopefully encourage you to move on to a lifelong relationship with a budget, even if you evolve to using a different system.

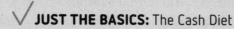

JUST THE BASICS: The Cash Diet

In case you just skimmed that section or want to refer back to this in the future, here's an overview of how to successfully utilize a Cash Diet budget:

→ Do weekly check-ins on your budget to assess how much you have left for the month.

→ Leave a $100 buffer, especially during your first attempt at a Cash Diet. Odds are that you will forget about a fixed expense that will hit halfway through the month. This buffer will help take care of that.

→ To prevent storing a bunch of money in your home—where it could be vulnerable to robbery, etc.—don't withdraw the entire month's amount all at once. Let the bank and FDIC insurance protect you and withdraw only the amount you can spend each week.

→ Any cash left can be rolled over to the next month, or you can really kick your financial skills up a notch and save the remainder.

The Tracking Every Penny System

Do you tend to get struck with that feeling of "What the hell did I spend my money on?!" each month? Then the Tracking Every Penny system is for you—at least for a while.

As with its cousin the Cash Diet, you should practice the Tracking Every Penny system of budgeting for two weeks at least once in your financial life. With Tracking Every Penny, you keep a meticulous record of every financial transaction instead of just saying, "I have $200 to spend this week" and spending only that $200. It's a strategy designed for those looking to regain control over their financial lives and/or those with intense type-A personalities.

The name says it all: you're going to record every financial transaction you make, down to the penny. You can customize this budget plan to suit your style of tracking expenses. For example, you can total your money spent at the end of each day or wait to crunch the numbers 'til the last day of the week. You might record your purchases by writing down each transaction (on your phone, of course; nobody does that pen-and-paper thing anymore). Or you may want to exclusively use one credit card for all purchases so you can just log into your account and make note of your daily or weekly transactions.

No matter which type of recordkeeping you pick, this budget works only if you're diligent about recording every penny you spend. Plan to reserve at least 20 minutes at the end of each day or about an hour on a weekend day to sit down and enter all your transactions into a spreadsheet, Google Doc, or app. You should be able to track by date, item purchased, and total cost, with a sum total at the bottom that shows just how much you've spent to date. You can even take it a step further and break it down by categories, such as money spent on food, bills, debt, pets, clothes, and entertainment.

Using budget trackers can help automate some of the process and perhaps even streamline beautiful charts and graphs of your spending if that's something that gets you jazzed about handling money. (Suggestions for apps that let you create such records appear at the end of this chapter. Though let's be honest: if charts are your thing, you're probably already working with some sort of intense budgeting strategy.)

After updating your spending in your preferred tracking method (I like using an Excel spreadsheet myself), be sure you have an accurate understanding of your remaining budget for the week or month.

Then it's time for some simple analysis—which is where those online charts and graphs can come in handy if you elect to use budgeting software. The Tracking Every Penny budget not only prevents you from overspending, it also enables you to notice patterns in your spending you either didn't know existed or want to focus on changing in lieu of redirecting those funds to other money goals.

The simplest way to perform this analysis if you aren't using an online tool is to create the categories mentioned above and do a weekly check to see whether the amount you're spending actually aligns with your perception of how much you routinely dish out for things like groceries, happy hour, or impulse buying a video game or a new pair of shoes. You can even go a step further and create subcategories, such as, in the food category, money spent on groceries versus money spent going out to eat.

I encouraged my first post-college roommate to participate in this practice when she was looking to free up some additional funds in her budget in order to pay for yoga teacher–training classes. Within a week she came to me dumbfounded, saying, "I spend nearly $20 a week buying bottled water!" It had become a mindless practice to buy a bottle of water at a local Starbucks during her workday, and those overpriced bottles added up quickly. Just carrying around a reusable bottle of water at work added $80 a month back into her budget.

Tracking Every Penny should be a budget practice everyone tries at least once in their lifetime because it's an illuminating experience about how you *really* spend your money. You can practice all sorts of delusional techniques about how you value eating well and pride yourself on only making purchases you actually use, but when you notice you're buying two pints of ice cream a week and you never actually read the *USA Today* you pay for each morning, well, maybe your priorities and money aren't completely in sync.

√ JUST THE BASICS: The Tracking Every Penny System

→ Research various techniques for tracking every penny. Writing down purchases and matching them up against receipts may work for some, while others may prefer paying for elaborate budgeting software like You Need a Budget (YNAB.com) or utilizing free options like Mint.com.

→ This strategy is worthless without analyzing what you're spending your money on, so be sure to mark down what the purchase actually was and not just the cost.

→ Tracking your spending by the penny will enable you to properly audit your spending habits and find where you may have been unknowingly hemorrhaging cash.

→ Don't give up if you forget to track for a day.

The Envelope System

The Envelope System is the Cash Diet system plus structure. The Cash Diet allows for a more flexible spending system in which you can buy what you want but have to go on lockdown only once the money is gone. The Envelope System dictates how much you can spend in certain categories.

This can be done digitally or with physical envelopes. Personally, I find the latter to be more motivating, but again it is potentially problematic to keep that much cash stashed in your home.

Take some time to sit down and write out your financial responsibilities and priorities into categories that will become envelopes. Common envelopes include rent/mortgage, utilities, transportation, cell phone bill, student loans, other debts, food, pet and/or kid, emergency fund, retirement, and entertainment.

$ *I highly recommend that you arrange for your savings and retirement funds to be pulled out of your paycheck before they hit your bank account. This money should be getting routed into a 401(k) or 403(b) or savings account so that you aren't tempted to ignore saving for a month.*

Once the envelopes are defined, it's time to fund them. Determine how much money out of each paycheck should be going into your various funds. Do you get paid biweekly and your rent is $800? Then $400 of each paycheck goes into the rent envelope.

The underlying principle is to never borrow from one envelope to beef up another. Once you're tapped out in one envelope, then you're done being able to spend in that category for the remainder of the month. So, for example, it'd be a good idea not to blow your food fund too early in the month on expensive dinners out with your crew. The only situation in which this may be forgiven is if you decide to skim off the top of the entertainment envelope to throw more at debt or savings goals. Leftover money can either be kept in the envelope to allow for more spending in the coming month, or it can be routed to a savings goal or debt repayment or shoved in a fun fund envelope.

$ *Some personal finance gurus will advise—or rather mandate—that you not have a fun fund while you are paying down debt. I'm a more practical millennial who would prefer you don't yo-yo diet with your finances. Having* *a small fun fund you can use to make a splurge purchase or go out with your friends ($50 or less each month if you're paying off debt) sometimes will keep you from falling off the wagon and blowing your budget out of the water out of frustration at having to live a fun-deprived, hermit-like lifestyle.*

The Traditional Envelope System

The pre–Internet age version of the Envelope System involved physical envelopes—do those even exist anymore?—stuffed with cash. You can certainly still partake in the old-school method, just like I did during those early days in New York, but be wary about having too much cash sitting around your apartment. You could always do a Digital and Traditional hybrid in which you withdraw the money you need each week, like with a Cash Diet, and put it in the corresponding envelopes. This mitigates the risk of roommates with sticky fingers, someone breaking into your apartment, or you just being totally irresponsible and misplacing a wad of cash.

The Digital Envelope System

Look for an app or budgeting software specifically catering to the Envelope System style of budgeting, like Mvelopes.

The more hands-on approach, if your bank allows for it, is to create subcategories in your checking account or to just create multiple checking and savings accounts. Each account should be labeled just like its physical envelope counterpart.

You may not have a debit card for each account, or you may not want to manage 10 debit cards to make sure you're always pulling from the appropriate fund. This means you will need to be proactive about transferring between accounts or putting it all on a credit card and moving the earmarked money from individual accounts to the one that is linked to pay off your credit card. Just be sure you know how many transfers you're allowed to make each month, because you don't want to have to start paying to move your money around.*

There might even be a separate digital version you've found that works

---

* Most savings accounts are restricted to six transactions per month before you have to pay a fee and the account is converted to checking. This is not a bank rule but rather a federal regulation (Federal Regulation D Reserve Requirements). You can usually transfer as much and as often as you'd like with checking accounts, but always read the fine print.

best for you but that's similar to the Envelope System. I encourage you to develop your own method, so long as it keeps you on track for your financial goals and you're still diligently saving each month.

THE ISSUE WITH THE ENVELOPE SYSTEM

You need a buffer. The notion that all your expenses in each category stay fixed from month to month is ludicrous. Rolling over your surplus from month to month can help mitigate this risk, but you may also want an entirely separate envelope that's just called *buffer*. The trick is that you can access it only for necessities, not because your friends want to take a cruise to the Bahamas.

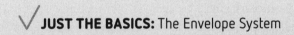 **JUST THE BASICS:** The Envelope System

→ The Envelope System is similar to the Cash Diet, but with structure about how much you can spend in certain categories.

→ Each envelope is labeled for a specific part of your budget, such as rent, student loans, emergency fund, pets, etc.

→ Once you've spent all the money in an envelope, then you're tapped out for the month. No borrowing from one envelope to fund another.

→ It's possible to do the Envelope System digitally, but you need to be on top of your game if you plan to segment all your money into various checking accounts or subcategories.

BUDGET 201 OPTIONS

Tracking every penny or strictly using cash are great training wheels for getting financially empowered. One of these budgeting styles might stay your personal preference as you pay down debt, try to hit savings goals, or just because you find it effective. However, you don't have to be tied to either one forever. As you become more financially fit, you may choose to evolve to a less time-intensive and strict budgeting style.

Percentage Budgeting

One of the more effective and less stringent budgeting methods—the percentage budget—often outlines three main categories for your cash: fixed costs (50 percent), financial goals (20 percent), and wants or flexible spending (30 percent).

In a Pleasantville version of the universe, these three groups are easily funded only by your net income—that is, after you've paid taxes and contributed to your retirement fund. The money that hits your checking account is what you use to fund your 20 percent savings goals, while 50 percent more than covers your housing, transportation, and debt costs, and the remainder funds your day-to-day living.

In reality, you might be chuckling to yourself at the notion of *only* spending 50 percent on your fixed expenses, especially if you're sitting in an apartment located in a major city. Your rent alone might be 50 percent of your salary, and that doesn't include paying utilities, taking care of your transportation, and, of course, paying down those student loans.

The idealized version of Percentage Budgeting should be your goal, but in the meantime, it's fine to develop your own reasonable percentages for those three major categories. Reasonable is not spending 40 percent on fixed costs, 55 percent on flexible spending, and 5 percent on meeting financial goals. When you create your own percentages, it's also important to reevaluate them as you pay down debt, progress in your career, and increase your available income. Here is an example.

Dwight lives in New York City and earns $45,000 a year. After taxes and his 401(k) contribution, Dwight earns $31,800 a year and gets paid $2,650 monthly. He pays $1,350 a month for rent, utilities, and his MetroCard. An additional $250 a month goes toward student loans. His fixed expenses cost him $1,600 (approximately 60 percent). He has already put 7 percent toward his retirement account, and he tucks $200 a month into a savings fund with the goal to have six months' worth of living expenses set aside (approximately 7.5 percent of financial goals).

Contributing 20 percent to savings would leave Dwight with only $520 to spend each month on living. While this is technically doable, Dwight prefers to be realistic and puts approximately 7.5 percent into savings, leaving just over 30 percent (or $850) for flexible spending.

When he gets his next promotion and raise, Dwight plans to keep his fixed expenses and flexible spending the same and put the difference toward financial goals, thus changing his percentages to better align with the ideal.

√ **JUST THE BASICS:** Percentage Budgeting

→ You should strive to keep fixed expenses at 50 percent and split the remainder as 20 percent toward savings and 30 percent toward daily living.

→ Adjusting percentages to better fit your current living situation is acceptable, but the budget should be modified as you continue to earn more.

→ Retirement contributions don't count toward the 20 percent in savings. Consider only your non-retirement contributions and post-tax income—in other words, the money that actually hits your checking account.

Zero-Sum Budgeting

The black belt of budgeting tactics, the Zero-Sum Budget uses last month's income to pay for this month's expenses. It enforces the notion that all your dollars should be assigned a "job" and is the foundation for the popular budgeting tool YNAB (You Need a Budget), one of many budgeting apps you could use. This method is the one to learn if you're a contractor or freelancer with sporadic income.

Using last month's income to pay for this month's expenses may sound ludicrous to you, especially if you have a tendency to borrow from your next paycheck before it hits your account (usually done on credit cards). This is why you can't just switch over from another budgeting style or never budgeting in your life to suddenly being flawless with Zero-Sum Budgeting.

The Zero-Sum Budget is one of the most effective ways to break the paycheck-to-paycheck cycle as well as aggressively pay down debt and hit other savings goals.

There's something empowering about working these steps by hand, so go get a notebook—for real—and a pen. Let's get to work!

Step 1: Know Your Income

For salaried employees, step 1 is simple: just pull your paychecks. I'd advise looking at your actual paystub so you see how much is leaving in taxes, how much is getting routed toward retirement funds, and how much is actually arriving in your bank account. For freelancers, this number can fluctuate drastically from month to month. You may have a $10,000 August and then a $4,000 September. This is one reason using last month's income to pay this month's expenses is a wise strategy; you'll never be praying for outstanding payments to make it into your mailbox or hit your PayPal account. Okay, that's not entirely true. You'll always be on the hunt, but it's a less stressful experience.

Step 2: Crunch Your Bills and Lifestyle Costs

Salary or sporadic income doesn't play an integral role in this step. You need to sit down and write out your expenses and the attached price tag. Take more than a few minutes to write this list. In fact, take a first pass and then walk away and come back later. You probably forgot a recurring cost (like buying toilet paper) during your first pass.

Robin is a 27-year-old woman working as a reporter for a local news channel. Here's what her monthly expenses look like, including an estimate for fluctuating categories like gas and utilities.

Rent—$950
Student loans—$300
Health insurance—$120
Renter's insurance—$20
Auto insurance—$95
Car payment—$115
Gas—$40

Utilities + Internet—$75

Cell phone—$85

Streaming TV services—$8.99 (let's be honest, she still uses a few of her ex-boyfriend's accounts too)

Groceries—$375

Household goods—$30

Miscellaneous self-care costs—$100 (you know, the shampoo/waxing/ hair styling products/makeup/face creams/lady sanitary care, etc. The pink tax isn't cheap.)

Entertainment—$250

Retirement contribution—$200

Emergency fund—$150

Robin's grand total: $2,913.99

Robin earns $3,700 after taxes, so there's $786.01 left unaccounted for. It's time to give those dollars a job.

Step 3: Employ Your Dollars

Once you've taken a look at your current expenses, it's time to assign each dollar a job so you're spending your entire paycheck. This sounds delightfully exciting, but "spending" also refers to stashing away cash for the future. Robin won't be getting a pass to go "Treat Yo Self" on mimosas and fine leather goods.

Instead, her budget may turn into something like this (the asterisked items are where the unemployed $786.01 got put to work):

Rent—$950

Student loans*—$651.01 (+$351.01)

Health insurance—$120

Renter's insurance—$20

Auto insurance—$95

Car payment*—$300 (+$185)

Gas—$40

Utilities + Internet—$75

Cell phone—$85

Streaming services—$8.99

Groceries—$375

Household goods—$30

Miscellaneous self-care costs—$100
Entertainment—$250
Retirement contribution*—$450 (+250)
Emergency fund—$150

Now Robin is zeroed out each month. She will continue to pay more than the minimum due on her car until the loan is paid off, and then that $300 can be redirected toward her student loans and savings goals.

Step 4: Evaluate Your Spending Categories

In the Robin example, she's fortunate to have a surplus. This means her budget can easily be retooled to zero out each month, but in many cases the amounts owed eclipse the money being earned each month.

If you crunch your numbers and realize your bills and general costs imperative to life outweigh your cash flow, then it's time to evaluate your spending categories. One of the easiest ways to do this is to track exactly where you really are spending money.

Step 5: Time to Get Your Penny Tracker On

The Penny Tracker budget style may not speak to you, but it's a crucial element in building a strong foundation for your Zero-Sum Budget. The Penny Tracker method should be used for one month minimum, but two to three months is ideal in order to account for any potential outliers from your single month of monitoring transactions.

The Penny Tracker also helps ensure you're staying within your predetermined limits for the month. This does require checking in, so it would be wise to have a standing date with your money each week, or even each night, to run the numbers.

Step 6: Prioritize Your Categories and Trim the Fat

A month or more of tracking every penny can easily help you home in on those problem areas. It's the financial equivalent of looking in the mirror and bashing yourself for your physical features, except this one is arguably healthier if you're able to use it as motivation for change.

Food and entertainment are some of the easiest categories to slash—part of the reason lattes and cable get so much bad press (literally) in the personal finance world.

Ditching cable or diligently brown-bagging your lunch and forgoing a daily coffee run will certainly pad your bank account, *if*—and this is a big if—you make the effort to re-route the funds in another direction. Forgoing one cost and then failing to put the additional money in another bucket makes the sacrifice pointless because you will wind up spending that money you saved on something else. For example, you can tack the extra $20 a week from ditching a coffee run onto your monthly student loan payment or increase your monthly retirement contribution. You might fall on your face a few times in the beginning, and that's okay. You'll learn which areas need a little padding each month to ensure you don't overspend and which routine purchases you may be able to eliminate entirely.

Now, if you relish your daily latte or can't imagine life without ESPN or knowing what the Real Housewives are up to, no judgment. You simply need to figure out another place to scale back your spending.

This practice should help you focus your money toward what's actually important in your life. Here's hoping it's paying down debt and protecting your future self with consistent retirement contributions.

Step 7: Get a Month Ahead
Now that your dollars are assigned jobs to zero out your budget for good reason—not because you went on a spending spree—it's time to get a month ahead so you're using last month's income to pay this month's bills. It's the entire point of the Zero-Sum Budget.

You may pull a month's worth of living expenses out of a savings account; however, you should avoid raiding an emergency fund to jumpstart your Zero-Sum Budget. If you do use savings to get started, then be sure to quickly replenish the money you withdrew.

A month's worth of living expenses available outside of an emergency fund is a luxury for many a millennial, so if it feels completely unattainable, then start putting aside a little at a time. This could mean it takes six months before you're fully one month ahead—but you'll get there. Not to mention that the practice of staying within your spending categories, tracking pennies, and trimming the fat starting now could push you to save more aggressively than you think is even possible as you read this sentence.

Step 8: Always Run the Numbers and Adjust Accordingly

This budget is hands-on, which means you need to be checking in weekly, perhaps even daily, as you work toward getting a month ahead. It's imperative you know exactly how much you earned last month, so you can adjust your categories accordingly. This is why the Zero-Sum Budget is ideal for freelancers and helps destroy paycheck-to-paycheck living.

Just be sure the categories you're adjusting are the non-essentials. If you're making $1,000 less in June than you did in May, your entertainment budget should be taking the hit and not your savings or debt-slaying categories.

√ **JUST THE BASICS:** The Zero-Sum Budget

→ Know your income first and then crunch the numbers to determine your cash flow each month.

→ Assign each dollar in your budget a specific job, so that at the end of the month it zeros out—but this means saving too and not spending all your money!

→ Your goal is to work toward using last month's income to pay this month's expenses in order to break that paycheck-to-paycheck cycle.

THERE'S AN APP FOR THAT

Finally we come to what you were probably thinking throughout this entire breakdown of budgets: *Is there an app for that?*

In most cases, yes, there is an app for that. In fact, there are scores of existing personal budgeting apps, and new ones are being added all the time.

Many of these—like two of the biggest ones, Mint.com and YNAB—provide the option to link your bank accounts, credit cards, and even investments together in one place in order to analyze your cash flow and your overall financial picture. They are simple and eliminate the need for you to proactively track down this information during your weekly self-run budget audit. It sounds like a semi-lazy-but-striving-to-be financially-savvy millennial's dream, right?

In many ways, these are helpful. But if you're thinking of going the app route, here are two big potential issues to watch out for:

1. *Cash needs to be updated by hand:* You have to manually enter into the app anything you pay for in cash. Perhaps you don't use cash and never carry it, but on the off chance it still plays a role in your life, then you'll need to track those expenditures by hand.
2. *Cyber security breaches:* Read the fine print before linking an app to your financial accounts. Many banks have started cracking down, saying you will be responsible for losses resulting from linking a third-party platform (aka a budgeting app) to your bank account. The app is also likely to provide fine print stating it isn't liable for losses due to a security breach.

You should research and read reviews before choosing an app, investing your time in setting it up, and, perhaps most importantly, linking your financial accounts to it. That doesn't mean you need to avoid all apps and budget software, but be proactive about protecting yourself. Set up alerts on all your credit cards to let you know when transactions occur. Check in on your bank accounts daily. Maybe even link only one checking account from which you do the bulk of your spending, so that if you're hacked, the loss is mitigated. It won't give you a comprehensive net worth overview; that might be worth doing by hand.

GO TAKE ACTION!

Before you lose that burning desire to get your financial house in order, you should probably put this book down and set up a budget. The first option you try might not be the best for you, but at least you're taking actionable steps to break free from the shackles of debt and ditch that paycheck-to-paycheck lifestyle.

Already got your budget mojo? Give yourself a gut check to see if maybe you can step it up a level. For example, I think I'm going to go run some numbers for that Zero-Sum Budget I've been creating for myself.

Chapter 5

Picking the Right Financial Products (aka The Chapter in Which This Book Pays for Itself)

"*. . . AND WE'LL GIVE YOU a free credit score!*"

Sadly, for a money-loving nerd like myself, it didn't take much creative advertising to get me, at age 24, to choose the first financial product I signed up for that wasn't simply a default to what my mom and dad used. Until that point, I had banked only where my parents did because it was easy, and this may be what you've done too. After a bit of a scare over having a "thin file" when I tried to check my credit score via Credit Karma, the idea of getting monthly access to a credit score was enough to get me to apply for a credit card.*

But it took me two more years to open a new bank account because I did research instead of just sticking with the bank my family used. This move happened after I realized $10,000 in savings could earn $100 instead of $1 in interest each year just by switching banks. #WorthIt

No matter your level of financial know-how and expertise, we can all go on autopilot by just staying with what we know or what our parents use when it comes to actually picking our financial products—checking and savings accounts, credit cards, and even your lenders for auto loans, personal loans, or mortgages. For example, it made more sense for our parents' generation to keep banking products in the family as most of the time there were fewer options available to them, so they couldn't shop around in the same way we can today. But thanks to the Internet and the subsequent rise of Internet-only banks, as well as online comparison tools that help you find the right financial products for you, you don't have to use financial products just because Mom and Dad did or because there's a branch on your block.

---

* Learn more about thin files and credit scores in general in chapter 6.

For a generation reared on the idea of being able to comparison shop with a few taps on our phones or getting products for cheaper online than in brick-and-mortar stores (thanks, Amazon), many of us are still oddly fixated on needing a physical bank to store our money.* This problem is that traditional brick-and-mortar banks often nickel-and-dime us, particularly when money is tight. You'll learn more about how and why that happens later in this chapter. Even if you never enter the bank, there's some sort of safety-blanket notion about it standing there proudly in your neighborhood, guarding your money deep in its iron-clad vaults. Spoiler: your money doesn't stay tucked away in the bank, but we'll get to that in a bit.

It's time to nix this superstition for the sake of your wallet. There's nothing wrong with sticking to the old-school way of banking, but you first must understand the financial repercussions of that decision. In this chapter, we'll walk through how to determine if your current financial products are the right fit and, if they aren't, how to find a better alternative.

 ## SOME BASICS TO KNOW WHEN CHOOSING FINANCIAL PRODUCTS

→ Make sure your bank has FDIC insurance (this means you're protected up to $250,000 should your bank go under).

→ You don't need to pay unnecessary fees on a checking or savings account, such as maintenance, annual fees, minimums, and overdraft protection. There are ways to avoid those that we'll explore in this chapter.

→ Your savings account should be earning an interest rate of at least 0.75 percent APY. The common offer of 0.01 percent is a joke—both you and your money deserve better.

→ Credit card rewards are worth it only if you avoid both overspending and paying interest.

→ Ditch credit cards with an annual fee and find a card that rewards your regular spending, which might be a basic, flat-rate card.

---

* For the sake of simplicity I am using the term *bank* throughout most of this chapter. However, credit unions are also viable options for your financial needs.

UNDERSTAND WHAT FDIC INSURANCE MEANS

Browse a bank brochure (if you've stepped into a time machine) or scroll down to the bottom of a bank's Web page and you're sure to find the bank's name followed by "Member FDIC."

If you can't find this statement anywhere on the bank's promotional material or Web site, then get out of there or, more realistically, click out of the browser as quickly as you can. You should be putting your money only in an account with an FDIC-insured bank, meaning it is insured by the Federal Deposit Insurance Corporation.

Why You Want FDIC Insurance

Most of the major banks, especially the "name brand" ones you'd think of if asked to name a bank, are FDIC insured. It's important to have FDIC insurance in order to protect your deposits. If you use a non-insured bank and the bank fails, then you'll have a hard-to-impossible time recovering your funds.

FDIC insurance also denotes a more reputable bank or credit union. Why bank with an institution that doesn't protect you? It's like dating someone who refuses to use birth control—you know it's a terrible idea, even if it feels good at the time.

You can usually see on a bank's home page if it's FDIC insured, but you can also use the FDIC's BankFind tool: https://research.fdic.gov/bankfind.

What Does FDIC Insurance Cover?

The simple way to think about your coverage is that it insures money you've stored away in a bank account, not money you've invested. Covered accounts include:

→ *Checking accounts:* Where you keep your daily-use money.
→ *Savings accounts:* Where you keep money you don't need right away (plus, you can make only six withdrawals from this account per month by federal law).
→ *Money market deposit accounts (MMDA):* Basically a checking-and-savings hybrid. These accounts typically earn more interest than a checking account, but there are also restrictions on how much you can deposit and/or withdraw each month.

→ *Time deposits such as certificates of deposit (CDs):* A certificate of deposit offers you a higher interest rate, but you have to lock the money up for a predetermined period of time. Taking it out sooner means potentially paying a penalty and losing some of the interest you earned. For example, you might earn 1.50 percent APY—but you have to deposit at least $1,000 and keep it in the account for a minimum of two years to earn and keep all the interest.

→ *Negotiable Order of Withdrawal (NOW) accounts:* Truthfully, I'd never heard of this type of account before writing this book. However, it's similar to a checking account except you likely earn a higher interest rate, but you may have to give written notice before you take money out—sometimes even as much as seven days'.

→ *Cashier's checks, money orders, and other official items issued by a bank:* You'd likely need these to prove that your check is good for the funds on a large purchase; for example, sometimes a landlord may ask for a cashier's check for the security deposit on your apartment when you move in. Basically, these are like the bank giving the official stamp of approval that the funds are there so the check won't bounce.

What Doesn't the FDIC Insure?

The simple answer is: your investments. Common investments include the following:

→ Stock, bond, and mutual investments—all of which you can learn more about in chapter 15.

→ Life insurance policies.

→ Annuities: Invested lump sums of cash that are meant to provide a monthly stream of income in the future, usually in retirement.

→ Municipal securities: In short, a bond (buying of debt) from a state or local government.

→ Safe-deposit boxes or their contents: The boxes stored in bank vaults where people keep valuables. You've probably seen this in a movie.

→ U.S. Treasury bills, bonds, or notes.*

---

* These investments are backed by the full faith and credit of the U.S. government but are not FDIC insured.

Important Things to Know About FDIC Insurance

→ FDIC insurance is automatically guaranteed if you're banking with an insured financial institution. You don't need to sign up or send in paperwork to get it.

→ In 2016, you're insured up to $250,000 total per bank (not per account). Creating two $250,000 savings accounts at the same bank does not mean you get $500,000 covered. You could deposit $250,000 with one FDIC-insured bank and $250,000 with another, though, to get $500,000 in coverage.

→ You can learn more about insured deposits at https://www.fdic.gov/deposit/covered/categories.html.

There's no point banking with an institution that fails to provide you with FDIC insurance when so many banks are FDIC insured so that you're protected. We certainly hope banks won't fail, but you just never know. So why not protect yourself and up to $250,000 of your money? If you find out your bank isn't FDIC insured, move your moolah to one that is, and do it today. You and your money deserve it.

CHECKING ACCOUNTS: TIME TO DITCH THOSE BANKING FEES

Raise your hand if you ever paid at least one of the following for your checking account: overdraft fee, non-sufficient fund (NSF) fee, annual fee, low-balance fee, monthly maintenance fee (seriously—what's the point of that one when we're already letting them keep our money?), or lost-card fee.

Feeling a little smug because you've managed to avoid all those? How about an ATM fee? The odds are you've probably been hit by one of these. But if you're thinking a small $2.50 ATM fee now and again is no big deal, think again. It can be expensive to bank with a traditional, big-name institution. This is particularly true if you're a low-deposit customer (you don't have lots of money stashed away), especially one with a tendency to overdraw your account. Luckily, you don't have to stay there. I'll show you how to avoid all these fees going forward.

Fees You Shouldn't Be Paying

BANK ACCOUNTS	CREDIT CARDS
Annual fee	Annual fee
Maintenance fee	Activation fee
Minimum-balance fee	Monthly fee
Overdraft fee	
Overdraft-protection fee	
Early account closure fees	
Lost-card fee	
ATM fees	

$ *According to the Consumer Financial Protection Bureau, in December 2015, banks earned 11.6 billion—let's say that again, 11.6 BILLION—dollars in revenue from overdraft and NSF fees.*[1]

The frustrating part of these fees isn't so much that they exist—banks are for-profit institutions, after all, so they've got to make money somehow—but rather that these costs are being triggered by doing something as simple as slipping under $1,500 in an account for a single day in a month. It's one thing to charge someone who consistently overdraws on their existing funds. That's a sign that they probably aren't managing their money well and could be a liability. But asking a person who struggles to maintain a minimum daily balance of $1,500, but perhaps could maintain a lower balance more easily, to pay $12 or $14 to use the bank's essential services could mean the difference between them paying a bill on time or having a nutritional meal on their table. College students, young professionals, people in poorer areas, and those in a paycheck-to-paycheck cycle tend to be the ones hurt most by this type of fee structure.

---

* Banks with more than $1 billion in assets and that offer consumer deposit accounts are required to report overdraft fees and NSF fees separately on their quarterly public financial statements.

Ditch the Fees

There is absolutely zero need for you to be paying a majority of these fees. Overdraft protection is one of the most outrageous fees. It's charging you $12 for "protection" as an automated transaction to move *your own money* from savings to checking when you overdraw your account. The bank doesn't normally charge you to move *your own money* from savings to checking, so why now and why so much? Credit unions are often just about as bad as the traditional brick-and-mortar banks when it comes to overdraft fees.

Here's what you should expect from a checking account:

→ No annual fee.
→ No monthly maintenance fee.
→ No minimum amount required to avoid fees.
→ No overdraft-protection fee.
→ No fee charged when you use an ATM outside of your bank's network, plus a reimbursement of the fee levied against you by the ATM you're using. (As a bare minimum: a certain amount of ATM fees should be reimbursed per billing cycle—e.g., $10 worth.)
→ A bank gets "bonus points" if there's no cost to replace lost or stolen debit cards.

Here's what you should expect from a credit card:

→ No annual fee: no matter your credit score, there are reputable cards with no annual fee.
→ No activation fee: This is such a scam fee. Don't use a credit card company that asks you to pay any sort of activation fee.
→ No monthly fee.
→ Simple way to make online payments.
→ Easy-to-understand terms.

Where Do You Find These Mythical, No-Fee Checking Accounts?

Internet-only banks often provide the most competitive deals. You may hear them called online banks, which is also true, but Internet-only is more accurate. These are the financial institutions with no or very few brick-and-mortar locations. Google can be your best friend when you're searching for these banks, but some notable checking account options that have been on the market for at least several years include:

→ Ally
→ Bank of Internet USA
→ USAA (you need a military affiliation)
→ Charles Schwab

However, big banks are starting to take notice, and some are responding to the appeal of the Internet-only banking experience. Capital One offers the Capital One 360 account, which is a no-fee account so long as you use a Capital One ATM.

The potential downside of Internet-only banking is if you deal primarily in cash for your job or tend to receive a lot of cash (e.g., tips as a bartender). Many Internet-only bank accounts do not provide a solution for the cash-deposit dilemma. Capital One 360 does offer the ability to deposit cash at select ATM. This does, however, seem like a pain point that will begin to be rectified in the coming years.

ATMs are another issue. Most Internet-only banks operate within a network of ATMs for free, such as the Allpoint network, but those aren't always readily available, and (in my personal experience) taking money out at a convenience store or similar type of ATM opens you up to thieves stealing your information with a skimming device and taking $600 out of your checking account. This is why it's best to go into a physical bank branch if you want to withdraw cash but have an Internet-only bank like Ally, Charles Schwab, or USAA that reimburses some or all ATM fees.

SAVINGS ACCOUNTS: YOU DESERVE MORE THAN 0.01 PERCENT APY

I made the bold claim that purchasing this book would pay for itself in this chapter. One of the ways in which I can help you make that happen is by convincing you to switch savings accounts. First, let's dig into why it's complete shenanigans if a bank gives you only 0.01 percent APY, which stands for *annual percentage yield* and factors how often interest is applied to a balance (e.g., daily or monthly or annually).

What Banks Are Really Doing With Your Money

You log in and see the balance of your savings account. Logic would follow that the money is just sitting there patiently waiting to be spent. It's *your* money, after all, and you deposited it into *your* savings account. Of course it's waiting for you. You might go so far as to picture a Gringotts Wizarding Bank situation with a cart moving at breakneck speed through a series of complex tracks until it arrives safely at your vault. Alas, you'd find your vault wanting, because banks don't just leave your money sitting pretty.

Sorry for the spoiler alert, but the funds you deposit into a bank are used to make loans to other customers. And you can be sure those customers are paying way more than 0.01 percent in interest. The bank is using your money to make an auto loan to the guy down the street who just rolled into the neighborhood on a new set of wheels. The bank uses your money to make a loan to someone else with a 3 percent APR (annual percentage rate) and thanks you by giving you only 0.01 percent.

Now, if you're already banking with an Internet-only bank and earning a minimum of 1.00 percent APY, then well done for treating your money right! Skip to the next section and maybe you'll learn how this book can pay for itself there. Otherwise, here's my case:

You're currently banking with a big name (or local) bank, likely because Mom and Pops banked there and set you up with an account or because it's the closest to your home. Those bank accounts are probably only offering you somewhere in the 0.01 percent to maybe 0.20 percent range.

If you save $2,000 for a year at 0.01 percent APY, you will earn you a whopping 20 cents! You can't even get another eight minutes in the dryer at my laundromat for that amount. But if you put that $2,000 in a savings account earning 1.00 percent APY annually . . . bam, you've got an extra $20, and this book paid for itself! (I wasn't kidding when I said this chapter would help you do that.)

How Those Banks Afford to Give You 1.00 Percent APY

I know what you're thinking: the way banks handle the APY, it feels like a gimmick, and frankly, it can be sometimes. Online banks will routinely fiddle around with the APY on savings accounts. One month it's 1.05 percent APY, and two months later it drops to 0.75 percent. It's actually within the bank's right to do this—but that doesn't mean you should hang tight at your measly 0.01 percent rate with your current bank because another bank might change from 1.00 percent APY to something a little bit lower. Because 0.75 percent still *crushes* 0.01 percent.

Okay, I'm coming off my soapbox to explain how Internet-only banks can afford to offer 1.00 percent APY and higher. This isn't to say brick-and-mortar banks aren't offering the higher interest rates. Some actually are; however, with them you'll usually find far more hoops to jump through in order to earn those interest rates.

Internet-only banks don't have to buy land, build a brick-and-mortar location, hire staff, pay property taxes, and cover hefty electric bills. This one simple, effective cost-cutting measure yields immediate results to put in customer pockets. And it's not a shabby marketing strategy to get millennials such as ourselves to switch over.

You also know the money is safe because you checked that it's FDIC insured, right?

Considering how often banks can, and do, change interest rates, and considering that this book is in print and not a blog post I can update monthly, it's a bit hard to give you recommendations for accounts with the highest interest rates today. You can google "highest-interest savings accounts" and be directed to a few answers. Be sure to consider other factors—like fees, customer service, and ease of use—before just picking the account with the absolute highest rate. At the time of writing, I've used Ally Bank for its 1.00 percent APY. It's not the highest on the market right now (1.05 percent is), but the customer service is excellent, and that's worth .05 percent to me.

It also doesn't take much effort to open a new account and move your money. A bank representative at the new bank would be happy to assist you; just be sure you know the account and routing numbers for your current account. Assuming that your current account is not overdrawn (aka does not have a negative balance), then there should be no repercussions from moving your money and closing the account. Just make sure that if you had any bills automated to pay from the old account, you quickly update the information to be linked to your current bank. Leaving an old, empty account open could also end up costing you money if that old account had minimum-balance requirements, so it would be best in that case just to close it down.

Once you've got your checking and savings all squared away, it's time to evaluate your credit cards.

FIND REWARDS THAT WORK FOR YOU. BUT DON'T SPEND FOR THE REWARDS.

Credit cards are one of my favorite financial tools. I've exclusively used credit cards to build my credit score (learn more in chapter 6). Rewards points have gotten me two round-trip airline tickets to Italy and multiple domestic trips. I've done much of my Christmas shopping by leveraging money I earned just by using my credit cards for everyday purchases. Given enough time, I could likely come up with an "Ode on a Credit Card." None of my credit cards have cost me a penny in interest. This is important. So important I'm giving the point its own line.

Using a credit card for rewards but overspending and therefore paying interest nullifies the point of earning rewards!

Your credit card needs to maximize rewards on your existing spending categories. The first step is to identity what type of rewards card you need.

The Common Reward Structures

→ *Rotating categories:* Rotating categories often work on a quarterly structure and usually offer 5 percent (or something similar) for three months before changing. For example, January to March is 5 percent cash back on transportation, including gas and public transit passes, but it rotates in April to June to earning 5 percent on dining out and movies. All other spending typically earns 1 percent cash back. One common trap with these cards is they require you to "opt-in" ahead of time in order to earn the 5 percent rewards, otherwise it's 1 percent for you.

→ *Flat-rate:* The simplest of rewards structures, the flat-rate card gives you a set percentage of cash back on all your purchases. Two percent back is often the highest you'll see, with 1.5 percent being the other common contender. These cards are perfect for the credit card user who wants to go on autopilot when it comes to rewards and isn't concerned about maximizing them all the time.

→ *Sign-on bonus:* A sign-on bonus is often coupled with another form of reward, but it's used to lure you in. "Spend $3,000 in the first three months and we'll give you 30,000 bonus miles" is the type of advertising you'll see for a sign-on bonus card. This type of reward is common among travel hackers looking to earn miles for flights or free hotels. Your card usually comes with other rewards, like two times points on all airline purchases, and all other dollars spent earning you a mile per dollar.

Finding the Best Rewards Card for You

The best rewards card for you is the one that won't tempt you to overspend. It's easy to fall to temptation with a credit card because the limit is often much higher than we can actually budget for each month. So it gives you the ability to make a purchase, but you can't always pay it off in full at the end of the month.

A flat-rate card is the easiest to use and often a solid beginner card. It can then be coupled with other cards to eventually maximize your rewards potential—just as long as you always pay your bill on time and in full.

The Card for Every Category Strategy

A basic cash-back card earning a minimum of 1.5 (but preferably 2) percent is a strong foundation for starting your rewards game. The next level is to couple it with one or two other cards that provide higher cash back in categories where you're already spending money on a consistent basis, such as groceries, gas, travel, dining out, etc. Matching all your spending to the highest reward category maximizes the cash back you earn on every dollar spent—but this approach can be time-intensive and is best utilized by those who are well-versed in credit cards and who always pay their bills on time and in full.

No matter how experienced a credit card user you are and which strategy you decide to utilize, just keep repeating the mantra to never spend more than you can afford to pay off on time and in full each month. You do not, should not, would not want to carry a balance on a credit card.

Churning Credit Cards

Travel hacking—aka churning cards, which is frequently opening and closing credit cards just to get the sign-on bonus—is one way plenty of people explore the globe without paying much out of pocket for the trip. Travel hacking as a subject could be a stand-alone book; I'll address it enough to say that while it's quite possible, it's also an advance-level move. Please don't jump from opening your first credit card account to build up your credit history right into trying to churn cards for miles or hotel points. Establish an excellent credit history first and a strong-enough credit score to withstand applying for (and closing) multiple cards within a calendar year.

For those planning to open a credit card because a flight attendant made an announcement that filling out the application meant 50,000 miles after you spend $3,000 in three months—just make sure you normally spend $3,000 in three months on a credit card (rent probably doesn't count).

Travel hacking sounds glamorous, but don't fling yourself into the deep end of the credit card swimming pool after a huge meal and with no understanding of how to even dog-paddle. Trust me, the credit card companies aren't going to serve as a lifeguard.

Remember, earning rewards should not change your spending habits for the worse.

Okay, now you're ready to make some changes to your financial products. How do you find out your options?

HOW TO FIND FINANCIAL PRODUCTS

Google can be your best friend, but the Web sites below also reputably rank products.

→ MagnifyMoney.com
→ NerdWallet.com
→ Bankrate.com

Just keep in mind that most of these companies pay the bills by earning referral fees from the financial institutions they send customers to. Because of this, some Web sites rank by the product that pays the highest referral fee on top and not because it's the best fit for you. Read through reviews before selecting a financial product, and read the fine print (or at least skim the details) before applying.

WHAT TO REMEMBER ABOUT DITCHING FEES AND SAVING MONEY

→ FDIC-insured banks all the way. Otherwise, don't even play.

→ Stop paying silly fees on your checking accounts, and switch banks now.

→ You should be earning a minimum of 1.00 percent APY on your savings accounts.

→ Only spend on a credit card what you can afford to pay off. Paying interest nullifies the point of earning rewards.

Chapter 6

Credit Reports and Scores:
The Report Card for Life

EXHAUSTED, SWEATY, AND FEELING DEFEATED by New York City real estate, my first grown-up roommate, Anna, and I flopped into two tacky chairs in yet another broker's office. We'd been scouring the streets of Astoria for two weeks and were running out of time to find a place before my Craigslist sublet ended and the lease on her current apartment ran out.

After a third roommate decided to nix her plan to move to the Big Apple, we suddenly found ourselves, on June 25, scrambling to find a two-bedroom apartment with a July 1 move-in date. Desperate, and a little scared, we took any meetings we could get with a broker or even a semi-safe-looking landlord from Craigslist. Like I said, we were desperate.

The current broker, an elderly Russian woman with the handshake of Ronda Rousey, interrupted my fantasies of sleeping in a bedroom of my own with a demand for $30.

"We need to run your credit reports and get your credit scores," she informed us.

Sitting in that ugly, red pleather chair, I first learned about the importance of being in the 700+ Club.

(Already feeling daunted by this chapter or just looking for the 411? Flip to the end of this chapter for the fast facts about credit scores.)

WHY CREDIT SCORES AND REPORTS MATTER AND WHO USES THEM
You may think it's the credit card companies, mortgage lenders, and car dealers of the world who would be most interested in your credit score and report. Unfortunately, that just isn't so. The reach of a credit report and score extends far beyond your attempt to get someone to believe you're qualified to borrow money.

The credit report is used as a way to judge your levels of responsibility—or really gauge just how well you're succeeding at adulting. Potential landlords may run a credit check to look for red flags like a history of missed payments or a heavy debt load compared to your income (also known as the debt-to-income ratio).

You may have heard that employers check your credit score, but this isn't true. Employers pull the credit report, which doesn't actually come with the credit score.

$ *Employers get a truncated version of your credit report, which is called an Employment Insight Report. It's less information than what both a lender and you would get if you pulled your own report. It never, ever contains your credit score.*
—Rod Griffin

Rod Griffin, director of public education for Experian, explained to me the two main reasons why an employer would want to pull your credit report.

1. You will manage the company money in some way, so the company wants to ensure you handle your own finances well.
2. Employers also use the credit report to verify your identity and protect themselves from fraud.

Bonus reason: Government agencies may use a credit report for security purposes. If you're under financial stress, as indicated by a high debt load on your credit report, then you may be more susceptible to bribes or more easily become a threat to national security.

WHAT'S THE DIFFERENCE BETWEEN MY CREDIT SCORE AND MY CREDIT REPORT?

Credit scores get most of the attention. They're the scantily clad Victoria's Secret models, while the credit report is the salads, juice diets, and Cross-Fit workouts the models did to look so alluring. You appreciate and gossip about the end product, but what it took to get there is far more important.

The credit report contains the information used to generate your credit score. The credit score is the simple, easy-to-understand piece of information we can all use to judge each other, even though the report is really what matters most.

$ *A credit score is not like an odometer on a car. A credit score represents a snapshot of the information on your credit report at that moment in time. The next time a lender or business requests a report and a score, they get a brand-new credit report and a brand-new credit score.*

—*Rod Griffin*

WHAT'S ON MY CREDIT REPORT?

Credit reports contain a detailed history of the ways in which you've interacted with credit and debt. Each of your applications for a credit card is noted, and those notes stay on your report for two years.[1] That auto loan you took out is on your report and it's chronicled each time you stay current on your payment.

It isn't all gold stars and participation trophies on your credit reports. The negative bits get on there too. Late payments, delinquent or defaulted loans, items in collections, unpaid tax liens, bankruptcy, and foreclosures will all be recorded on your credit report and damage your credit score. The one month you overextended yourself in college and forgot to make the payment on your credit card will stay on your report for seven years from the date of the first missed payment or, in technical credit bureau jargon, the original delinquency date.[2]

You're being tracked each time you interact with a line of credit. A line of credit doesn't only mean how many credit cards you have open but also refers to:

→ Student loans
→ Personal loans
→ Auto loans
→ A mortgage
→ Or almost any other type of debt. Payday and title loans are often not reported to the credit bureaus while you're in good standing, but they will be reported if you default and the debt is sent to collection.

All this information is collected by the three credit bureaus: Experian, Equifax, and TransUnion. However, not all lenders will report to all three bureaus, so it's possible your information will vary from one credit report to another. Sound odd? It kind of is, but it's the way the system works.

Mindy applied for a mortgage from NoMoreRenting Mortgages, but NMR reports only to Experian. A few months later, Mindy diligently pulled all her credit reports and saw her student loans on all three, but her NMR mortgage is only on Experian, and her credit card reports only to TransUnion and Equifax.

Unfortunately, you have no control over how your information is reported, and lenders are rarely quick to tell you which credit bureau they will use. This makes sense for the lender because if you have a bad mark on your Experian report but it isn't reported on Equifax and TransUnion, then you're likely to scope out lenders that pull only Equifax or TransUnion reports. Lenders are not too keen on giving you that kind of upper hand. The best way to deal with this uncertainty is to simply treat your credit well—and you're about to find out how.

UNDERSTANDING HOW A CREDIT SCORE WORKS

To understand what your credit score is and why it exists, let's take a stroll down credit score history lane. Lenders used to have an incredibly subjective way to determine whether or not you'd be a responsible borrower: a gut feeling. Okay, it was a little more nuanced than that because you would have to go in and have a conversation with a banker and make your case for them lending you money. But it really did come down to whether or not the banker felt in his gut that you could repay the loan.[3] Considering that this was the model pre-1960, it didn't exactly give equal lending opportunities to women and minorities.

In 1956, two gents named Bill Fair and Earl Isaac got together and decided that it was about time business decisions stopped being made based on subjective feelings and that perhaps data could be utilized instead. The two developed a credit-scoring model based on which behaviors made someone a credit risk and which indicated responsibility. This model debuted in 1958 for American investments under the name the Fair Isaac Corporation. A form of those names that may sound more familiar to you is FICO®. After much reconfiguring, credit scores more akin to what we're familiar with today were released in the 1980s.

Why Your Credit Score Even Matters

Think of a strong credit score as an insurance policy for your financial life. A strong credit score proves to a lender that you're reliable, which directly correlates to favorable loan terms.

For example, at some point you're probably going to need to borrow money to buy a house or a car or to refinance student loans. When that day comes, you want to have a high credit score so you'll be eligible for the lowest possible interest rate on the loan. Low interest rates mean you'll pay far less money in interest over the course of the loan than you would with a higher rate. That's more money in your pocket for doing whatever you want (like saving it, or using it to pay off a debt faster, or, I suppose, taking that trip to Paris). A healthy credit score makes the rest of your financial life more affordable by providing access to loans at low interest rates.

A *high credit score* will result in low (or lower) interest rates on any money you borrow. A *low credit score* will mean high interest rates on loans or potential outright rejection of your loan applications from lenders.

Perhaps you'll be one of the fortunate few who legitimately never need to borrow money for a mortgage or a car or to refinance existing debt to a lower interest rate. You may, however, want to use a credit card.

Those who don't necessarily need to borrow can leverage a reputable credit history to get the best reward credit cards.* The best credit cards with top-notch rewards—the kind that enable you to book flights to Italy and pay for hotel rooms or just get cash back for your regular spending—are available only to people with strong credit scores. (You will, of course, pay those cards off on time and in full, so you keep that score high and never go into debt for rewards.) A credit card is also the easiest way to build your credit history without ever paying a penny in interest. More on that later in the chapter.

Just as a high credit score grants you the password to an exclusive club of low interest rates, a low credit score shoves you into a room with sleazy salesmen looking to peddle high-interest-rate junk like payday loans at 300 percent APR. When you find yourself in a financial pickle and need money fast, you will likely just have to take what's available to you. This is how so

---

* Go back to chapter 5 if you didn't already read about picking the best financial products.

many people end up with subpar financial products like title loans and payday loans. It's difficult to get approved for a personal loan with a decent interest rate or a credit card when you're chained to a score of 600 or below. Even dipping under 650 could land you in a tough spot. This is why I say a strong credit score is similar to having an insurance policy on your financial life. You don't want to have to borrow, but if you need to, then you have non-predatory options with reasonable interest rates (like personal loans from a reputable lender or a line of credit from your credit union or community bank).

How Do They Determine Your Credit Score? The FICO Score Range

For simplicity's sake, we're going to focus on the base FICO credit score when discussing how to decode these numbers that determine much of your financial fate.

The base FICO credit score uses a range from 300 to 850. Just like pretty much anything in life (except golf and darts) the higher the score, the better you're doing. The low end of the spectrum indicates you're a higher credit risk to a lender. This could be because you have limited or no credit history or because you've missed payments and have items in collections.

800+: Exceptional
750–799: Excellent credit
700–749: Good credit
640–699: Fair credit
580–639: Poor credit
Below 580: Bad credit

Your goal should be to join the ranks of the 700+ Club—not to be confused with that oddball evangelical talk show. A 700+ credit score tells lenders you have a history of making wise choices when given access to credit and that you make your payments on time.

For the overachievers, particularly those who got irked when everyone in class got a blue ribbon just for participating in the fun run, you can aim to get above an 800. It's mostly bragging rights, because once you are safely into 700 territory, you start to gain access to top-tier financial products.

So what happens when you check your credit score and you don't actually have one? Yeah, that's a thing.

What the Heck's a "Thin File"?

I'm the type-A, overachiever type who still enjoys getting a gold star from the dentist, so it should be no surprise that I was an early adopter of tracking my credit score for free on sites like Credit Karma.

Except my first experience with Credit Karma resulted in a harsh rejection. After filling out all the personal information and answering a bunch of questions to prove my identity, up popped a screen telling me I had a "thin file." No score, just the words "thin file."

I felt slighted by the almighty beings that preside over personal finance and the Credit Karma algorithms. I'd spent four years diligently using a credit card for the sole purpose of having a reputable credit history and thus a good credit score. I'd already gotten my first adult apartment in New York City based on said score (and my ability to actually pay rent). So what the heck, Credit Karma?

After hours of nerding out on message boards and even calling my credit card company, I got to the bottom of the "thin file" debacle. It appeared my single credit card didn't report to all three credit bureaus, and the bureau tied to Credit Karma had zero information about me, the A+ credit card user.

A thin file can also be the result of no or minimal credit history. You may be in the process of building—or rebuilding—your credit and there simply isn't enough information on your credit report to generate a score.

Don't panic over your thin file and immediately start applying for a bunch of credit. Keep steady at using one or two credit cards wisely and making payments on any existing loans. This strategy will build a strong credit history, and you'll have a credit score in no time.

$ *Student loans help build your credit score if you pay them on time and never let them default or become delinquent. However, if you are in college and aren't making payments, then your student loans aren't helping you build credit until you graduate and start forking over money each month. Just having loans in your name isn't enough. The credit bureaus need to see that you're making payments and keeping your loans in good standing.*

One potentially worrisome reason for a thin file could be a mistaken death. If you have years of credit history under your belt and pop up as having a thin file, or one or more of your creditors marked you as deceased on an account, then you should pull your credit report immediately. It's not unheard of for the credit bureaus to mistakenly mark someone who is still roaming the earth as deceased.

Now that you understand where your credit score stands—or why you don't have one yet—let's look into how it got there.

How a Credit Score Is Determined: The Five Factors

There are five factors used to determine your credit score.[4]

1. *Payment history (35 percent):* Make your payments on time and in full, and the lenders, the credit bureaus, and your credit report and credit score will all be happy. I can sense you about to roll your eyes because if it were just that simple, no one would ever have credit card debt. Fair enough. What happens if you can't afford your payment?

    Obviously, your goal should always be to pay off credit cards on time and in full each month. However, if you've put yourself in a bind and are unable to make the full payment by the due date, then you need to at least pay the minimum due to count as making an on-time payment. However, keep in mind that carrying a balance from month to month will ultimately send you into a downward debt spiral.

    Should you ever feel you're unable to make the minimum payment to a credit card company, personal loan provider, student loan servicer, or mortgage company, you need to pick up the phone and call. This isn't a case where it's better to ask for forgiveness than permission. Explain your situation and see if a deal can be worked out during your short-term budget crisis. Don't expect this to work more than once. And it will be effective only if you have a history of on-time payments.

2. *Amounts owed (aka utilization; 30 percent):* Amounts owed often goes by the far more exotic name of utilization: the amount of available credit you spend.

    When a credit card lender extends you a line of credit, there is the not-so-secret hope that you'll buy far more than you can afford; then you'll make only the minimum-due payment, causing you to rack up interest. This is why you're lured in with sign-on bonuses of a $100 statement credit for $2,000 of spending in the first two months or

30,000 miles for $3,000 of purchases in the first three months. It's also why you're given a credit limit of $4,000 a month, even though you earn only $45,000 a year.

The credit bureaus want you to resist the temptation to buy the latest Apple product and Kanye's recent fashion creation. Using 30 percent or less of your credit limit shows restraint and responsibility. Staying in the single digits makes the credit bureaus weak at the knees.

$ *Utilization is calculated as the percentage you use of your total available credit limit. Leslie has three credit cards with the following limits: $3,000, $5,000, and $2,000. She spends $1,500 a month on just one card. Leslie is 15 percent utilized because she used $1,500 of her total $10,000 credit available. However, Griffin explains that maxing out a single card still doesn't look attractive and can ding your score. Do yourself a favor and keep your balance at a maximum of 30 percent on both individual and total credit limits.*

Spoiler: Don't stress too much over these next three factors. Keep your eye on the prizes of payment history and amounts owed.

3. *Length of credit history (15 percent):* This section is easy to handle with a two-step process.

→ Step 1: Use your credit.
→ Step 2: Don't die anytime soon.

Boom. Nailed it.

Okay, it may be slightly more formulaic. The third step would be to keep your oldest line of credit alive for at least the early years. If it's a terrible, fee-riddled card with less appeal than going back to using a flip phone, then I give you permission to ditch it, but not until you've secured yourself another credit card with no annual fee.

An active credit card is the simplest way to keep your length of credit history healthy. Installment loans like a car loan, a personal loan, or a student loan will eventually be paid off and then ultimately roll off your report. A credit card will usually stay on your report as long as it's open and active.

4. *Credit mix (10 percent):* As the name implies, this factor is the diversification of your lines of credit (e.g., having credit cards, an auto loan, some student loans, and a mortgage). I abhor this factor because it makes you think it's a requirement to have a credit card, an auto loan, a student loan, and a mortgage to build a strong credit score. *False.* You can use one credit card with no annual fee, make every payment on time and in full so you're never paying interest, and have a high-700s credit score. How do I know? That's what I did. (All right, I admit that's a #Humblebrag. #SorryNotSorry.) If you have trouble getting an installment loan (such as an auto loan) from a lender because you've only ever used credit cards, then take the time to shop around. Not everyone will give you a tough time because you've lacked a credit mix.

This is crucial information because it's likely you'll come across a well-intentioned friend or a misinformed family member who will tell you it's important to have diversity of credit—someone who encourages you to take out a car loan, even when you can buy in cash, or argues that you shouldn't aggressively pay off your student loans because paying them off quickly will "hurt your credit score" since they will roll off your report sooner. Shut it down.

There isn't a need to take out multiple forms of credit just for the sake of building a credit score. By all means, get an auto loan if you need to buy a car and can't afford to pay the total amount for it up front. Or take your time paying off student loans if it means being able to also balance other important financial goals like saving for retirement and building an emergency fund. But do not generate debt just for the sake of a credit score, as it's not worth it when you have the option to do it interest free. (Skip to "The Quick Way to Get Results" if you want to learn more.)

5. *New credit (10 percent):* This final factor tracks your applications for new credit because FICO states that research has shown that if you open a bunch of cards quickly, then you're a greater risk (aka you probably won't repay your debts on time or at all).[5] It's only worth a measly 10 percent of your credit score, but, man, can this factor really get people's panties in a bunch! You may have resisted applying for a credit card, student loan refinancing, or a personal loan due to

an intense fear about hurting your credit score. Stop stressing. Again, let's note it's worth only 10 percent.

$ *People always worry about inquiries for new lines of credit when they really don't need to. Hard inquiries will always be the very last thing that affect your ability to apply for credit. An inquiry by itself will never cause you to be declined if everything else is in great shape. Unless you're applying for a whole lot of credit at once, which is a big sign of risk, there isn't a need to worry.*

—Rod Griffin

Before you put this book down and run to apply for those four credit cards you've been eyeing because you recently heard about the world of travel rewards, give me a moment to explain.

Applying for a new line of credit will often result in what is called a *hard inquiry* on your credit report. This inquiry typically lasts on your credit report for two years, but FICO factors such an inquiry into your score for only 12 months.[6] An inquiry for a product like a credit card usually drops your score by only a handful of points—we're talking about 10 at most. Unless you're shopping for a mortgage soon, in which case you want the highest possible credit score, a 10-point drop in your score probably won't be a make-or-break factor when applying for a loan. The exception, of course, is if you're right on the edge of dipping into poor credit score territory (i.e., being in the low 600s).

If you apply for only one credit card and then behave responsibly—i.e., spend less than 30 percent and pay it off on time and in full—you'll see your score start to rebound in just a few months. You can also mitigate your risk of rejection by seeing if the company offers the ability to check if you're pre-approved. While pre-approval isn't a guarantee you'll officially be approved, it does indicate a higher likelihood.

Even though inquiries can ding your credit score, they shouldn't prevent you from shopping around to find the best deal on loans (not credit cards, but loans).

If you're shopping for a loan and want to find the best deal, then Griffin recommends comparing all the offers within a 14-day window, which is within a 30-day rolling period, and while you'll see all the inquiries, they will only be weighted as one by the scoring system.

However, if you get a little trigger-happy and start treating credit card applications like Tinder dates before cuffing season, that's when you start to look risky to potential lenders. A spike in applications for credit has the same stench of desperation as your ex from three years ago who keeps creepily liking all your Instagram posts.

This isn't a perfect science for consumers. Your score may drop more than 10 points when you apply for a credit card—or perhaps less, because other factors come into play, such as the length of time that passes between now and when you opened your last line of credit.

Ron has a 760 credit score and applied for a credit card in March. He saw his score drop down to 752, but he kept his utilization below 10 percent, and by June his score had gone up to 765. Then his girl-friend, Diane, asked him to take a trip to the Grand Canyon and suggested they get a different credit card to earn miles from the sign-on promotion. Ron applied for the new credit card in June, and his score went down to 740 because the back-to-back applications for credit cards made his potential risk as a borrower go up.

Ron may have dropped to a 740, which feels significant from a 765, but he's ultimately still sitting on a healthy credit score.

What Isn't Part of Your Credit Score

Your net worth and salary have no bearing on your credit score. You could be earning $25,000 a year with $10 in savings and have an 800 credit score, or you could be Warren Buffett/Bill Gates/JayZ & Beyoncé kind of rich but have a 520 credit score.

Here are other pieces of information excluded from your FICO credit score:[7]

→ Race
→ Age
→ Religion
→ National origin
→ Gender
→ Marital status
→ Employer

→ Occupation
→ Interest rates you're being charged
→ If you're in credit counseling
→ Child support or alimony payments

Okay, you understand the five factors that go into a FICO credit score and how to determine if your score is healthy (700+, baby!). It's time to tackle a slightly more complicated reality: there are actually tons of credit scores—and why that shouldn't bother you.

THERE IS MORE THAN ONE CREDIT SCORE

Not only is there more than one credit score; there are scores of scores. (Sorry, couldn't help it . . . I love wordplay!)

There's a different FICO score for each of your credit reports. There's a FICO score for auto loans, mortgages, personal loans, credit cards, and more. Then there are the other types of credit scores entirely, like Vantage-Score, and some models that banks create on their own.

$ *There are a lot of different credit-scoring models, for the same reason General Motors doesn't just produce one car with one set of options. While all credit-scoring models do pretty much the same thing, just like cars are cars no matter the model, there are different versions because lenders have different needs. A credit union, usually a small lender, has a very specific type of customer, and so credit scores are developed to predict the risk of that particular member group. A national bank issuing credit cards is going to have a much different type of customer base, so risk factors will be different, and they'll use a different credit-scoring model.*

—Rod Griffin

Luckily, there's one simple way to avoid stressing about all these credit-scoring models and fretting about which score a potential lender will use to determine whether you are worthy of borrowing their money: just don't. Realistically, we all still do anyway, so Griffin devised a way to minimize fretting for himself, and it might work for you too.

Griffin goes so far as to not check in on his credit scores regularly because, he says, what you really need to be concerned with is your credit report. This is because every single credit-scoring model uses the information from your credit report to make its score, so if your credit report is strong, then you can rest assured your score will correlate, regardless of which model is being used.

THE QUICK WAY TO GET RESULTS (NO, THIS ISN'T A DIET AD, I PROMISE)

It isn't shameful to admit you love knowing the lifehack to credit success. It's why you always click on those articles like "10 Habits of the World's Richest People" or "5 Tricks to Make You Her Best Lover." Well, consider this the "3-Step Process to a Mind-Blowing Credit Score."

1. Make one or two small purchases on your credit card each month to keep your utilization ratio low (extra gold stars if you keep it below 10 percent). Sure, you can make more purchases if you want, but one or two small ones are enough to ensure that you use the credit limit but don't overspend.
2. Pay off all your bills on time and in full.
3. Rinse and repeat.

This method is specific to credit cards as a means to building a beach-body-ready credit score. Factoring in student loans, auto loans, or any other installment debt you may have is equally simple: make your monthly payment on time.

Combine your monthly installment payment with the responsible use of a credit card—and no lender will be able to resist you! However, you need to be able to resist your lenders. Continuing to take out loans or spending more when your credit limit is increased is how consumer debt creeps up.

I'M WORRIED ABOUT HURTING MY CREDIT SCORE

(Spoiler: It's not a trophy!)

"But doesn't applying for credit hurt my score?"[8]

Yes, applying for a line of credit does indeed ding your credit score. But if you're so concerned about a little blip or going from an A+ to an A, then you're missing the point entirely. A strong credit score helps make the rest of your financial life both simple and more affordable because it opens up the world of low-interest-rate loans and credit cards with no annual fees.

Sitting on a strong credit score and refusing to use it when you need to is like putting a dog in a purse—ridiculous.

Now don't think that I'm encouraging you to just apply to a bunch of credit cards and seek out loans you don't need. Quite the contrary. I do believe in protecting your credit score for most of the year, but I'm also a devoted fan of taking that trophy off the shelf and using it as leverage when necessary.

It could be necessary if you get yourself into a bind with credit card debt and need to use a balance transfer or a personal loan to reduce interest rates and pay it off. It could be necessary if you have had a secured card to build your credit history and you're now ready to graduate to a big-boy credit card (maybe even one with rewards!). It could be necessary if a pipe bursts in your house around the same time you get laid off from work and your emergency fund is already dangerously low so you'd rather get a low-interest-rate personal loan to patch the pipe instead of depleting your savings entirely. Or it could be necessary because you're a diligent user of credit who has never once been in debt and figured you'd go ahead and get a rewards card offering enough miles to get a round-trip flight to Europe.

Use your credit score to your advantage when you need to because it isn't a trophy to be kept on the mantel, where it will just collect dust.

WHERE DO I GET MY CREDIT REPORTS (AND ARE THEY FREE?)?

Any butterfly-hairclip- and cargo-pants-wearing tween near a television during the early aughts will remember a catchy jingle declaring you should go to freecreditreport.com. Catchy as the jingles were, freecreditreport.com and similar sites are not your answer for checking your credit report.

The answer comes from the government-endorsed annualcreditreport .com.

Annualcreditreport.com is the official site to get access to a free copy of your credit report from each of the three credit bureaus (Experian, TransUnion, and Equifax) once per year. You are entitled to a free copy of your report under federal law, so don't let any site/app/financial advisor tell you you're required to pay. You will not be asked to plug in your credit card information on annualcreditreport.com.

You can get all three credit reports at once or you can space them out during the year. I recommend downloading one every four months as a proactive way to keep an eye on your identity and monitor for fraud.

Remember, this is just your credit report, and it will not come with your official FICO score attached. You can learn how to get access to your credit score(s) in just a moment, but let's wrap up this credit report chat first.

HOW DO YOU DECIPHER THIS CREDIT REPORT?

You don't have to have any special training to read your personal credit report.

—Rod Griffin

According to Griffin, you actually get access to information lenders don't usually see, such as soft inquiries. Soft inquiries are when you apply to see if you're approved for credit, but the lender promises no hard pull will be done to your report. (A *hard pull* or *hard inquiry* is a type of credit check that could cause your credit score to drop. A *soft pull* or *soft inquiry* doesn't affect your credit score or go on your credit report.) Like that time you were seeing if a personal–loan lender would give you $3,000 for a Eurotrip that seemed like a great idea seven drinks in at 3 a.m.

Griffin advises you go directly to the sources and pull your credit reports from the credit bureaus because asking for a copy from a lender may yield some confusing results. Experian, for instance, has worked hard to make it easy for you to understand your credit report by providing information in the most simplistic way possible, as in: here's your account, the account number, your balance, your available limit, and whether or not you're paying on time. Lenders, however, may have their reports coded specifically to work with their computers, or they may combine information from multiple credit bureaus, making it far more difficult to read.

SOMETHING'S NOT RIGHT ON THIS REPORT! WHAT DO I DO?

One of the many important reasons to keep an eye on your credit report is in order to detect fraud or just a plain ol' clerical error. The credit bureaus aren't flawless. If you pull your report and find an error, you can take these steps:

1. *Dispute an item:* This can be done via snail mail (but why bother?) or online. Each credit bureau's process is somewhat unique, but you'll

be prompted to provide information about why the item is an error, and then the credit bureau will reach out to the lender. The lender has 30 (or, in some cases, 45) days to respond to the dispute. You'll be notified after that time period if the investigation clears you or still finds you liable for the item.

2. *Put on fraud alert or credit freeze:* It takes a bit of effort to determine if the error is on the report as a result of a clerical error or because you're the victim of fraud. Just to err on the side of caution, you may want to put a fraud alert or credit freeze on your report. A *fraud alert* notifies a potential lender pulling your credit report to verify the identity of the person requesting credit in case it's a fraudster. A *credit freeze* puts your credit reports on lockdown. A creditor can't access your report unless you "thaw it" by telling the creditors to temporarily or permanently lift the credit freeze, which usually includes a passcode given to you by the credit bureaus. A fraud alert is usually free, while a credit freeze may cost you a small amount (often around $10 per bureau) depending on your state. You may get a free credit freeze if you are the victim of identity theft.

HOW DO I GET MY CREDIT SCORE FOR FREE?

FICO credit scores are the Coca-Cola formula of the financial world. For the most part, you still have to pay to get access to the Coca-Cola, but you can have Mr Pibb, Kirkland Cola, or many other similar-tasting versions of your credit score, just not the real thing.

Credit Cards

Credit card providers are listening to consumers' demands for access to their credit scores, and many are now offering it as a perk. If you get a no-fee credit card offering access to your FICO score and you pay off the bill on time and in full, then you'll be getting free access. If you pay an annual fee for the credit card, then you are technically paying for access to your credit score. But hey, you might also be getting a free checked bag every time you fly, so maybe it's a wash. These scores are typically FICO scores generated from a specific credit bureau.

You should check with your bank and credit union to see if free credit score access is being offered but you simply haven't found it yet.

Free Credit Score Web sites

Credit Karma is to free credit scoring what cat videos are to the Internet. (Did you just get SAT chills from this analogy? I did.) There are also other helpful Web sites available for finding your credit score, but Credit Karma is certainly one of the largest and most informative.

You may have heard the term *FAKO score* in relation to Credit Karma and similar credit score education Web sites. A FAKO score is often used to describe a credit score that simply isn't the official FICO score. However, times have changed, so non-FICO scores can be completely legitimate and are even used in lending decisions.

Credit Karma utilizes TransUnion and Equifax's VantageScore 3.0 as well as credit reports from both bureaus.[9] The access to weekly versions of your credit report is one of the biggest perks of using Credit Karma.

Credit Karma doesn't charge you for credit scores or reports, nor do you have to keep track of a free trial period. It generates revenue from advertisements and affiliate links. You will get ads for certain financial products, such as credit cards and personal loans. In turn, Credit Karma will get a kickback if you click through and purchase the financial product. This isn't to say that Credit Karma is pushing unnecessary or ill-fitting products on you, but do keep in mind that the suggestions on the site are affiliate deals.

Other Web sites to check your credit score for free include:

→ Credit Sesame. You can get your free TransUnion credit score, but the bigger perk is Identity Theft Protection. Credit Sesame offers up to $50,000 in identity theft insurance and the opportunity to speak with an identity restoration specialist for free when you enroll in its Free ID Theft Protection program.

→ Quizzle. You can get access to an updated free VantageScore credit score and a TransUnion credit report every three months.

→ Credit.com. You'll get access to your Experian credit score and your VantageScore 3.0 credit score.

Before you whip out your phone and start researching how to find your free credit score and download your credit report, take a few minutes to ensure you don't fall into the trap created by one of the common myths about credit. I bet you've heard of at least one of these myths before—and may even believe them.

DON'T BELIEVE THESE CREDIT MYTHS!

Myth: *Checking my credit report will hurt my score.*
Truth: No, checking your own credit report(s) will not harm your credit score. It's a smart move for you to be proactive and check your own credit reports from each of the three credit bureaus at least once a year, as allowed by law. You can do this by going to annualcreditreport.com.

Myth: *A potential employer can check my credit score.*
Truth: Your potential employer can run your credit *report*, and only with your permission. The employer will not be gaining access to your credit score and will receive a truncated version of your actual report.

Myth: *I should carry a balance month to month on my credit card.*
Truth: *No!* This is my pet peeve about credit scores. You absolutely, 100 percent, unequivocally *do not* need to carry a balance on your credit card to build and maintain a strong credit score. Instead, you should utilize no more than 30 percent of your available credit limit and then pay it off on time and in full when the bill comes due. This myth is likely rooted in a misunderstanding of the fact that you do need to show utilization on your credit card bill.

If you make a purchase on your credit card but pay it off before the end of the billing cycle, then your credit card bill says you've made $0 in purchases and owe $0. Even though you actually used your credit card, the credit bureaus often just see the report that you used $0. This might sound like you're super-responsible, but in reality all they see is, "Hey, this person might not be responsible as a borrower because she's not even using her card to prove she can handle paying it off on time."

What you want is for your credit card statement (the bill) to show at least one small charge, and then as soon as the bill comes in, you pay it off on time and in full. This way you're proving that yes, you can handle using the credit card but you're also not paying any interest to the bank.

Myth: *It's good to max out my card or get close to the limit.*
Truth: Similar to the perversion of carrying a balance, some credit card users believe it shows more responsibility to use as much of the

credit limit as possible and then pay it all off. That's like saying it's a good idea to see how many Thai chilies you can stuff in your mouth. (One's enough, trust me.) Keep your utilization at 30 percent of your total available credit limit or less. Preferably less.

Myth: *Just use a prepaid card or a debit card.*
Truth: Prepaid cards and debit cards are not reported to the credit bureaus; therefore, they do not help you establish and build a credit history. So sure, you can use prepaid cards or a debit card as long as you will never need access to credit. Some of you may be able to buy a house with a suitcase of cash, or you may never need a personal loan to cover an unexpected emergency. It's a great life goal to be able to pay for everything outright in cash, but it may not only be unrealistic but also a gamble. Having a strong credit score is like having an insurance policy. You don't want to use it, but it can help prevent a world of financial pain when you need it to. You can use a mix of credit and debit cards, but I also caution you to be careful about where you swipe your debit card and which ATMs you use. Debit cards leave you far more vulnerable to thieves because they enable people using skimmers (devices used to steal your card information) to gain direct access to your bank account.

Myth: *Don't accept a credit limit increase.*
Truth: This depends completely on your ability to handle credit. A credit card company offers you a credit limit increase as a way to lure you into spending more with the hope that you'll ultimately spend more than you can pay off in a month and therefore carry a balance. Carrying a balance and paying interest is one way to keep the lights on at the credit card company headquarters.

Be honest with yourself. If you have never overspent on your card and always make your payments on time and in full, then accepting the credit limit increase is fine. The increased limit will also help boost your credit score even if you don't end up spending more because it automatically drives down your utilization ratio. You have more available credit but still spend the same amount of money. However, if you tend to overspend on your credit cards, then don't take the risk of an increased line of credit luring you into debt.

Myth: *Never close your oldest credit card.*

Truth: You may outgrow that first credit card you received as you gain access to cards with better reward plans or higher credit limits. However, closing it means you'll eventually lose all the positive history associated with said card, and it could also reduce your average length of credit history (which makes up 15 percent of your credit score). This can make people feel a bit panicky about closing accounts.

There's two ways to approach this issue:

1. Keep the card and just use it to pay a small monthly charge like a Netflix account and then have it set to automatically pay off. If you keep the card and never, ever make a charge, then the credit card company may eventually close it down due to inactivity.
2. A potential small dip won't be a big deal if you close the card because you have so many years of healthy credit history with other cards and lines of credit, plus your credit score is well into the 700s.

GRIFFIN'S GUIDANCE: Credit History Advice from an Expert

Here are tweet-size tidbits of advice from the expert featured in this chapter, Rod Griffin, director of public education for Experian.

→ Credit reports and credit scores are two different things. The report informs the score, but credit scores aren't part of a credit report.

→ Credit history plays an important role in your adult life, so building and protecting your credit is a valuable asset.

→ You never need to carry a balance on a credit card. You do need to make all payments on time.

→ Use 30 percent of your available credit limit at most, and always strive to pay it off in full.

→ Credit scores never prevent anyone from getting a job because lenders get a version of your credit report, not your credit score.

> → Don't stress about which credit score is used. Focus on a strong credit report, because the report informs all credit-scoring models.
> → Understand your risk factors when you check a credit score, as they are just as important as the number itself.

Part of the issue for us millennials is simply that we're young and haven't had credit history for a long time. Each day improves this.

WHOOPS, I MISSED A BILL AND IT'S IN COLLECTIONS— WHAT DO I DO?

Fewer things destroy your credit quite like an item going to collections. According to a Consumer Financial Protection Bureau (CFPB) report from 2014, an estimated 43 million Americans have medical debt in collections.[10] That's just medical debt. We're not even talking about unpaid cell phone bills, missed student loans, delinquent car payments, angry landlords, or missed utilities bills from when you thought you'd successfully taken your name off the electricity bill before you moved.

Suffice it to say, it doesn't take much for one small misstep to happen and for an item to be sold by the company you owe to a collection agency (aka end up in collections). Collection agencies buy old, defaulted debts and then try to come collect them from you—sometimes in rather aggressive ways.

Unfortunately, items in collections are the credit report equivalent of plagiarizing a term paper: there is a zero-tolerance policy, and your grade is going to get tanked. You're more or less giving the middle finger to your lenders and saying to the credit bureaus, "Hey, I'm completely unreliable because I don't uphold the end of my agreement to pay back what I borrowed." (That's them judging you, not me.) The version of your story doesn't matter, even if it's completely legitimate and your lender got shady. Once an item is in collections, then it's time to figure out how to deal.

There are a few ways you may find out an item has been discharged and sent to collections.

1. Old faithful: You get a call from a collection agency.
2. The awkward turtle: You attempt to submit payment and are told your debt has been discharged and sent to collections.
3. The gut punch: You dutifully check your credit report and discover an item in collections, or you check your credit score and see that it dropped 70 to 100 points overnight.

HOW LONG WILL THIS HAUNT ME?

Negative information, even items in collections, will eventually roll off your credit report. But it takes seven years from the date of the original delinquency (the first time you missed your bill) for the item to be removed from your credit report.[11] That's seven years that this will impact your credit score and credit reports. Even if the item didn't get reported to collections until four months after the date of the original delinquency, it should still be removed from your report when it was first late and not when the lender charged it off.[12]

Other dates to know if you get yourself into a financial pickle:[13]

→ Foreclosures: deleted after seven years.
→ Chapter 13 bankruptcy: deleted seven years from the filing date.
→ Chapter 7 bankruptcy: deleted ten years from the filing date.
→ Civil judgments: deleted seven years from the filing date.
→ Unpaid tax liens: may be deleted after ten years from the filing date, but could stay on indefinitely.
→ Paid tax liens: deleted seven years from the paid date.

BUT THIS DEBT ISN'T MINE

Did you find an item on your credit report or get a call from a collection agency about a debt you know for a fact isn't yours? Don't mess around, because the clock is ticking to get this resolved.

First, you need to request a debt validation notice within 30 days of first being notified about the item in collections. Your debt validation notice request should be sent to the collection agency via certified mail so you have proof you sent it; keep a paper trail through the entire process and take copious notes during phone calls. The letter should tell the collection agency that you want documentation to verify the debt is yours as well as information about the original creditor (the company that charged off the debt).

The collection agency is not allowed to continue making contact with you until it can prove the debt is indeed yours by sending verification of the debt, often the associated bill.

Missing your 30-day window gives the collection agency the go-ahead to assume the debt is indeed yours and to come after you for the money.

The CFPB provides a template letter that you can use to send to collectors when disputing whether a debt is yours.[14]

SHOULD I PAY OFF THE DEBT?

Paying the item in collections does not automatically remove it from your report, but it will be marked as a "paid collection," which may curry some favor with future lenders. Making a partial payment could result in "partial payment" being reported as well.

Some collection agencies may engage in a practice known as "pay for delete." This is what we'll call an ethical gray area. It is against credit reporting agencies' policies to remove a reported item in collections. However, there are companies that advertise pay-for-delete services—for a fee, of course. There are also success stories on message boards like Reddit about people succeeding with negotiating a pay for delete with a collection agency as part of the agreement to pay the debt. Before you get excited about using this practice, just remember that there is no guarantee of success (even if you pay a third party), and it does go against credit bureaus' policies.

CONSIDER NEGOTIATING

Collection agencies buy your debt for pennies on the dollar. This knowledge gives you the beautiful gift of leverage. A $400 doctor's bill might be sold to a collection agency for $75. The collection agent is coming for you to pay the full $400, but he's probably working on commission, so getting even $175 from you is going to be a profit, especially if you're willing to pay a lump sum immediately and not be on a payment plan. This is why you can play a little bit of hardball to negotiate on debt you're willing to pay.

Be warned: collection agents are not always the nicest—or most reputable—human beings, at least at work. They may be delightful people otherwise. Any deal you strike with a collection agent should also be given to you in writing with an agreement that your debt will be marked paid in full, even if you negotiate a lower settlement than the full amount of the bill. You don't want to be tricked into making a partial payment, have it documented as such, and then have the remainder sold off to another collection agency, which is a relatively common practice. Like I said, these guys are not always the most trustworthy.

HOW TO PAY AN ITEM IN COLLECTIONS

You should never pay a collection agent with a debit card or directly out of your bank account. The full sum may be removed, even if you agreed on a lower amount, and you don't want money "accidentally" being taken at a later date.

Less risky options include:

→ Open a checking account just to pay the collection item: Use an account that won't charge overdraft fees in case the collection agency tries to charge you more and overdraws the account.
→ Money order or certified check: You should also send this through certified mail so you can receive confirmation that the collection agency got the check.

Keep in mind: if you owe debts on delinquent taxes, alimony, child support, or federal student loans, then your federal benefits, such as Social Security or veteran's benefits, may be garnished.

I HEARD TALKING TO A COLLECTION AGENCY OR ACKNOWLEDGING MY DEBT RESETS THE CLOCK

This conversation is a little bit tricky because the statutes of limitations for items in collections vary state by state. The statute of limitations rule (or SoL) protects you from being sued over your debt after a certain period of time, which can range from three to ten years. You should also check your credit card agreement to see if the SoL is governed by a specific state that's not where you reside in order to extend the option to sue.

One sneaky tactic the collection agency might employ is to sue you over time-barred debt after the statute of limitations has run out, or to just try to get you to admit it's yours. If you're sued, you'll need to show up in court and present SoL as a defense; otherwise, there could be a judgment against you. You should also consult an attorney if you're feeling overwhelmed with the legal issue and sense that the collection agency may be trying to pull a fast one with a legal loophole.

The statute of limitations may reset on the debt with the collector if you acknowledge the debt as yours or make a payment, but it won't reset the clock for falling off your credit report. So regardless of when you talk to the collection agency, that original debt is falling off within seven years and 180 days from your first default.[15]

DO I HAVE RIGHTS WHEN DEALING WITH A COLLECTION AGENCY?

Collection agents do the financial equivalent of slut shaming to try to get you to pay; you do, however, have certain rights as outlined in the Fair Debt Collection Practices Act (FDCPA).[16]

Collection agencies cannot be abusive, harassing, or unfair in their attempts to strong-arm you into forking over money.

Here's a sampling of rights you are provided under the FDCPA:

→ A debt collector can call you only between 8 a.m. and 9 p.m.

→ A debt collector may not contact you at work, or at all, if you ask him in writing to cease communication. This can be legally broken only if the collector calls to say there will be no future contact or to say he is filing a lawsuit. This doesn't void your debt; it just stops the onslaught of calls.

→ A debt collector cannot contact anyone other than you (e.g., employers, neighbors, friends, family, etc.) or share information about your debt. However, it can contact third parties to get your contact information.

→ A debt collector must provide you with a written validation notice within five days of his first contact with you. The validation notice contains the name of the creditor, how much you owe, and how to dispute the item if you don't think it's yours. You will need to dispute the collection in writing—again, do it via certified mail—within 30 days of getting the validation notice.

→ A debt collector cannot claim you'll be arrested if you don't pay the debt or pretend to be law enforcement in conversations with you.

As with many laws of the land, your own state may have specific rules about how collection agencies may or may not interact with you, so make sure to do your research.

You can report any collection agency in violation of your rights under

FDCPA to your state attorney general's office, the Federal Trade Commission, and the Consumer Financial Protection Bureau.

HOW CAN I IMPROVE MY CREDIT SCORE AND HISTORY AFTER A COLLECTION ITEM?

An item in collections doesn't hold the same weight for the full time it remains on your credit report. There will be a dramatic impact at the start, but within a couple of years it won't be such an anchor on your credit score. You can also counteract the negative information by pumping positive information into your report. Be sure to stay current on all future payments. Keep your credit card utilization below 30 percent. And don't go applying for a bunch of credit all the time—it makes you seem desperate.

You can learn more from the Federal Trade Commission (https://www.consumer.ftc.gov/articles/0149-debt-collection) and the Consumer Financial Protection Bureau (www.consumerfinance.gov).

You've learned just about everything there is to understand about credit scores, credit reports, and how to protect your credit history. Take a few minutes today to use one of the free credit score tools and see how you're doing, as well as to pull a copy of your credit report. You may surprise yourself and have some serious bragging rights already.

QUICK SUMMARY FOR UNDERSTANDING, BUILDING, AND MAINTAINING A HEALTHY CREDIT HISTORY

→ There are three credit bureaus: Equifax, TransUnion, and Experian.

→ Your goal is to be in the 700+ credit score club.

→ Always pay your credit card off on time and in full.

→ Lenders aren't required to report your information to all three bureaus.

→ Routinely monitoring your credit score is a simple way to detect identity theft.

→ Pulling your own credit report doesn't harm your credit score.

→ A *soft pull* lets a lender get a peek at your report without harming your credit score, while a *hard pull* leaves an inquiry on your credit report and results in a small dip in your credit score.

→ Shopping around for the best rate on a mortgage, auto loan, or personal loan will result in just one hard inquiry on your credit report if you do it within a 14-day window. The credit bureaus understand you're just looking for the best deal.

→ Don't stress so much about hard inquiries on your credit report because your credit score isn't a trophy; it's meant to be used to get you better financial products.

→ Items in collections will tank your score at first but won't hold such a strong weight the entire seven years they remain on the report.

→ You can negotiate with a collection agency, but be careful about how you pay off the bill.

→ Collection agencies can't harass you, and you should report any mistreatment.

Chapter 7

Wait, I *Shouldn't* Just Pay the Minimum Due on My Credit Card?

YOU MAY REMEMBER the first week of college as a time of excitement mixed with anxiety and peppered with a befuddling new amount of freedom. My first week of college featured a swinging pendulum of nerves ranging from anxiety to extreme homesickness and back again.

The anxiety came from living 7,223 miles from and 12 hours behind my family. I tried to figure out life in upstate New York (real upstate, not Westchester upstate) while my parents and sister lived in Shanghai, China. FaceTime was not yet a thing, and calling directly from my pink Motorola Razr would cost about the same as the GDP of a small country, so I wallowed in a lot of self-pity and worry.

Finances played a large role in my daily fretting. If anything disastrous were to happen, would I be prepared? This very question may have been part of my dad's logic when he told me to get a credit card. A credit card that sat unused in my wallet for months.

My wallet suddenly transitioned from containing brightly colored bills displaying Chairman Mao's face to primarily carrying two pieces of plastic: a debit card and a credit card. But I'd exclusively used cash while living overseas, and the notion of swiping plastic felt wrong. As if I could easily blow through my money without noticing (which you can).

Except I knew I had to force myself to start using the credit card. Each time a cashier asked "Debit or credit?" I heard my dad's voice in my head: "Use your credit card once or twice a month to make a small purchase and pay off the bill on time and in full."

He'd given me this advice in order to build a strong credit score—frankly, at the time I still wasn't sure what that meant—but I listened to him anyway. Once or twice a month, I would use the credit card to make a purchase, and I'd pay it off in full as soon as the bill came in. It only took a month after college graduation to realize that this strategy had served me well.*

The first rule of using a credit card: Pay it off on time and in full.

CREDIT CARDS 101: PAY. IT. OFF. (YES, *EVERY* MONTH)

Credit cards are now one of my favorite financial tools. Using a credit card wisely can earn you a high credit score without paying a penny in interest, like you would with a loan.

The right way to use a credit card is simple: Don't charge more than you can afford to pay off every single month. Then *pay it off.*

How a Credit Card Company Makes Money

In theory, a credit card offers you access to a monthly loan. The credit card company gives you a piece of plastic that allows you to make purchases up to a predetermined limit each month. You buy what you want or need that month and pay the credit card company back for the amount you spent in one of the following ways:

→ Pay the entire bill when your statement comes in.
→ Just pay the minimum due.
→ Pay an additional amount above the minimum.

The credit card company is hoping you'll overspend and be unable to pay your bill in full at the end of the month. Why? Unlike with actual loans, which have a set monthly payment, a set timeline for paying off the loan, and agreed-upon interest each month, a credit card company makes money only when you trip up and pay less than the full balance due. How? Because you'll owe interest on the amount you don't pay back.

$ *A credit card is a good financial tool only if you pay it off on time and in full every month. Never carry a balance month to month.*

It's incredibly lucrative for a credit card company when people just pay the minimum and start accumulating interest on the outstanding balance.

---

* This story is shared in chapter 6 if you skipped ahead.

If a company is willing to let you pay off the card without any interest, earn rewards, and never fork over money for an annual fee, then the folks who are paying interest must really be generating a hefty profit, and it doesn't hurt that merchants also pay credit card companies each time you swipe at checkout.

Carrying a balance on your credit card is a waste of money and an easy way to slide into a debt trap that feels impossible to overcome. Interest rates on credit cards can be north of 20 percent, and many cards come with a penalty APR clause, which means you can get slapped with a higher interest rate if you're late or miss a payment. Spoiler: you don't need to carry a balance month to month to build your credit score (see chapter 6 for more details).

You also want to be careful about picking the right credit card for you. You don't need a card riddled with fees, especially an annual fee.

WHAT IT MEANS TO PAY ONLY THE MINIMUM: A MILLENNIAL HORROR STORY

It's really easy to get confused the first time you open up a credit card bill. Right there in bold it says "minimum due." Usually this is the first line item on your bill, even above the total due. It's almost as if that's what you're *supposed* to pay. It's not. It's what the credit card company *wants* you to pay. You're supposed to (and should) pay the full balance due.

Paying the minimum due is giving the credit card company the smallest amount possible to keep yourself from being considered late and missing a payment. It's also a way to start incurring a lot of debt quickly. Not to mention, you're going to be paying way more for your items than you actually intended.

Kenneth recently moved to New York City for his dream job working for a TV show. His meager salary makes it hard for him to make ends meet, so he decided to use his credit card, with a 21 percent APR, to purchase a high-end TV. He rationalized this purchase by arguing that since he works in TV, he should have one. His credit card has a $2,000 limit, and the TV cost him $1,200. Kenneth got his bill and saw "minimum due: $33," which felt very manageable. If Kenneth kept paying the minimum due, it would take nearly five years and cost him $724 in interest to pay off that TV. If Kenneth had just increased the payment to $50 a month, then it would've only taken him about 2.5 years and cost $370 in interest to pay off his TV.

The minimum payment is usually 1 percent to 3 percent of the total balance due. It may also be the greater of either a set dollar amount—say $35—or the percentage of your total balance.

Another not-so-fun fact about the minimum payment is that it's typically applied to the portion of your bill with the lowest APR, which is one reason why it can feel like you're throwing money at a debt that's never going down. Why is it that credit cards can have multiple APRs? Because there are different APRs on various credit card transactions you might make. For example, if you took out a cash advance and are unable to pay off your purchases, then your cash advance and purchases would have two separate APRs. However, according to the CARD Act of 2009, credit card companies are required to apply anything above the minimum amount due to the balance with the highest APR.

Failure to understand the impact of just paying the minimum due can cause a lot of pain, both financially and emotionally. No one wants to be buried under the weight of credit card debt.

BEATING THE BANKS AT THEIR OWN GAME

You need to stay on high alert for other ways your credit card company will be looking out for #1 (spoiler: that's not you).

Promotional Rate

You might sign up for a card in order to take advantage of a promotional offer. It could be 0 percent APR on purchases for the first 12 months, or you might be using a balance transfer to pay off debt. It's not necessarily a bad idea to take advantage of these offers, as long as you have an actionable plan and are able to pay off the balance by the end of your 0 percent offer. Make note of exactly when the promotional period ends and whether or not the interest is waived or deferred.

Waived or Deferred Interest

Waived interest means you won't be on the hook to retroactively pay any interest if you're unable to pay off the balance before the promotional rate ends. *Deferred interest* means you would need to pay back interest that accumulated from the first day you opened the card until today. Store cards are notorious for offering deferred interest. If you can pay off your balance before the end of the promotional offer, then you're off the hook. But if you have even just a small amount remaining, you're going to owe interest for the full amount of time you've had the card.

Fees, Fees, Fees

Always understand your fee structure before signing up for a card. Is there an annual fee that's waived in year one? Then make a note of when that annual fee kicks in; calendar alerts are quite efficient. Do you have to pay penalty fees or foreign transaction fees, balance transfer fees or cash advance fees? Don't make a move with your card before you understand if it will incur an extra fee.

Increased Interest Rate

The credit card company has every right to hike your interest rate if you slip up, even just once. Being as much as a day late on a payment could mean getting put on the high end of your APR range. It may return to a lower APR after you make on-time payments for six months or more, depending on your cardholder agreement.

Increased Credit Limit

This sounds like a perk for you, and in some ways it can be. An increased credit limit comes after you've been a good boy or girl with your credit card for a while. However, it's also the credit card company saying, "You're so great with handling your credit card that you can certainly afford to charge a little more! Go on, try it out." Don't. Instead, keep your spending the same, and the fact that your credit limit has increased but your spending hasn't will immediately reduce your utilization ratio and help improve your credit score.

Opt-in for Reward Categories

It's a pain to have to opt in to receive your 5 percent rotating bonus category (or whatever percentage your credit card company offers). Be sure to sign up for all the alerts so you don't miss the opt-in window and get iced out to earning only a measly 1 percent. It's certainly an easy way for a credit card company to get away with not paying out all its advertised rewards.

SET UP ALERTS!

Most credit card providers give you the option to set up alerts about your credit card activity via e-mail or text message or, if you really want to be informed, both. The reason for setting up alerts for your credit card activity is twofold:

1. You get bugged with each transaction and get daily or weekly reminders of your overall balance so there's no way to get punched in the mouth by your credit card bill at the end of the month.
2. You immediately know when someone is trying to scam your card for a huge shopping spree—or, in one of my strange experiences, a sub from Jersey Mike's in Georgia.

Credit card companies usually make it quite simple to set up alerts and don't charge for the service. They're all quick to remind you to check and see if your cell phone carrier charges for texts (because it's still the early 2000s apparently). For most millennials, setting up text alerts is a free and easy way to monitor not only your spending habits but the security of your credit card. And as a person who has dealt with credit card fraud no fewer than three times, it's a major plus to get out ahead of the situation.

I KEEP GETTING REJECTED FOR A CREDIT CARD. WHAT SHOULD I DO?

You need a strong credit history to get approved for a credit card, but a credit card helps you build that stellar credit history. It's the financial world's mind-boggling version of the "chicken or the egg" scenario. But don't worry, you won't need to get all Philosophy 101 with a credit card application in order to get approved for a card.

Get a Secured Card

Credit card companies offer a beginner-level credit card known as a secured card. This is particularly useful for recent college graduates who never applied for a student credit card. While credit card companies seem more than happy to offer college kids access to a line of credit, there's no "I'm working my first job and trying to be a grown-up" card that's easily accessible.

$ *Mitigate the risk of rejection by seeing if you're pre-approved for a credit card. Many of the major credit card companies offer the option to check if you're pre-qualified (or pre-approved) online. Just google the name of a credit card company you're interested in and "pre-qualified" to find these landing pages. You'll need to input your name and address and the last four digits of your Social Security number. Being pre-qualified doesn't guarantee you'll get the card, but it reduces the risk of rejection. It also won't harm your credit score to check.*

You'll need to plop down a deposit in order to open your secured card. The amount required varies based on the credit card company but usually ranges from $50 to $200. The deposit typically serves as your credit limit and is refundable *if* your card is in good standing when you close it down. Failure to pay your bills means relinquishing your deposit and doing absolutely nothing to build your credit history. #DoubleFail

HOW TO PROPERLY UTILIZE A SECURED CARD FOR QUICKEST RESULTS (BECAUSE WE ALL KNOW MILLENNIALS JUST WANT INSTANT GRATIFICATION)

1. Put down your deposit, and make sure you know your credit limit. In this example, it's going to be $200.
2. Use your secured card to make one small purchase each month. You can even keep the card out of your wallet entirely and just set it up to pay a small, recurring monthly bill like Netflix (assuming you're the chump who actually pays for Netflix and not the one poaching it off your boyfriend's best friend's ex-girlfriend's parents' account).
3. Never use more than 30 percent of your limit, so no more than $60 of a $200 limit.
4. Pay off the card on time and in full each month. If you've been told to carry a balance, then someone lied to you. Read chapter 6 about how to build a credit score.
5. Monitor your credit score by using one of the many free

tools available, such as Credit Karma, Discover's Free Credit Scorecard, and Capital One's CreditWise. Both Discover and Capital One allow you to use these tools without being a customer.

6. Once your credit score creeps above 680 or you suddenly find that you're starting to get pre-qualified letters in the mail, then apply for a regular, unsecured credit card. Just be sure to properly vet the card because you may get some crappy offers early on. It should be a card with no annual fee and no activation fee.

7. Wait until you've been approved and received your new, no-training-wheels-needed credit card before calling your current company to close down your secured card and receive your deposit back.

REWARDS SOUND GREAT, IN THEORY

Credit card companies offer rewards as a way to lure you in. No tears will be shed if you end up overspending and interest begins accruing. This isn't to say all credit card companies are strangers pulling up in a creepy van with tinted windows offering you candy while asking for help trying to find their lost puppy. Well, some are definitely that way, but not all.

Reward credit cards can be a strategic way to hack free flights, earn cash back, or even deposit extra money into investment accounts. However, for every person you hear about who uses rewards to fly to exotic locations and stay in posh hotels, there are people who have found themselves in horrific credit card debt because they didn't understand the rules of the game.

Don't focus on rewards early on in your financial journey. First master a basic, no-frills credit card with no annual fee. If you survive at least a year making the payments on time and in full (both on time *and* in full is important here), then you can consider moving on to a rewards card.

Once you're ready to take advantage of rewards, be sure to return to chapter 5 and learn more about how to utilize them without getting yourself in debt.

$ *Credit card companies offer rewards as a portion of the interchange fee they charge merchants to accept credit cards. Store owners usually pay banks a fee of around 2 percent per transaction to accept credit cards, and credit card companies sometimes use this to fund your rewards programs.*

IT'S BEEN A ROUGH MONTH. CAN'T I JUST CHARGE THIS TO MY CARD EVEN IF I CAN'T AFFORD IT?

The short answer to this question is no, you can't.

Okay, that's not entirely true because, yes, you are capable of charging unexpected expenses to your card, but you probably shouldn't.

Credit cards can be, and often are, a fallback for unexpected expenses, except that this option comes with a hefty price tag. Having an emergency fund even when you're in debt is incredibly important for this reason. *(Not sure how to start building an emergency fund? Flip to chapter 10.)*

Sometimes the credit card feels like the only option if your savings funds have been depleted and a true emergency arises—we're talking a hospital visit or a tire blows out on the freeway. There's no time in that moment to shop around for a personal loan and find the lowest possible interest rate for your debt. So yes, in some rare instances the card is going to get charged.

But if you're going to make that fateful swipe, then you best be putting together a game plan as soon as that happens. Check your interest rate, and do the math on how long it will take to pay down the balance. Consider if a balance transfer is a legitimate option, or perhaps a personal loan; see chapter 8 for details. Start making payments above the minimum due so your money isn't just getting thrown at the accumulating interest.

One proactive approach to avoid using credit cards as a crutch in a pinch is to apply for a personal line of credit with a bank or credit union. A personal line of credit provides access at any time to a predetermined amount of money. It sounds like a loan, but it's more similar to a credit card. You aren't actually borrowing until you use the personal line of credit. Just having the line approved and in place as an option, much like having a credit card in your wallet, can provide you with a sense of security; it isn't a loan until it's used. And it's not a loan unless you request access to your personal line of credit. Also, as with a credit card, there may be an annual fee.

Do some rate shopping before you actually commit to a personal line of credit, and be sure to explore the rates with community banks and credit unions. Make sure to find one with no pre-payment penalty and no collateral needed. There's a huge *but* with this approach. Do not get this line of credit if you think it will tempt you into borrowing when you don't *need* the money but just *want* the money. I'm looking at you, person with a trigger-happy finger in Etsy storefronts or always eyeing Apple's latest release.

WHAT HAPPENS WHEN I CAN'T AFFORD TO PAY OFF MY BILL?

Getting in the habit of paying off your credit card bill on time and in full can save you hundreds, perhaps even thousands, of dollars, but it might be too late for you already. If you're struggling with a life of rapidly unmanageable credit card debt (or any credit card debt at all), then the next chapter is for you. We'll go over what to do if you find yourself in this situation and how to get out of it (and hopefully, after reading this book, stay out of debt).

$ *Your monthly credit card statement will have information about the APR you're currently being charged.*

"USING A CREDIT CARD" CHECKLIST

- ❑ Only charge what you can afford to pay off each month.
- ❑ Pay your card on time, on the due date listed on the statement.
- ❑ Pay the amount due in full every month.
- ❑ *If* you find, one month, that you need to charge more than you can afford to pay off, then always pay as much above the minimum balance due as possible.
- ❑ You can use a secured card to begin establishing credit if you're unable to get approved by lenders for a regular, unsecured card.
- ❑ Set up account alerts to notify you of your balance and when a transaction occurs.
- ❑ Rewards should complement your spending habits. Don't change your spending to earn rewards.

Chapter 8

Yikes, I Already Have Consumer Debt. What Now?

YOU'RE MORE LIKELY TO FESS UP that you have a guilty pleasure Nickelback playlist on Spotify than admit to carrying consumer debt.* After all, it's all "bad debt" since it doesn't provide long-term value. You can brush off student loans as "good debt" with long-term value because at least those were investments in your education and hopefully in a successful future. But credit card debt can be read as a reflection of your character: a lack of willpower, an inability to understand how to keep your finances in check, an insistence on living beyond your means. You might think it means you're all of these things and worse. But don't worry, you're hardly alone, and I'll show you how to get back on track in no time.

STOP FEELING SHAME, BECAUSE YOU'RE NOT THE ONLY ONE

This certainly isn't an area in which you want to excel, but it may comfort you to know that you might just be aggressively mediocre in the world of consumer debt. According to 2015 data released by the Federal Reserve, the average American between 18 and 65 carries $4,717 of credit card debt.[1]

The reason it's important for you to know this is so we can start to remove some of the stigma and shame around carrying credit card debt—and then prevent it from happening in the long run.

One way to be preventive is to understand the basics of how credit

---

* Consumer debt comes from purchasing items that will not appreciate over time (like a house would) and that, therefore, start to drain your finances. Credit card debt and auto loans are common examples.

cards work (be sure to read chapter 7) and another is to understand how to deal with your cash flow and budget correctly (chapter 4). But if you're past the point of prevention, then let's discuss how to get you safely away from the stranglehold of your credit card companies and their devastatingly high interest rates.

This process will require diligence, patience, fortitude, and pretty much every other motivational platitude you've seen on a poster in the hallways of your office. Basically, it will require you to suck it up, track your spending patterns, pick up another stream of income, or drastically nix your currently unsustainable lifestyle. It's time to get your act together or just sink deeper into debt. Let's talk about how this is possible.

HOW BAD IS THE SITUATION?

"Face the numbers," says Michelle Singletary, nationally syndicated personal finance columnist and author of *The 21-Day Financial Fast: Your Path to Financial Peace and Freedom.* "It sounds so simple, yet so many people only kind of know their debt situation, but they don't know the numbers. They don't really know what's going on because they haven't listed anything."

One method for hitting the reset button on your financial habits is to participate in a financial fast, not unlike the Cash Diet described in chapter 4. Singletary's inspiration for the 21-Day Financial Fast came from her ministry providing money-education courses to a women's group at her church. The 21-Day Financial Fast is in fact modeled after her church's food fast, the Daniel Fast, which provides a foundation for a spiritual quest.

Singletary wondered if this mentality could be applied to fasting from consuming instead of abstaining from indulgent and excessive food. The financial fast is designed to encourage you to purify your money habits by taking time to stop and reflect on whether your funds are actually going toward what matters most, as opposed to mindless consumption.

THREE OPTIONS FOR DITCHING YOUR CONSUMER DEBT

You certainly don't want to open your credit card bill and realize that you charged way more than you can afford to pay off this month, but sometimes it happens. If you've fallen into a revolving debt cycle, here are three strategies you can choose from to get yourself out of the hole.

Option 1: Pay It Down the Old-Fashioned Way—Debt Avalanche or Debt Snowball

As you're creating the list, call lenders to see if they'll reduce the rate.
—*Michelle Singletary, author of* The 21-Day Financial Fast

Once you've decided a balance transfer or a personal loan isn't the right fit—or the banks and lenders have determined that for you by rejecting you—your options quickly narrow down. Before you're tempted to skim off the top of 401(k) savings or dash down to that storefront that promises "Quik Kash Now" with no credit checks required, it's time to visit the Debt Avalanche and Debt Snowball strategies.

Both versions are effective ways to pay off debt and require similar amounts of financial grit and determination. One makes more mathematical sense, while the other provides the psychological boost you just might need.

As you read more about these techniques, please keep in mind that personal finance is nothing if not *personal*. The rational part of your brain may scream at you to go the mathematical route to pay less interest, but if you're someone who needs to see quick results (which, let's admit, is most millennials), then the mental boost method may be the one that actually keeps you on track.

Debt Avalanche: The Mathematically Correct Strategy

The Debt Avalanche is often referred to as the "right way" to pay down your debt. It is the option that leaves the most money safely in your bank account instead of in the hands of your debtors. However, it could also be the option that's most likely to lead you back to your life of overspending. You may feel like it's taking forever to make any progress on your debt repayment, so what's the point?

Here's how it works.

Step 1: Write a list of your debts, arranging them from largest interest rate to smallest interest rate. As mentioned in chapter 7, you can find information about the APR on your cards on your monthly statement. Don't rank debts by the balance due, but focus instead on the interest.

Also include the minimum payments due on each amount. For example, Pete and his wife, Paula, have the following debt:

Debt	APR	Balance	Minimum Due
Town Bank Credit Card	25.99%	$3,000	$90
Orange Store Credit Card	24.50%	$700	$25
Follow Bank Credit Card	18.00%	$1,200	$36
Student Loan	4.29%	$10,000	$103

Step 2: Evaluate how much you have to put toward all your debts each month. Yes, this means putting together a basic budget so that you know your cash flow. Refer to chapter 4 if you're unsure about how to make a budget.

If you're seriously interested in getting out of debt quickly, then every extra dollar you have after paying bills, buying food, putting money in a retirement fund, and saving at least $1,000 in an emergency savings fund needs to be going toward your debt. The truly committed may also figure out how to start earning more money by whatever (legal) means necessary.

Step 3: Pay the minimums across all your balances to ensure that you stay current, but any extra dollars go toward the debt with the highest interest rate. Pete and Paula owe $254 a month at minimum, but they've run the numbers and determined they can afford to put $330 toward their debt each month. Here's how the revised table should look:

Debt	APR	Balance	Minimum Due	Monthly Payment
Town Bank Credit Card	25.99%	$3,000	$90	$166
Orange Store Credit Card	24.50%	$700	$25	$25
Follow Bank Credit Card	18.00%	$1,200	$36	$36
Student Loan	4.29%	$10,000	$103	$103

Step 4: The debt at the top of the list gets knocked out, and you combine that monthly payment with the next minimum payment due . . .

and so on until the debt is completely eliminated. For the sake of simplicity, we'll say that Pete and Paula's other debts stayed at the same amounts despite making the minimum payment due.

Debt	APR	Balance	Minimum Due	Monthly Payment
Orange Store Credit Card	24.50%	$700	$25	$191
Follow Bank Credit Card	18.00%	$1,200	$36	$36
Student Loan	4.29%	$10,000	$103	$103

Debt	APR	Balance	Minimum Due	Monthly Payment
Follow Bank Credit Card	18.00%	$1,200	$36	$227
Student Loan	4.29%	$10,000	$103	$103

Debt	APR	Balance	Minimum Due	Monthly Payment
Student Loan	4.29%	$10,000	$103	$330

Debt Snowball: The "Makes My Brain Happy" Strategy

Debt Snowball is often the favored method for paying down debt. Popularized by the well-known personal finance expert and radio show host Dave Ramsey and used as the foundation for his recommended debt repayment plan, this strategy emphasizes little victories to keep you motivated. In clichéd terms: it's the same thing as trying to lose weight. Seeing a little movement on the scale gets you hyped to keep watching your diet and exercising. Getting weighed day after day and not losing an ounce makes you want to shove a brownie in your face and drink all the beer within relative proximity.

The Debt Snowball strategy does have you end up paying more in interest, *but* it could keep you on target to actually pay off the debt in the first place. If you'll respond better to this method, it'll actually save you money, because at least the debt will eventually go away entirely.

Step 1: List your debts from the smallest balance to the largest balance. Pay no mind to interest rates. You should also include the minimums due, just like with the Debt Avalanche approach. Here are Pete and Paula's debt in Debt Snowball format:

Debt	APR	Balance	Minimum Due
Orange Store Credit Card	24.50%	$700	$25
Follow Bank Credit Card	18.00%	$1,200	$36
Town Bank Credit Card	25.99%	$3,000	$90
Student Loan	4.29%	$10,000	$103

Step 2: Crunch your numbers to see how much you have to put toward your debts each month. Just like with Debt Avalanche, this means putting together a basic budget so you know your cash flow. Refer to chapter 4 if you're unsure about how to make a budget.

All the surplus money you have after paying bills, feeding yourself, putting money in a retirement fund, and saving at least $1,000 in an emergency savings fund needs to go toward your debt. Freelancers may want a little extra padding in that emergency savings fund considering the volatility of your monthly pay.

Step 3: Pay the minimums across all your balances to ensure you stay current, but any extra dollars should go toward the smallest debt first. Pete and Paula owe $254 a month at minimum, but they've run the numbers and determined they can afford to put $330 toward their debt each month. Here's how it should look:

Debt	APR	Balance	Minimum Due	Monthly Payment
Orange Store Credit Card	24.50%	$700	$25	$101
Follow Bank Credit Card	18.00%	$1,200	$36	$36
Town Bank Credit Card	25.99%	$3,000	$90	$90
Student Loan	4.29%	$10,000	$103	$103

Step 4: The first debt listed gets knocked out, and you combine that monthly payment with the next minimum payment due, just like with the Debt Avalanche method. You continue to do this until you've "snowballed" to the largest debt. For the sake of simplicity, we'll again

say that Pete and Paula's other debts stayed at the exact same amount despite making the minimum payment due.

Debt	APR	Balance	Minimum Due	Monthly Payment
Follow Bank Credit Card	18.00%	$1,200	$36	$137
Town Bank Credit Card	25.99%	$3,000	$90	$90
Student Loan	4.29%	$10,000	$103	$103

Debt	APR	Balance	Minimum Due	Monthly Payment
Town Bank Credit Card	25.99%	$3,000	$90	$227
Student Loan	4.29%	$10,000	$103	$103

Debt	APR	Balance	Minimum Due	Monthly Payment
Student Loan	4.29%	$10,000	$103	$330

Step 5: Do a happy dance because the debt is gone!

$ *Michelle Singletary, the personal finance columnist, notes that the experts who usually advocate the Debt Avalanche method tend not to work in the trenches with people's budgets on a regular basis. In her extensive experience, those who try Debt Avalanche are not as successful as those who do Debt Snowball (or, as she calls it, the Debt Dash). It's really about behavior over math, and knocking a debt out quickly is far more inspiring than logically knowing you're paying less interest.*

Option 2: Balance Transfer

It's quite possible you've gotten an e-mail, a physical piece of mail, or even a pop-up when you log into your credit card portal offering you a balance transfer. Annoyingly, these offers keep on coming even when you don't have credit card debt.

A balance transfer allows you to move your outstanding credit card balance with Bank A to a new card with Bank B. Bank B will offer you something like 0 percent APR for 18 months with a 3 percent fee if you transfer your debt. The reason you'd want to move your debt is because 0 percent APR means that you aren't getting charged interest and every penny from your monthly payment will be applied to the principal debt.

Frank collects hats and ended up $4,000 in credit card debt when he overindulged in his hobby. Bank A charges him 17 percent APR a month on his $4,000 in debt. He pays $170 a month toward his card, but it feels like the debt never gets smaller. At this rate, it will take him nearly 2.5 years and cost him nearly $900 in interest to pay off his credit card. He takes an offer from Bank B to move his debt to a card offering 0 percent APR for 18 months. He'll pay a 3 percent fee to move the debt ($120), and the card will charge him 18 percent interest after the promotional period ends.

Even with the 3 percent fee, Frank pays only $180 in interest and fees and is done with paying off his debt in 25 months. That's a savings of nearly $720. Frank could even pay it off in 18 months and pay only $120 in fees if he increased his monthly payments from $170 to $230.

Why would a company be interested in taking over your credit card debt? Because debt is hugely profitable to the banks, and the bank is willing to make a bet that you're going to screw up and stay in debt, thus owing them interest. In the bank's mind, you've already messed up before to get into debt in the first place, so why not again?

$ *Do not use this option if you think for one moment you'll be tempted to spend on the balance transfer card or continue to spend on your old credit card. It's not worth adding more debt.*

You may already be writing off this option because applying for a credit card will ding your credit score. Yes, there will be a dip in your credit score when there's a hard inquiry. But if you have a strong credit score, particularly a 700+, then why not use it to help you get out of debt? Besides, aggressively paying down debt and decreasing your utilization ratio (the amount of available credit you're using) will help your credit score rise to counteract the small dip from a hard inquiry. However, if your score is below 680, then don't apply for a balance transfer as the decision will not be likely to go in your favor. Ideally, you should have a 700+ score when applying.

Because no one likes rejection, especially if it dings your credit score without even the benefit of a credit card, there is a way to mitigate the risk of banks swiping left on you. You can check to see if you're pre-approved for a credit card. Many of the big credit card companies (think Discover, Citi, Chase, Capital One) offer the ability to see if you're pre-approved without harming your credit score. There is not a 100 percent guarantee you'll be approved, but it's pretty likely if you're pre-approved. You can find these pre-approval portals thanks to your trusty friend Google. Just plug in "pre-approved for [insert name of credit card company here] credit card."

Taking a balance transfer offer can be a risk, so you need to be aware of a few common traps to avoid in order to successfully pay off your debt before the 0 percent APR promotional period ends.

You need to be a new customer. Bank B is willing to offer you 0 percent APR because it's trying to lure business away from Bank A. That means you cannot transfer your balance between two cards at the same bank. This is a general rule of thumb, but you're almost always going to get a better deal if you move banks entirely. There's no real incentive for a bank to offer you a 0 percent APR deal between two cards when it has your debt already.

- Don't try to move your debt between two cards at the same bank.
- The best deals are reserved for new customers of the bank.

Complete your balance transfer ASAP. Most offers give you 60 days to transfer your balance over to the card before you forfeit the promotional offer. However, your clock on the offer starts right away, so waiting 60 days means losing two months of your 0 percent promotional period.

- The clock on your balance transfer starts ticking immediately, so if you wait to transfer, you've squandered valuable time to get debt free at 0 percent APR.

- Waiting 60 days or more to transfer could mean you lose your promotional rate.

Always pay on time. Missing a payment due date could cause you to lose your promotional offer and get chucked into the penalty APR group, which is usually north of 20 percent.

- Late payment = no more promotional offer + penalty APR

Make a realistic, actionable plan to pay it off. This step should really come before you take out the balance transfer in the first place. Do the math and see how much you need to pay each month in order to hit $0 by the time your 0 percent promotional period ends. The math on this is basic. Just take your outstanding balance plus any fee you need to pay to complete the transfer and divide that total by the number of months the offer is valid.

- You're more likely to succeed if you have a plan to pay off the debt before you get the balance transfer.
- The goal is to have the debt gone before the promotional period ends, so you need to pay above the minimum due.

Don't spend on the card. Complete the balance transfer and stick that credit card in the literal or figurative freezer and don't spend a penny. Sure, the offer might say you have 0 percent APR on the transferred balance (or balances) *and* 0 percent APR on new purchases for a set period of time. This tactic is the bank equivalent of twirling a ridiculous mustache and tying your bank account to the railroad tracks. Spending is an easy way to trip you up and keep you revolving on your debt, unable to break the cycle and pay off the transferred balance. Like I said, debt is really profitable for banks.

- Repeat after me, "I will not use this card to make purchases. I will not use this card to make purchases."

Is the interest waived or deferred? Waived interest means you're completely absolved from paying any interest, even if you fail to pay off the credit card before the end of the promotional period. There's no retroactive interest owed. This is not the case for deferred interest. Deferred interest offers will charge you retroactively for all the interest that accrued during your repayment of the debt. You would need to pay back interest that accumulated from the first day you opened the card until today. Store cards are notorious for having deferred interest offers. If you can pay off your balance before the end of the promotional offer, then you're off the hook. But if you have even just a small amount remaining, you're going to owe interest for the full period of time you've had the card.

- Misunderstanding the difference between waived and deferred interest could risk completely losing all the benefits of the balance transfer.
- Deferred interest means if you don't pay off the existing balance by the end of the promotional period, then you owe back *all* the interest.
- You want waived interest: even if you don't pay off the balance, you still don't owe back interest.

Still have debt left? You may not receive a credit limit big enough to roll over all your debt, or paying it off before the end of the period could be impossible for your budget. You could do multiple balance transfers and either apply for two or three right in the beginning (advisable only if you're well into the 700+ credit score range), or you could chip away at your first segment of debt and roll any remaining principal balance to a new offer at the end of your first promotional period.

- You may not be approved for a limit large enough to move all your debt, but even a portion at 0 percent is better than all of it at a high interest rate.
- Consider multiple balance transfers if you're interested in moving all the debt over and you're sure it won't tempt you to spend.

Know yourself: Is this really a good decision? A balance transfer can be a great resource *if* you don't have issues with overspending. If the credit card debt is a result of a shopping addiction or a general failure to budget well, then applying for another credit card probably isn't the right move and could end up landing you in even more debt. Seriously reflect on why you have the debt, and evaluate if a balance transfer could end up causing more financial trouble instead of solving a problem.

- Be honest: Will a credit card, even with good intentions, send you deeper down the debt hole?

Option 3: Personal Loan

A balance transfer may sound like tempting fate if you've already had issues with credit cards. Or you just may not be motivated enough to keep searching out the best balance transfer deal and moving your debt toward the end of the promotional period. It's understandable; simplicity takes a lot of stress out of debt repayment. Personal loans can afford you that simplicity.

$ *"I want you to feel pain," says Singletary, who recommends not consolidating each of your payments into one debt, but paying them off individually. "Once you feel the pain, you don't go back."*

A personal loan can be used to pay off your cards and therefore consolidate your debt into one payment with, hopefully, a lower interest rate. Personal loans with single-digit interest rates are available to those with high credit scores, a healthy credit history, a strong record of employment, and a debt-to-income ratio of less than 40 percent. Going into the low double digits (e.g., 12 percent) for a personal loan isn't necessarily a bad thing, but run the numbers and make sure the new interest rate is lower and will save you money compared to your existing rates.

Going the personal loan route means having a built-in plan for when you'll be debt free because the loan comes with a term. You make set monthly payments, and it's easier to understand exactly how much is going to the principal versus interest, unlike the complexities of paying down credit card debt.

A personal loan may look something like this: $5,000 for 24 months at 6 percent APR with a monthly payment of $221.60. Making that payment means you will be debt free at the end of 24 months. You could even pay a little extra each month or make a few larger payments during the year (perhaps at bonus time) in order to pay off the loan before month 24.

How to Get a Personal Loan

You don't need to go to a traditional brick-and-mortar bank or credit union in order to get access to a personal loan. Instead, you can just apply from the comfort of your couch, thanks to the glories of the Internet. It's not just for binge-watching TV shows, people!

The first step to getting a personal loan is to shop around. Yes, during this process lenders will pull your credit report. Some lenders will do what's called a *soft pull*, so it won't harm your credit score for them to see if you're pre-approved and what your rate would be. Others will do a *hard pull*, which causes a ding on your score. Don't let this freak you out and prevent you from shopping around for the best rate. Doing all your shopping for a loan within a 14-day window is weighted as only one inquiry on your credit report. The credit bureaus understand you want to shop around to find the best deal, so you won't be harshly penalized. However, taking out multiple personal loans in a month is an entirely different story.

Before you plug in your Social Security number and other valuable information, it's important to make sure you're dealing with a reputable lender. Do a quick Google search to see if the lender is associated with any scams, and check with the Better Business Bureau.

You're going to need documentation to prove your income, so be prepared to fork over a tax return or pay stub. If you earn irregular income, then you may need to provide your tax returns for the last two years.

What to Watch Out For
Personal loans are generally a bit less trap- and fee-riddled than balance transfers. However, there are still some shady players with a few tricks up their sleeves. Here are ways lenders can get a little more for themselves:

Origination fee
→ An origination fee is a percentage of your loan that you pay when it's first disbursed.
→ If you borrow $5,000 with a 3 percent origination fee, then your fee is $150.
→ Often this fee is taken out of the loan before it's deposited into your bank account, which means you'd actually get $4,850 in your account.
→ This is not considered a shady practice, as long as the lender is up front about charging an origination fee, but you might be able to get a loan that doesn't charge this fee.

Pre-payment penalty

→ Pre-payment penalty fees are charged when you get aggressive about debt repayment and pay off your loan before the end of the term.

→ Paying the loan early ticks off lenders because they're losing money—the interest you would've been charged had you hung on until the end of your term.

→ Like the origination fee, it's not considered a shady practice if you understand it's part of the loan deal, but you can probably find a loan without pre-payment penalties.

Pre-computed interest

→ Pre-computed interest ensures that the lender still gets that sweet, sweet interest rate money even if you make large payments to aggressively pay down your debt quickly.

→ The simple (aka normal) interest method will charge you based on the principal balance still owed each month. This is why paying off your debt early saves you money.

→ Pre-computed interest charges interest based on the original terms of the loan.

→ Making early or large payments up front just means more is going to interest initially, which ensures the lender still gets the interest payments he anticipated upon giving you the loan.

→ Don't get a loan with pre-computed interest if you plan to try to pay off the loan before the end of your term.

Add-on insurance

→ Always be wary of an upsell.

→ The lender may try to sell you on additional policies for a monthly or annual fee, like unemployment or credit insurance, which is designed to help you if you find you can't pay the loan.

→ It sounds like a great option, but do you really need to be paying a monthly premium for this protection in case you happen to lose your job during the term of your loan?

→ Perhaps putting the cost of the premium in an emergency fund is a better use of your money.

Above all, *know yourself and be honest with yourself about your habits.* Will you use this properly? It's easy to fall back on personal loans to subsidize lifestyle inflation, especially if you qualify for a low interest rate option. Don't eye a personal loan to fund your lifelong dream of going to Oktoberfest or seeing the pyramids. Definitely don't use personal loans to buy an engagement ring or to invite an extra 100 people to your wedding. Personal loans can be ideal in the case of an emergency situation, or a necessary home renovation, or to aggressively pay down high-interest debt. Otherwise, don't add to your debt burden.

WHAT YOU SHOULD AVOID

Borrowing money could lead you toward some rather unsavory, potentially even predatory, businesses. There tends to be a correlation between the accessibility to cash and the cutesiness of a business name (think throwing in a K where a C or Q should be) with high interest rates and less than favorable terms for you, the borrower. Lenders offering fast cash or no credit checks should also be approached with the same caution you'd use when deciding if the person you were matched with on your dating app actually looks like the picture or won't spike your drink when you visit the bathroom.

\$ *"If you're working with anyone, then it needs to be via the non-profit route," says Singletary. You can find a certified and reputable non-profit credit counselor near you by looking on https://www.nfcc.org.*

There are two common types of lending you should avoid during both your debt repayment and the rest of your life:

→ *Payday loans.* A payday loan is a short-term loan that's supposed to cover your financial bind and get repaid on—you guessed it— payday. For this reason, the term on most payday loans is two weeks. However, if you can't repay the loan by the end of the 14th day, then you may need to "roll over" your loan, which means taking out a new loan to cover the first, and thus the vicious cycle of payday lending begins. Interest rates on payday loans, when annualized, often end up well into the hundreds range. Yes, hundreds. You could be paying 300 percent APR on a loan, primarily because it was designed to be taken out for only a couple of weeks and not a year. It seems like a quick and easy fix for a money problem, but for most people it ends up being hundreds or thousands of dollars spent in fees. A 2014 report from the Consumer Financial Protection Bureau showed that more than 80 percent of payday loans are not paid off within the 14-day period.[2]

→ *Title loans.* Title loans are similar to payday loans, but this time there's collateral if you don't pay. The collateral is often handing over the title to your car or motorcycle. Title loans are typically also short-term loans (usually about 15 to 30 days) with steep interest rates. Twenty-five percent for a one-month loan annualizes out to a 300 percent APR. Failure to pay this loan can result in your car being repossessed, which often means you then can't get to work to earn the money you need to dig yourself out of the hole.

STILL IN A BIND? HERE ARE SOME LAST-DITCH OPTIONS.

Unfortunately, there may be times when you're in such a tight bind that your only choice is to turn to a lender that's actually willing to take a chance on giving you money. Should this be your scenario, then consider these options:

→ *Charitable assistance:* The rise in online crowdfunding has increased your ability to get a helping hand from complete strangers. It isn't uncommon for families and individuals in need to use sites like GoFundMe to get through a bind. There are also charitable organizations both online, like Modest Needs, or in your community, such as the Salvation Army, Catholic Charities, or United Way.

→ *Borrowing from a loved one:* Asking friends or family for money can ultimately destroy relationships, so if you're going to do it, then do it right. Ask for the exact amount you need, draw up a contract for the two parties, and determine a payment plan—even if you're told, "Don't worry about it." A plan takes some of the stress off both parties because your loved one, the lender, doesn't have to feel awkward about asking when you'll start paying back the loan, and you, the borrower, don't have to get defensive.

→ *A cash advance:* I dislike adding this option, but I also recognize that this could be a last option and still potentially cheaper than a payday or title loan. Using a credit card to withdraw cash in order to pay off another debt is the financial equivalent of sending a nude pic via Snapchat. You think it's going be no big deal until someone takes a screenshot and plasters the image on another social media platform. In the moment, a cash advance sounds like an easy out, and in some cases, the math adds up that it's a better alternative than a payday loan. Similar to a payday loan, the interest starts accruing immediately, so this isn't like other credit card charges for which you get a grace period.

Cooper needs $500 to pay some old parking tickets and get the boot taken off his car.[3] He knows he can pay this amount back in four weeks after two paychecks, but he needs his car in order to get to work. He uses a cash advance to take out $500 at 24.99 percent APR with a 3 percent transaction fee ($15).

A payday loan would cost him $15 per each $100 he borrowed ($75) and he'd need to roll over the payday because he couldn't pay it off within two weeks, which would mean incurring another $75 charge at minimum. Cooper would already be paying $150 to borrow $500 for a month.

The credit card company charges 24.99 percent annually, so his 30-day charge will cost 0.068 percent per day (24.99 percent/365 days). $500 × 2.04 percent APR = $10.20 in interest.

Assuming Cooper can pay off the cash advance on time at the end of the month, it would've cost him $15 fee + $10.20 interest = $25.20. This pales in comparison to the payday lender fee.

Be warned that adding a cash advance to existing credit card debt is a painful decision to reverse. In fact, your cash advance may not be paid off until you've paid off existing debt, which leaves it sitting there accruing dangerously high interest rates while you slowly chip away at your current principal balance.

→ *Do your research.* Before you use a cash advance, take the time to understand how much it will cost on your credit card. You have access to this information in your cardholder agreement, or you can call the company directly.

→ *What's the interest rate?* A cash advance interest rate is almost always higher than the rate you'd pay on regular purchases. Know exactly what you'll be paying to get quick access to cash and how much that will cost you for 30 days, 60 days, 90 days . . . you get the picture.

→ *Know the fee.* With very few exceptions, credit card companies charge a fee on top of the interest rate (and the potential ATM fee) when you use a cash advance. There may be a flat-rate fee, or it may be a percentage of your transaction. For example, with a 3 percent transaction fee, a $500 advance would carry a $15 fee. Do the math before you do the deed.

→ *Avoid an ATM fee.* Should you elect to use a cash advance, try to use it without also having to pay an ATM fee. This means using a bank that matches your credit card provider, if possible.

→ *Don't take a penny more than you need.* Don't compound your pending debt problem by thinking, *What's a little more?* Take out the bare minimum you need to get yourself through an existing bind, and have a plan to pay it off before you stick your credit card into the ATM.

→ *Can you pay it back?* Be honest with yourself. Can you pay back this amount efficiently?

YOU CAN'T SUCCEED WITHOUT CHANGING YOUR HABITS

You can have all the information available about how to successfully pay down your debt—all the strategies, hacks, tips, and tricks—but it comes down to you. There's no filter to swipe over your bank account and make those negative numbers seem aesthetically pleasing. Can you seriously change your spending patterns?

One of the major roadblocks Michelle Singletary consistently witnesses is the desire to get rid of debt without changing any behaviors.

Once you make the commitment to get debt free, Singletary says you have to think of debt as "the monkey on your back." It's imperative you stop piling on—that is, stop spending so much!

FIVE ACTIONABLE STEPS TO CRUSH YOUR CONSUMER DEBT

1. *Forgive yourself:* Singletary suggests you start your journey to crushing consumer debt by forgiving yourself. Then move to the toughest step.
2. *Face the numbers:* Singletary notes that most of the people she works with don't really know how deep the debt goes because they haven't written it all down. You need to take the time to list every bit of debt and get an intimate understanding of your situation.
3. *Pick a method:* It can be Debt Snowball, Debt Avalanche, a hybrid, or just a balance transfer to ditch that bit of credit card debt you're still carrying. Identify what's likely to work best for you. Be honest about it and then go for it.
4. *You can do it on your own:* There is no need to be paying a debt relief company.
5. *Stick with it:* This is the simplest and yet toughest step. You need to stick to your action plan, but don't be afraid to pivot to a new method if your first one isn't yielding results.

Chapter 9

Student Loans: How to Handle Them Without Having a Full-On Panic Attack

THE DEPOSIT HAD BEEN SUBMITTED to secure my seat in the 2007 freshman class of a relatively well-known liberal arts school in North Carolina. I'd already started flipping through course catalogs and wondering whether or not I'd want to pledge a sorority (it seemed like the proper "American thing" to do). After spending eight years living in Asia, the prospect of returning to the United States and living more than 7,000 miles away from my family both thrilled and frightened me.

But in the midst of wondering if my reference points from *One Tree Hill* and *The O.C.* would help me acclimate back to life in the States, my father called a meeting.

My father often refers to himself as the villain in the retellings of my financial experiences, but he was a villain in the most loving of ways. Both he and my mother used tough love to ensure that my sister and I were raised to understand that hard work equated to purchasing power. Most ten-year-olds don't think, *It will take me three days of caring for the neighbor's devil-cat Bonnie in order to be able to purchase the new Christina Aguilera album*. But that's how I thought (and it was totally worth Bonnie's hissing and litter box to be able to listen to "Genie in a Bottle" on repeat).

I sat down across from my father at our formidable dining room table.

He looked me square in the eye and slid a bill across the table. After years of being required to pay for 50 percent of anything I wanted, I should've anticipated his next move.

I always knew I'd be financially responsible for a portion of my education, but I'd naïvely neglected to ask just how much was expected from me. Admittedly, I sort of thought my parents were bluffing and would generously fork over the more than $200,000 it would cost to send me to my chosen university.

Looking down at the itemized bill, I saw just how much it would set me back to attend college. My contribution would be a staggering $80,000. I didn't qualify for financial aid, and there were no scholarship offers. For a declared theater and journalism double major, this felt like an absolutely insurmountable sum to pay back with my estimated future wages.

I looked at him and said, "So what are my options?"

Then he slid another bill across the table.

I could go to college and come out debt free, if I went to St. Bonaventure University. St. Bonaventure is a small Catholic college in western New York. My mother and all eight of her siblings went there. My grandfather had been a revered English professor and golf coach there for half a century (yeah, as in 50 years).

As if it were a sign from the college admissions overlords, an academic scholarship to St. Bonaventure was in play. It wasn't a scholarship I'd specifically applied for, but rather a bundle of academic scholarships based on my transcript and one for being a legacy kid that covered—you guessed it—50 percent of tuition.

Assuming I kept the scholarship all four years, my parents would pay the other 50 percent, and I could avoid the dreaded curse of student loan debt.

We've reached the part of the story where I'm an ungrateful brat and run upstairs crying and slamming my door . . . several times, for good measure, I should add. Instead of being grateful that my parents could afford 50 percent with ease, I felt resentful they weren't willing to pay for my education in full.

But I couldn't hide up there and rage at them forever. Instead, I dried my tears and made the kind of rational decision I'd been taught to make since the Krispy Kreme donut incident of my youth (it's in chapter 1, if you missed it). Sure, I could have picked my original school and accepted the financial responsibility of student loans. But in the end, I elected to graduate debt free.

So, why do I know anything about student loans and why should you bother to continue reading?

Reason 1: Because I'm on a mission to stamp out financial illiteracy in our generation, which means I had to become an expert in all things student loans.

Reason 2: If you skip ahead to chapter 12 ("Getting Financially Naked with Your Partner"), you'll get to learn all about the risk of catching debt in your relationship. Like a majority of our generation, my partner has significant student loans, to which I will be yoked if we decide to get married. Learning the ins and outs of all things student loans has become imperative to my future budget.

Ahead you'll also find inspiring debt payoff profiles as well as expert advice from Andrew Josuweit, the 29-year-old CEO of Student Loan Hero, a company he founded to help his fellow millennials understand how to successfully pay off their student loans.

Josuweit graduated with an economics degree from Bentley University in 2009, in the depths of the recession, with $74,000 in student loan debt spread across 16 loans that were a mix of federal and private co-signed student loans. Unable to find a stable, full-time job at first, Josuweit put his loans into deferment and forbearance (explained later in this chapter) and even defaulted on some, which led to his principal debt ballooning up to $107,000. In an excellent display of millennial ingenuity, Josuweit took his struggle with student loans and combined it with his entrepreneurial spirit to launch the site Student Loan Hero. Instead of aggressively paying down his debt, Josuweit invested in himself and his business, choosing to see the extra $33,000 in interest he accrued as his version of paying for graduate school. He eventually paid off his debt faster than the standard 10-year repayment plan, and he made his last student loan payment by September 2016.

So let's figure out how you can handle your student loans without having a full-on panic attack.

SITUATION #1: I HAVEN'T GRADUATED FROM COLLEGE YET

If you're fresh out of high school or still looking to fund your college education, then there's time to avoid making some critical financial mistakes when it comes to student loans.

Federal versus Private Student Loans: Which Should You Choose?

Federal! You should always choose federal student loans. The government is a far more benevolent lender than private entities, which means you stand to receive certain perks on federal student loans. These perks will be explained in detail as you progress through this chapter, but highlights include:

→ Subsidized loans (some federal loans don't accrue interest while you're in school)
→ Grace periods (getting to delay making your first payment)
→ Deferment or forbearance (continuing to delay payment with permission from your lender)
→ Income-driven repayment plans (only paying what you can afford)
→ Student loan forgiveness (as beautiful as it sounds)

Private lenders are far less willing to let you prorate your payments based on salary. The way they see it, it's not their fault you took out $85,000 in student loans and then decided to teach in an underfunded school district because the movie *Coach Carter* just really spoke to you. Some lenders may be kind enough to extend you a grace period for six months, but when it's time to pay up, your lender doesn't care that teaching in a qualifying public school means you'd be eligible for student loan forgiveness with the federal government. Private lenders want to be repaid in cold, hard cash, not service.

$ *Student loans are extremely difficult to discharge, even in bankruptcy. Don't anticipate that even extreme measures can relieve you of this millennial hell.*

Unfortunately, it isn't always possible to completely finance your education with federal student loans. Or perhaps you've already signed on the dotted line with a private lender and are just trying to figure out how to make those loans affordable.

Luckily for us millennials, the glories of technology provide more than just immediate dating opportunities and a car at the tap of a button. A rise in the number of marketplace lenders willing to refinance student loans at lower interest rates can make those private student loan payments far more affordable. (Skip to the "The ABCs of Refinancing Student Loans" section later in this chapter if you don't care to learn more about federal student loans.)

Handling Co-Signed Student Loans

Carrying private student loans almost guarantees that your parents will need to co-sign on your loans. If you aren't able to pay, then the lender will collect from your parents. Failure to pay not only damages your credit history but also starts to ding your parents' as well. Naturally, this has the potential to cause both emotional and financial problems for you and your parents.

Andrew Josuweit faced the emotional impact of handling student loans after he couldn't afford to make payments and the lenders came calling on his parents. In order to prevent co-signed loans from causing tension in your own relationship with your parents, Josuweit recommends taking these steps:

→ Sit down with your parents and talk about your student loan situation.
→ Determine who is responsible for which loans. Some parents feel strongly about helping their children pay for college; other parents may require their offspring to pay back all the loans.
→ Go over your career plans and goals, and detail what you want to do and how you plan to get there.
→ Set realistic income expectations.
→ Create an action plan with your parents about how the loans will be paid off.
→ Be honest with one another.
→ Discuss what will happen if you can't make a payment.

You may also want to look into a basic term life insurance policy depending on how much debt your parents co-signed on and the policy of your lender. There is a possibility that if you were to die prematurely, your parents would still be on the hook for paying off your student loans. Federal loans are discharged in the case of death, but not all private lenders offer this yet if there is a co-signer. Be sure to check your policy to know if your parents would still be required to pay out the total, and decide if a basic term life insurance policy is appropriate for you.

Make Payments While You're Still in School

There's no mandate that you must wait until after you graduate from college to start paying back your loans. Making payments while you're in school doesn't do any harm. If you make a payment, you're not required to keep making payments consistently or lose your grace period. You could make one big payment at the end of each summer after working or even after the holidays if you got cash as a gift or a bonus from a job. Putting even a little money toward your loans could seriously reduce your post-graduation stress, especially if your loans are subsidized.

There are essentially two kinds of federal student loans:

→ *Subsidized loans:* The federal government picks up the tab for your interest while you're in school and during your grace period.* Any payments made on these loans during college or in the grace period will chip away directly at the principal balance.

→ *Unsubsidized loans:* Such loans do not offer the option to have interest covered by the federal government. You will be responsible for all the interest that accrues while you're in school, during your grace period, and during the repayment of your loan. The interest that accrues while you're in school and during your grace period will capitalize (get added to) the principal balance of your loan.

Interest-only payments are a valuable way to reduce your total debt burden by putting money toward your loans while you're still in school. Payments made to subsidized loans will knock down the principal balance to make the debt feel more manageable after graduation, and interest-only payments on unsubsidized loans will minimize the amount of interest that accrues and then is added to your loan post-graduation. Either way, it reduces the amount you'll have to pay over the life of the loan.

---

* There are some exceptions, such as a Direct Subsidized Loan that was first disbursed between July 1, 2012, and July 1, 2014. You would be responsible for the interest that accrued during your grace period. https://studentaid.ed.gov/sa/types/loans/subsidized-unsubsidized#subsidized-vs-unsubsidized.

Wondering how you're supposed to magically come up with money to put toward loans while you're still in school? Try some of these:

→ Participate in a work-study program.
→ Become a resident assistant.
→ Work during the summer.
→ Explore paid internships (yup, those exist now).
→ Keep applying for scholarships each year of college.
→ Get entrepreneurial on campus (as long as you aren't breaking college rules).

$ *Take advantage of your on-campus financial aid office and set up a time to speak with someone about your loan situation before you graduate. They should be able to help decode anything confusing.*

SITUATION #2: I'VE ALREADY GRADUATED—WHAT NOW?

No matter where you are in the graduation experience—just walked the stage or trying to finish these payments years later—it's helpful to understand your options. There are different ways to handle your loans depending on if they're private or federal, what type of job you work, and how aggressively you want to pay down the loans. If you're well into your repayment experience, then skip down to the sections about payment programs and refinancing. Otherwise, first let's talk about how to find all those student loans.

JOSUWEIT'S ADVICE: Tough Love Edition

→ You can't ignore your student loans.
→ There are two main options for handling repayment:
  1. Figure out a way to make more money.
  2. Figure out a way to reduce expenses.

You can cut out lattes and brown-bag it to work, but those aren't going to produce the same sort of results as moving to a city with a lower cost of living, being smart about your career development, and even reducing your tax burden (like living in a state with no state income tax).

How the Hell Do I Find My Loans?

You probably started taking on loans at 18, which is not an age that is particularly well-known for its financial savvy and attention to detail. Don't freak out if you aren't sure where to find the paperwork on your loans or how to track them down.

Got Federal Loans?

The federal government makes it pretty easy to track down your student loans. Just log into the National Student Loan Database (https://www.nslds.ed.gov), select "Financial Aid Review," input the requested information, and your loans will pop up. You will need your Federal Student Aid (FSA) ID to log in.

Once you're in, here are the types of loans and servicers you're likely to see:

Name of Loan	Details of the Loan
Federal Perkins Loan	Funded by your college; you will need to demonstrate financial need.
Direct Subsidized Loan*	Funded by the U.S. Department of Education; interest is usually not charged while you're in school full-time or on a grace period or deferment. However, you do need to demonstrate a financial need.
Direct Unsubsidized Loan*	Funded by the U.S. Department of Education; interest is charged, but financial need is not a requirement.
Direct PLUS Loan	Funded by the U.S. Department of Education and available to parents of dependent undergraduate students as well as graduate and professional students. Financial need is not required.

Learn more here: https://studentaid.ed.gov/sa/types/loans.

Federal servicers (the companies in charge of handling your loans) include the following:

---

* Also known as Stafford Loans or Direct Stafford Loans.

Servicer	Web site	Phone
CornerStone	https://www.mycornerstoneloan.org/	1-800-663-1662 Armed Forces Members Hotline: 1-844-255-8326
EdFinancial	https://www.edfinancial.com/Home	1-800-337-6884
FedLoan Servicing (PHEAA)	https://myfedloan.org/	1-800-699-2908
Granite State (GSMR)	https://www.gsmr.org/	1-888-556-0022
Great Lakes	https://www.mygreatlakes.org/	1-800-236-4300
MOHELA	https://www.mohela.com/	1-888-866-4352
Navient	http://www.navient.com/	1-800-722-1300
Nelnet	https://www.nelnet.com/	1-888-486-4722
OSLA	http://www.osla.org/	1-866-264-9762 Service members: 1-844-835-7484
VSAC	www.vsacfederalloans.org/	1-888-932-5626

Got Private Loans?

Your best bet is to pull your credit report. Your loans should be reported on your credit report, even if you haven't started making payments. You can obtain a copy of your credit report for free by going to annualcredit report.com, a government-backed Web site. You're entitled to a free copy of your report from each of the three bureaus (Experian, Equifax, and TransUnion) once per year. Common private student loan lenders include Discover, Wells Fargo, Citizens Bank, and Sallie Mae.

The Grace Period: A Delightful Gift from Your Lender

A grace period provides you with a set period of time to find a job before you need to start forking over part of your paycheck to repay loans. This time period can vary but is often approximately six months.

The grace period generally begins upon graduation, but it could be used sooner if you:

→ Drop below part-time enrollment.
→ Leave school entirely (even if it's just for a semester).

$ *Paying even just a little bit each month during your grace period can help you offset some of the interest accruing or, even better, chip away at your principal balance if your interest is subsidized.*

In most cases, you get only one grace period per loan. That means if you drop below part-time enrollment for a semester or two and use the full six-month grace period, then your loan payments will come due a month after you officially graduate or leave school.

You can also lose your grace period if you consolidate (or refinance) your loans during the grace period.

There are some noteworthy exceptions to this rule:

→ *Military duty:* You're using a grace period but get called to military duty more than 30 days before the end of your grace period. You'll be granted another six full months upon your return.

→ *Return to school:* You left school but decided to re-enroll to at least part-time status before the end of your grace period. You will likely receive the full six-month grace period when you graduate or drop below part-time enrollment.

Not all federal student loans are eligible for a grace period. PLUS loans will not receive a grace period, and you need to check in with your school to determine the grace period on a Federal Perkins Loan.

Your lender may continue to pay the interest on subsidized loans during your grace period. Unsubsidized loans will continue to accrue interest during the grace period. This accrued interest will capitalize on your principal balance at the end of your grace period. Make sure to figure out which categories your loans fall into.

STUDENT LOAN PAYOFF PROFILE: Melanie Lockert

Melanie Lockert, freelance writer and event planner
Age: 31
Location: Los Angeles
Schools: California State University, Long Beach, and New York University
Major: Theater and Performance Studies
Student loan debt: $81,000 principal + interest for approximately $100,000 total
Time to pay off: 9.5 years

Melanie started out her college career knowing she'd need to finance her education without financial support from her parents. She borrowed $23,000 for her undergraduate degree from California State University, Long Beach, and then an additional $58,000 for her graduate school degree from New York University.

She spent the first five years after getting her undergrad degree just making minimum payments and treating her loans like any other bill in her budget, even when her income increased. Melanie entered the workforce for a few years after getting her undergrad degree and then decided to get her master's. She still paid on her student loans while in a one-year accelerated MA program for Performance Studies at NYU. After graduating from NYU and seeing the cost of her undergrad debt combined with her graduate school debt, Melanie decided to get serious about tackling her debt and paid off $68,000 in 4.5 years.

Strategies Melanie used to get debt free:

→ Left New York City for Portland, Oregon's lower cost of living.
→ Shared a studio apartment with her boyfriend to make the rent cheaper.
→ Cut expenses to the bare minimum, living like a broke college student into her early thirties.

→ Started side hustles, which led her to a new career in writing about money and event planning, often for financial services companies.

→ Put every tax return, bonus, and raise toward paying down her debt.

→ Tapped her emergency fund for the final payments just to get the debt down—a strategy she wouldn't advocate for others.

Melanie says, "Everything has changed [since I started my debt repayment journey]. I found a purpose. I created a new career. I learned how to make more money, which has given me a lot of confidence. I know that I can get through tough times and now realize how resilient I am."

Melanie currently lives in Los Angeles and is focused on re-building her emergency savings fund, saving for retirement, and building her career. You can learn more about Melanie's journey on her blog, DearDebt.com.

Delaying Payment Without Painful Consequences (Deferment and Forbearance)

The federal government doesn't stop the gift giving at grace periods. It actually provides struggling borrowers the opportunity to stop making payments on student loans.

Don't get too excited. There are some catches.

First of all, the ability to delay payments doesn't last indefinitely. You have a window of time, often 12 to 36 months, which depends on the type of deferment or forbearance.

Second, you have to prove your financial need, such as hardship from a job loss, illness, or military duty. Your student loan fairy godmother isn't just going to bequeath unto you the ability to stop repaying your debts.

Third, deferment and forbearance are not the same thing.

What's the Difference?

When given a choice, deferment is better than forbearance because it allows you to temporarily stop making payments, *and* the interest may be subsidized by the government.

Forbearance also provides the ability to stop making payments (or at least reduce them) for up to 12 months. However, interest will continue accruing, even if you are paying off a subsidized loan.

How Do I Enroll in Deferment?

You need to reach out to your loan servicer or, for a Perkins Loan, you need to contact the school you attended. Explain your situation and see if you qualify. Eligible reasons for deferment may include:

→ Enrollment at least half-time in college or trade school.
→ A period of unemployment or difficulty finding full-time work.
→ A period of economic hardship.
→ Being on active military duty or in the midst of the 13 months following your service.

As you can see, some of these are a bit subjective, and lenders aren't exactly eager to hand out deferments. If you don't qualify for deferment, then ask about forbearance.

$ *Call your loan servicer before you miss a payment. You lose a lot of leverage when you go into delinquency or default.*

How Do I Enroll in Forbearance?

There are two types of forbearance: mandatory and discretionary.

Your lender can decide whether or not to approve you under *discretionary forbearance* (includes issues like illness or financial hardship). *Mandatory forbearance* may occur under these conditions:

→ You're in the midst of a medical or dental internship or residency program, and you also meet certain requirements as defined by the program.
→ Your monthly payments are more than 20 percent of your total monthly gross income (if this is the case, you should jump to the income-driven repayment section in this chapter).
→ You're a recipient of a national service award and are serving in a national service position.

→ You're eligible for teacher loan forgiveness.

→ You're eligible for a partial repayment of your loan thanks to the U.S. Department of Defense Student Loan Repayment Program.

→ You're a member of the National Guard who has been called up, but you don't qualify for military deferment.

Even if one of these scenarios applies to you, you still need to call your loan servicer. *You won't automatically be enrolled in deferment or forbearance.* You also shouldn't delay in applying because you think maybe things will get better next month. If you're struggling now, go ahead and see if you're eligible for forbearance or deferment.

Failure to enroll in forbearance or deferment and then missing your payments is going to seriously screw with your financial life.

Delaying Payment with Painful Consequences (Delinquency and Default)

Asking for forgiveness instead of permission may work in certain circumstances, but not when it comes to missing student loan payments.

In other words, asking to miss a payment by enrolling in deferment or forbearance is one thing, but just skipping your monthly bills entirely is a bad move.

Ditching payments can annihilate your credit score and make your credit report a nightmare to clean up. Your future self would happily find a wormhole to come back and slap you across the face for ignoring your student loan bill.

When Am I Delinquent?

$ *Did something trip you up, and, despite your long history of making on-time payments, did you suddenly miss one? A goodwill letter, which asks for forgiveness and shows a track record of on-time payments, may convince the lender or servicer to remove the late payment from your credit report.*

It takes only one day. Your student loans are delinquent the day after you miss a payment. The loans stay delinquent until you're caught up. If you haven't paid after 90 days, your servicer will likely report the delinquency to the credit bureaus.

When Am I in Default?
Default status is attained when you fail to pay your loans for 270 days (330 days if you have a FFEL Program loan).

What Happens If I Default?
Default will not only rip your credit report to shreds (which could mean it will be hard to get credit cards, an apartment, a job), but also:

→ You lose your eligibility for deferment or forbearance or to enter into an income-driven repayment program.

→ Your wages could be garnished to repay a loan.

→ Your tax refund could be withheld to repay a federal loan.

→ Collection agencies might start calling.

→ You lose your eligibility to apply for any other federal student aid.

It's not a pretty situation.

If you're worried about missing payments because you simply can't afford to pay, then consider an income-driven repayment plan for your federal student loans.

WHAT MADE YOU REALIZE YOU WANTED TO GET RID OF YOUR LOANS ASAP?

There were all these huge, beautiful mansions on the water. I hadn't been on the water very much at all, and I really had never seen those kind of houses up close. I mentioned that I wanted to live in one of those someday, and Jim basically said: "You'll never live in one of those with $40,000 of student loans on a teacher's salary." Boom. That was it. I started making large payments the next payday.

—Bobby Hoyt, founder of Millennial Money Man;
he paid off $40,000 in 1.5 years on a teacher's salary.

What Is an Income-Driven Repayment Plan?
Remember when you used to watch TV on actual cable, and during the holiday season you'd hear commercials advertising the ability to buy pres-

ents on layaway? Just pay a little bit over time and eventually it's yours! I like to think of income-driven repayment plans as the layaway option for student loans.

Many (but not all) federal student loans are eligible* for income-driven repayment plans. These plans are not all created equally, but they all do help make your monthly student loan payment more affordable by capping the amount you have to pay as a percentage of your discretionary income. A formula is used to figure out your discretionary income based on how much of your adjusted gross income exceeds the poverty line as determined by your state. (It's okay if your eyes just glazed over.)

There are four main types of income-driven repayment plans:

1. **Pay As You Earn (PAYE)**

    Payment: Usually 10 percent of your discretionary income, but never more than you'd pay under the Standard Repayment Plan.

    Forgiven after: 20 years.

    Eligibility: Your monthly payment must be less than what it would be under a standard 10-year repayment plan. You must be a new borrower as of October 1, 2007, with a disbursement of a Direct Loan on or after October 1, 2011.

2. **Revised Pay As You Earn (REPAYE)**

    Payment: Usually 10 percent of your discretionary income.

    Forgiven after: 20 years for undergraduate, 25 years for graduate loans.

    Eligibility: Any borrower with eligible student loans.

3. **Income-Based Repayment Plan (IBR)**

    Payment: Usually 10 percent or 15 percent of your discretionary income, but never more than you'd pay under the Standard Repayment Plan.

    Forgiven after: 20 years for new borrowers, 25 for others.

    Eligibility: Your monthly payment must be less than what it would be under the standard 10-year repayment plan and be a new borrower. New borrowers pay 10 percent, while others owe 15 percent.

---

* Note on loan eligibility: Not all student loans are eligible for a repayment plan in their current state, but consolidating loans under a Federal Direct Consolidation Loan usually converts non-eligible loans to eligible status. Parent PLUS loans can even be eligible for ICR if consolidated.

New borrower status is determined if you borrowed on or after July 1, 2014.* It will be 15 percent if you're not a new borrower as of July 1, 2014.

4. **Income-Contingent Repayment Plan (ICR)**
   Payment: The lesser of either 20 percent of your discretionary income or what you would pay on a repayment plan with a fixed payment over the course of 12 years, adjusted according to your income.
   Forgiven after: 25 years.
   Eligibility: Any borrower with eligible student loans.

$ *Don't pay to have a third party handle your federal student loans. There are plenty of predatory services offering to enroll you in a "new" payment plan or forgiveness program—for a fee, of course. You can enroll in any federal program for free. Save the money and put it toward your loans.*

Those with FFEL loans can look into the much less publicized Income-Sensitive Repayment Plan. This program will decrease (or increase) your payments based on your income and are made for a maximum of 10 years—the standard repayment period.

You can use the Repayment Estimator from the Federal Student Aid Web site (studentloans.gov) in order to get a rough of idea of your new monthly payment.

How Repayment Programs Work

First, you consolidate your federal loan through the Federal Direct Consolidation Loan. Then you enroll in a repayment plan. There are regulations about which one you can join based on when your loan was disbursed.

Once enrolled, your payments are capped at 10, 15, or 20 percent of your discretionary income, depending on your program. You continue to make monthly payments. If you still have debt after 20 to 25 years (depends on the program), then the remainder is discharged.

---

* According to Studentaid.ed.gov: "For the IBR Plan, you're considered a new borrower on or after July 1, 2014, if you had no outstanding balance on a William D. Ford Federal Direct Loan (Direct Loan) Program loan or Federal Family Education Loan (FFEL) Program loan when you received a Direct Loan on or after July 1, 2014. (Because no new FFEL Program loans have been made since June 30, 2010, only Direct Loan borrowers can qualify as new borrowers on or after July 1, 2014.)"

As of now, the discharged amount could be taxable. However, the regulations around taxing discharged student loans are subject to change. What does that mean for you? About five years before your loans are subject to getting discharged (you know, like two decades from now), you should start saving some money for the tax bill so you aren't blindsided.

Do Payments Stay the Same During the Entire Repayment Period?

No, you'll need to reapply and submit information each year. Various factors can impact the size of your monthly payment, such as:

→ Increase or decrease in income
→ Marriage (and filing joint taxes)
→ Increased family size

Who Should Utilize These Programs?

Anyone struggling to meet the minimum payments on federal student loans should enroll. These programs are also ideal for those with high student loan debt but lower-paying jobs, who are therefore unable to repay the debt on a Standard Repayment Plan of 10 years. These programs won't necessarily be useful if you can pay off your debt in 10 years, because there won't be anything left to discharge.

Loan Forgiveness Programs

Once again, the federal government comes sweeping in as the sugar daddy of student loans. Okay, that sounds a bit gross. Let's go with "benefactor in exchange for many years of your labor."

There are several types of student loan forgiveness or loan cancellation programs available, but the underlying theme is exchanging years of work in some form of public service for discharged loans.

Like most student loan perks, this applies only to federal loans.

Public Service Loan Forgiveness (PSLF)

One of the most common forms of forgiveness is Public Service Loan Forgiveness. After you work in eligible public service positions for 10 years, the remainder of your debt will be forgiven. The program was founded in 2007, so at the time of publication the first wave of graduates is having loans discharged.

Those planning to enroll must do the following:

→ Consolidate your federal loans.
→ Get on an income-driven repayment plan.
→ Make 120 payments (10 years' worth).
→ Stay in eligible positions, such as working for the government or for an eligible non-profit.
→ Fill out and submit the appropriate paperwork every year.

For the procrastinators, know that you need to be meticulous about filling out your paperwork each year. You don't submit it until the very end of the 10-year period, but can you imagine trying to track down a boss from 10 years ago to sign off that you performed your job? Just get him or her to sign the form now, and be done with it!

Check with Your State

Some states provide niche forgiveness programs. Be sure to do your research early. You may even be eligible for a program that helps offset future education costs, such as graduate or medical school. Check your state's Web site (which should pop up if you google "[state name] student loan forgiveness program"). New York State, for example, offers the NYS Nursing Faculty Loan Forgiveness (NFLF) Incentive Program.

Check with Your School

Your university may also offer a forgiveness program. These programs, much like grants, aren't often highly advertised, so you'll need to check in with the financial aid office or ask around your alumni networks.

The ABCs of Refinancing Student Loans

Are you sick of only hearing about the perks of federal loans when you've shackled yourself to tens of thousands of dollars in private debt? Or maybe you have mostly federal loans but aren't eligible for any forgiveness programs and just want to pay down the debt as aggressively as possible.

Enter refinancing.

What Exactly Is Refinancing?

Your student loans carry a 7.05 percent APR (which is similar to interest but factors in an annualized fee) and are being serviced by Bank Bleeding-YouDry. The interest rate is 6.25 percent. Bank WeCareALittleMore is willing to offer you a rate of 3.50 percent if you move your debt over. So you take out the loan with Bank WeCareALittleMore and pay off the loan at Bank BleedingYouDry. You now just have the new loan at Bank WeCare-ALittleMore with a 3.50 percent APR, which means you can pay it off both faster and with less interest.

Who Can Refinance?

The student loan refinancing space is still fairly new, which means many lenders tend to be a little cautious with their underwriting (the criteria used to approve borrowers). Typically, you can get the best interest rates if you:

→ Have a 700+ credit score.
→ Have been employed for at least a year.
→ Have made at least six months of payments on your student loans.
→ Never missed a payment nor had loans in default.

Consequences of Refinancing Federal Student Loans

I know. I know. You're tired of hearing about federal loans, but let me just get this disclaimer out of the way.

If you refinance any federal loans, you will give up the perks associated with those loans. No option for income-driven repayment programs. No student loan forgiveness. No deferment or forbearance. It's game over. And much like accidentally leaving a red T-shirt in with your white laundry, there is no reversing the consequences.

Where Can I Refinance a Student Loan?

There are lots of start-ups providing refinancing. But you're a millennial—doing this entirely online without ever interacting with a real person shouldn't be a deterrent.

These quickly growing companies include SoFi, Earnest, DRB, and CommonBond.

You should always do your due diligence on a company before taking out a loan by reading reviews and checking with organizations like the Better Business Bureau to avoid scams. Then you should see which lender is willing to offer you the best rate.

Do I Have to Refinance All of My Loans?

No, you don't have to refinance all of your loans. For example, some may be federal on an income-driven repayment plan, while others are private with a high interest rate. You can refinance the private loans and leave the federal ones alone on the income-driven repayment plan.

What Are My Options If I Didn't Graduate but Have Student Loans?

Unfortunately, being in the position of carrying student loans without a degree is one of the least negotiable options. Federal loans could still be put on an income-driven repayment plan, but private loans are tough to handle as refinancing is likely not an option; lenders typically include having a degree as part of the underwriting criteria.

ANDREW JOSUWEIT'S ADVICE

→ Focus on increasing your salary as much as possible.
→ Consider going to community college for your degree or for the first two years before transferring to a four-year college program to complete your degree. This also should have a lower cost than attending a four-year school.

SIMPLE TRICKS TO REDUCE YOUR DEBT BURDEN QUICKLY
Trick 1: Pay Above the Minimum

For all the reasons outlined in chapter 10, digging out of debt efficiently means paying above the minimum due. Student loan payments are designed to get you to repay the principal balance plus interest during a set period of time (often 10 years). Every little bit you pay above the monthly payment will help shave time off your overall repayment journey.

In fact, a mere $10 more a month will save you hundreds of dollars and even take a year off your debt repayment timetable.

STUDENT LOAN PAYOFF PROFILE: Zina Kumok

Zina Kumok, freelance writer and founder of DebtFreeAfter
   Three.com
Age: 27
School: Indiana University in Bloomington, Indiana
Major: Journalism
Student loan debt: $28,000 ($24,000 in principal + $4,000 in
   interest)
Time to pay off: 3 years

Zina received scholarships and financial assistance from her parents but still needed to take out loans to cover the cost of out-of-state tuition at Indiana University. At graduation, Zina had $24,000 in principal student loan debt, only $4,000 shy of her starting salary. Even though she earned only $28,000 a year—and didn't have any savings—she still contributed $10 a month toward her loans. This seemingly insignificant sum shaved a year off her standard 10-year repayment plan.

"Once I saw how much money was going to interest," Zina said, "I became determined to pay off my loans as soon as possible. I hated feeling like I was chained down to my debt. Anytime I bought something, I thought about my loans and how that money could go toward them. I really felt trapped by my debt and that I couldn't live the life I wanted."

Zina embraced that trapped feeling and tapped into it as motivation to aggressively pay down her debt. "I started putting all my money toward my debt. Anytime I had a bonus, birthday check, or freelance assignment, I put that money toward my debt. When I got a small pay increase and moved to a cheaper city, I put the difference in my budget toward my loans. I did that again a year later when I moved in with my then-boyfriend and a friend of ours and put the rent difference toward my loans."

Then, on November 18, 2014, Zina logged into Nelnet.com to find her final payment on her loans and the words "Paid in full by borrower" displayed on the screen. Then she had to take out her dog and do the dishes, just like any other day. But a lot of things have changed for Zina since becoming debt free. "As soon as I became debt free, my then-fiancé (now husband) and I merged our finances. We used the extra money to save for an emergency fund and moving expenses. Now we're saving for a rental property we hope to buy in the next couple years that will bring in passive income."

Trick 2: Tell Servicer to Apply Any Extra Payment to Principal Debt

Your loan servicer can do something a little sneaky once you start to make those extra payments above your monthly minimum. Instead of applying that extra money to your principal balance, your loan servicer can apply it, first, to outstanding fees; second, to interest (including future interest); and, third, to your principal balance, which doesn't help you get out of debt efficiently. This is especially true if you have more than one loan with the servicer, because your servicer is probably spreading the love around instead of applying those extra payments where it's most beneficial for you. The best way to use your extra payment will be to focus it on one loan specifically instead of spreading it across the balances you owe.

$ *Be warned: You might see that you start owing "$0" a month because your extra payments have added up enough that you've paid ahead and covered the interest accrued since your last payment. Keep making payments. If you stop, then you'll just end up accruing interest again.*

Here's the plan of attack to counteract this devilish plot:

1. Decide which loan you want to prioritize for paying down, while still continuing to make minimum payments on all other loans. For the sake of simplicity, it may be easier to just decide whether you're going with the Debt Avalanche method or the Debt Snowball before contacting your servicer. We'll pretend you're doing a Snowball and Avalanche hybrid.

2. Send your servicer a formal letter (find a template option in the endnotes) via e-mail or old-school mail stating that you want any additional amount over your minimum payment to be applied toward the loan with the smallest principal balance.[1] If there are multiple loans with the same balance, ask the servicer to apply it to the loan with the highest interest rate. You should send this request via certified mail or follow up shortly afterward to ensure that it was received.

3. Track your loans each month to ensure that the payments are being applied properly and that your principal balances are actually starting to decrease.

4. Keep making those aggressive payments on a set schedule, even when you see that it's $0 due (despite still having a balance) or that your payment due date is suddenly months away.

Servicers don't hide the fact that they can apply payments in this way. See their Web sites:

→ FedLoan Servicing: https://myfedloan.org/borrowers/payments-billing/paying-ahead
→ Great Lakes: https://www.mygreatlakes.org/educate/knowledge-center/how-payments-are-applied.html
→ Sallie Mae: https://www.salliemae.com/student-loans/managing-your-loans/pay-and-manage-your-loan/payment-allocations/

Trick 3: Opt for Bi-Weekly Payments

If you get paid on a bi-weekly schedule, then you probably know that two months a year you get those sweet, sweet three-paycheck months. You can also leverage the weeks in a year to squeeze out an extra student loan payment. And no, it doesn't have to come out of your third-that-month paycheck.

Some lenders allow you to set up bi-weekly payments. You'll pay your student loan twice a month instead of once.

Don't worry, this doesn't mean you pay the minimum due twice. Instead, you split it in half. For example, if you owe $400 a month, then you'll pay $200 in week 2 and $200 in week 4, for a total of $400.

Using this repayment strategy actually forces you to make 26 bi-weekly payments, or 13 payments a year, instead of 12. It won't be an extra squeeze on your wallet either, thanks to those glorious three-paycheck months. This strategy is an incredibly beneficial way to pay off debt faster, especially if you can combine it with Trick 1 and pay a little (or a lot) more than the minimum payment.

Trick 4: Combine Debt Snowball and Debt Avalanche

Debt Snowball, the psychological path of paying off the smallest to the largest debt, and Debt Avalanche, the mathematical path of addressing highest-interest-rate loans before lower-rate loans, as outlined in chapter 8, helped Andrew Josuweit pay off his loans efficiently. While many people commit to one plan over the other, Josuweit used a hybrid method.

He found loans with high interest rates but smaller principal balances and focused on paying those down. This enabled him to get some of the financial win of paying off high-interest loans, while also having the psychological boost of paying off a loan quickly. He focused primarily on the Debt Snowball method to keep himself motivated.

> Figure out what your priorities are—mine were becoming debt free and traveling. Anything outside of that—such as going out, buying takeout, or shopping at full price—was out of the question. That doesn't mean I never did it, but it was something I actively avoided. Pick one or two other things to focus on besides your debt so you're not solely living a boring life.
>
> —Zina Kumok, paid off $28,000 of
> student loan debt in three years

GO MASTER THOSE STUDENT LOANS

Mix and match the tools outlined in this chapter to create the best strategy in your personal student loan situation. What worked for Bobby, Zina, Melanie, or Andrew may not be the perfect combination for you, but there's some perfect combination of extra payments, refinancing, income-driven repayment plans, and side hustling out there to help crush your student loans. At the very least, add an extra $10 to one of your student loan payments to shave off a year of time.

🔧 STUDENT LOAN ACTION LIST

❑ Find all your student loans.
  → Federal loans: National Student Loan Database (https://www
    .nslds.ed.gov).
  → Private loans: Pull your credit report (annualcreditreport.com).
  → Ask your parents; they might know where all the bodies are
    buried.
❑ Determine if your loans are federal or private.
  → Only federal loans will be on nslds.ed.gov.
  → A Federal Direct Loan, a Federal Perkins Loan, Direct Loan
    Consolidation, and a Stafford Loan are all federal loans.
  → Loans from major banks like Wells Fargo, Chase, Discover,
    and often even Sallie Mae are private.
❑ First-time payer? Connect with your servicer before the end of
  your grace period to find out the due date of your first pay-
  ment and the minimum due.
❑ Begin making *at least* the minimum payment due (the higher
  the better).
  → Remember, just an additional $10 a month can shave a full
    year off your total repayment term.
❑ Can't afford the minimum? Consider putting your federal
  student loans on an income-driven repayment plan such as
  IBR, REPAYE, or PAYE.
  → Your loans must first go through the Federal Direct Consoli-
    dation process.
  → You can initiate the process via your student loan servicer.
  → You will need to provide proof of income with old tax returns
    or a recent pay stub.
  → You never need to pay a third-party service to enroll you in
    one of these programs.
❑ Check if you're eligible to have your federal student loans
  forgiven through a program such as Public Service Loan
  Forgiveness (PSLF) or Teacher Loan Forgiveness.

→ Loans usually need to be on an income-driven repayment program to be eligible.

→ Determine if you truly plan to stay in that line of work for the required time period to benefit from forgiveness.

❏ Refinance your student loans if that makes sense.

→ You need to have graduated, have a steady source of income, and a 700+ credit score to be a contender.

→ Refinancing can reduce your interest rate and consolidate your loans into one payment, making it cheaper and easier to pay them back.

→ Refinancing makes the most sense for private student loans.

→ Don't refinance federal loans unless you've got well-funded emergency savings, are stable in your career, and have no plans to get loans forgiven.

→ Once you refinance federal loans, there is no going back. You lose eligibility for all federal perks like income-driven repayment and forgiveness.

RESOURCES TO UTILIZE

Student loans can be an overwhelming and constantly evolving topic. You can keep digging deeper by using these Web sites:

→ Federal Student Aid (http://studentaid.ed.gov)

→ National Student Loan Database (https://www.nslds.ed.gov)

→ Consumer Financial Protection Bureau (http://www.consumer finance.gov/paying-for-college/repay-student-debt/)

Chapter 10

I've Got Debt, So Why Should I Care About Saving? (Pay Yourself First)

EMILY GOETSCHIUS HAD A PLAN. She was going to be debt free, and fast—so she put every extra penny in her budget toward paying down her existing credit card and student loan balances. Goetschius, then a full-time college student, began accumulating credit card debt in a classic way: buying textbooks for classes. Despite having a part-time job at McDonald's during school to help bring in some money, Goetschius continued to use her credit cards as a cash flow reserve. Moments in her life like finishing up school, moving out of state, working a series of low-paying jobs, going back to school, getting divorced, and even covering groceries and basic toiletries became moments when she would dip into that reserve. No matter what, Goetschius dutifully made the minimum payments due on her cards in order to avoid negative marks on her credit report. But those balances kept rising.

In 2014, at the age of 27, Goetschius received a raise and could finally start covering her living expenses without the aid of credit. After crunching the numbers, she realized she could also put some extra money toward her existing debt. In the years since buying those first textbooks, her outstanding balances had accumulated to $4,198.17 across three cards with APRs ranging from 17 percent to 24 percent. By December 2014, she'd knocked her debt down to $1,193.14.

That's when it happened.

Goetschius had been so focused on her dream of escaping her debtors' clutches that she had completely ignored her savings account. Then, two days before Christmas, she walked out of her apartment, suitcase in hand, ready to drive home for the holidays—and discovered her car was not in the shape she'd left it in the night before.

Someone had slammed into Goetschius's car and fled the scene without filing a report or leaving their insurance information. That meant it was on her, and her auto insurance, to pay for the $4,000 of repairs. Her year of debt repayment success was reversed in one night because the lack of a savings buffer meant she had to finance her deductible using a credit card with a 17 percent APR.

By July 2016, Goetschius had brought down her debt to a mere $594.50 with a combination of the Debt Snowball strategy and a balance transfer, but she also changed her focus exclusively from debt repayment to simultaneously funding an emergency savings account.* The car accident inspired her to rework her budget in order to contribute 10 percent of each paycheck toward savings and contribute toward her company 401(k). Goetschius, now 29 and an archaeological field technician and corporate health-care administrator, even got a roommate so she could increase her debt contributions from $100 above the minimum payment due to $300.

Once her credit cards are completely paid off, Goetschius's next move will be to use either the Debt Snowball or Debt Avalanche approach to attack her student loans. But she won't stop saving this time. Goetschius plans to set aside six months of living expenses in her emergency savings fund so she can transition out of her job in health care to focus full-time on her career in archaeology.

LET'S GET THE CLICHÉ OUT OF THE WAY: PAY YOURSELF FIRST

"Pay yourself first" is the war cry of personal finance experts. It means the first thing you do with a paycheck is to save a chunk instead of waiting until the end of the month and hoping there is some left over. It's a tweetable but actionable piece of advice, and therefore also some of the most diluted advice you'll find on how to manage your money. While sound in theory, it seems absolutely ridiculous when you're looking at your credit card statement, student loan payment, rent bill, and all those other pesky money drains like feeding yourself. You feel fortunate enough to just break even at the end of the month, let alone start the month by tucking money away in an account you aren't supposed to touch.

Well, too bad.

Saving money prevents you from sinking deeper into debt by providing

---

* Both are explained in chapter 8.

a buffer when you hit a streak of bad luck and everything you own suddenly breaks. The other option is to finance your emergencies on a credit card and begin or continue the downward spiral of high interest and a principal balance that refuses to decrease.*

This is why financial professionals and enthusiasts everywhere, myself included, continue to chant "pay yourself first" as a mantra.

Paying yourself first also implies that you have some understanding of your cash flow, which means that, yes, you must set a budget.† A detailed understanding of how much is coming in and how much is going out enables you to find where it's possible to slash non-essential purchases, at least for now, and repurpose those savings to an actual savings account, which had better earn at least 1.00 percent APY (chapter 5 coaches you on how to pick the best financial products).

There's no harm in starting small, like $10 per paycheck. Saving less than what it costs to buy a craft cocktail in New York City may sound completely pointless, but it's more about forming the habit. There's no *Secreting* your way to success here. Wishing and visualizing fat stacks in your bank account will not fat stacks make.

The secret of saving money #1: Once you start living with 10 fewer dollars each month, you just adapt. The same then goes for $20, $50, even $100. Starting the process gradually reduces the pinch and makes it easier to keep saving.

Where to Find the Money to Save

There are ultimately two ways to dig yourself out of your current situation: Earn more, or spend less.

Okay, okay, I get that those are easy to say and not so easy to do. But while the first may not be a possibility right now, the second *is* completely within your control. When you start slashing your spending, there is a magical opportunity to start saving. The same goes for earning more, as long as your lifestyle costs don't inflate with your salary, but that may feel

---

* Dealing with consumer debt? Be sure to read chapter 8.
† Seriously, just do it. There are so many ways that certainly one will speak to you. Flip to chapter 4 in order to find your perfect strategy.

more insurmountable as a beginning step to increasing your personal wealth.

How to Automate Your Savings

Set up your "pay yourself first" contribution to route directly from your paycheck into your savings account. If you have strong self-control, you can nix automation if you must and just route the money directly as soon as your paycheck hits your bank account, but that does leave a lot of room for you to rationalize why you don't need to save so much this month. Those of you who elect not to automate savings from your paycheck should move the predetermined amount as soon as it hits your account. If you can, start by saving 10 percent of your monthly income, but if that feels too steep, just get into the habit of moving $5 or $10.

You can speak to your human resources department about getting a portion of your paycheck automated into savings: just arrive with your bank account number and routing number in hand. There's also a chance you can set this up yourself through whatever employee benefits portal may exist within your company. The final option is to have your bank set up an automatic transfer for you on a certain date and time. The only issue here is that you need to be sure the money will clear your account before the transfer initiates so you don't accidentally end up with an overdraft fee.

As you develop the habit of saving, you should also be giving those dollars a purpose. You can work your way up to saving for the down payment on a house or a new car, but you should be sure to start with building an emergency savings fund.

THE FIRST SAVINGS ACCOUNT YOU NEED: AN EMERGENCY FUND

The emergency fund is part of your overall savings strategy. You should have goals other than just a fully funded emergency savings account—like retirement—but this is a foundational part of your financial journey. Debt or no debt, the emergency fund serves as your panic box when the budget busters strike and leave your bank account drained. Murphy's Law naturally suggests the opportune time for such an attack to occur is exactly when you've just maxed out your credit card and need to wait another two weeks for a paycheck.

Classic financial wisdom dictates that at least six months of living expenses is a sound buffer against the threat of the unexpected, but alas, that's quite unrealistic for the student-loan-debt-burdened, underemployed millennial cliché. So here are the updated guidelines for a millennial's emergency fund:

→ *When you have debt: $1,000 minimum (if it's just you).* Whether it's student loans, consumer debt, or a fun mix, you need to have at least $1,000 squirreled away for when you get hit upside the head with the bad karma stick. And it's going to happen. If you have dependents, even a pet, I recommend doubling that minimum, or striving for $1,500. Things are going to unexpectedly happen to loved ones too.

→ *When you don't have debt (or it's highly manageable, low-interest debt): 6 months of living expenses.* Yes, the common advice still stands. Know how much you need to cover a month of basic living expenses—your thrice-a-week happy hours might need to get nixed in this scenario—and have at least six months of that number in liquid savings. That means not invested in the stock market and not contributed to your company 401(k), just sitting pretty in your savings account. When everything goes sideways, you really don't want to have to deal with selling off investments to pay rent.

→ *When you're a freelancer: 9 months of living expenses.* Everything is more expensive when you're your own boss. Health care, taxes, and even saving are up to you. And working with a variable income is stressful, so it makes sense to pad your emergency savings fund with more than you would as a traditional office employee.

And seriously, if that money isn't in an account with at least 1.00 percent APY, then I've taught you nothing!

The secret of saving money #2: Put your savings in an account you don't see when you log into your main checking account. This probably means using a different bank entirely. The out of sight, out of mind principle will apply when you feel a bit strapped for cash. This way your savings isn't sitting right in front of you saying, "Hey, you can skim some off the top here!" and it's easier to let it continue to accumulate.

THE FUCK-OFF FUND

In January 2016, an article on TheBillfold.com rocked the personal finance world. The story chronicles the journey of a recent college graduate who ventures into the world prepared for complete domination. She's got the job and the boyfriend and even knows self-defense because, dammit, she can take care of herself. But through a string of seemingly normal financial decisions (leasing a new car, going to happy hours, shopping for professional attire) she finds herself in an all-too-typical financial bind. Her boss starts to subtly, then overtly, sexually harass her, but she needs the job. Her boyfriend gets abusive, but he's covering the rent. Then the story flips, and the writer points out how if all those seemingly small decisions—like maxing out a credit card and leasing a new car instead of keeping the clunker—had been reversed, then the saved-up cash could've allowed the heroine to quit when the creepy boss made a move or eased the decision to leave the boyfriend behind for good.

It wasn't a revolutionary idea, but the emotions it invoked suddenly left even the most financially stable individuals scrambling to double down on savings. This account was cheekily named the Fuck-Off Fund. (Sorry, Mom and Dad, if you're reading this. But hey, we made it nine chapters without saying the F-word!)

"The Fuck-Off Fund is the money someone needs to be able to walk away from any terrible situation or person with two middle fingers in the air, if needed. And sometimes it is needed," explained Paulette Perhach, the 34-year-old Seattle, Washington–based writer who penned the original article.

$ *When we say "emergency fund," there's no emotion attached to it, because it's too vague. So while my Fuck-Off Fund is my emergency fund, calling it my Fuck-Off Fund reminds me of the power it gives me to choose my life and not be subject to the whims of others.* —Paulette Perhach

Perhach admits the story was inspired by her memories of feeling financially helpless when faced with adversity in her youth.

"My indebtedness muted me, a consequence I hadn't before considered when I was just being young and too 'fun' to care about debt," Perhach told me. "I couldn't say what I really wanted to say, and I wasn't being the kind of strong, independent woman I wanted to be. I hadn't realized, before, that I was leading myself into that trap. No one had ever warned me in this way before."

While the Fuck-Off Fund is really no different than an emergency savings fund, it's important to note that it's not just for women! Perhach says she wrote from a woman's perspective because, spoiler alert, she is one. But she's quick to point out that men can also find themselves in uncomfortable work and relationship situations. There's no gender bias when it comes to the importance of saving.

There's also no rule that it's either/or when it comes to savings accounts. You can certainly have an emergency fund earmarked for pending events—like the fact that I have two baby teeth, and one day they'll crack and cost me $5,000 per tooth to fix. Or you can have just one Fuck-Off Fund for whatever life throws your way. Or you can mix and match! One savings fund for pending doom (broken teeth) *and* one to be able to walk away from a douche partner or sketchy job situation, in case your teeth happen to break the same day your boss tries to feel you up.

HOW TO SAVE WHEN EVERY PENNY ALREADY FEELS SPOKEN FOR

Disclaimer: Before you get frustrated about your ability to save while reading the following list, beware that it sometimes takes a while before these tips yield any real savings. You may be faced with difficult situations before you're able to build any substantial emergency savings buffer. If this happens, you may have to make the call about which bill you can skip this month in lieu of paying something more important (like skipping out on your water bill in order to cover rent and a car payment). In these scenarios, it is best to ask for permission first. Call the company, explain your situation, and see if you can perhaps get a grace period. Then be sure to catch up as quickly as possible.

Know Your Cash Flow

There's zero way around this. You cannot understand your money and how to best manage it unless you have a detailed understanding of the inflow and outflow of your cash.

Start getting intimately familiar with your cash flow by writing out all existing expenses (even small ones like Hulu and Netflix, the salad you got for lunch, or the latest video game you bought).

Take a piece of paper and write your net take-home pay—the total amount of money that hits your checking account each month—at the top of that piece of paper.

Then list each monthly expense you pay, both fixed and variable.

→ Rent/mortgage
→ Internet/cable
→ Utilities (electric, water, gas, etc.)
→ Cell phone
→ Student loan payment
→ Transportation cost (car payment, gas, monthly transit card)
→ Health insurance
→ Car insurance
→ Renter's insurance
→ Groceries
→ Entertainment (Netflix, Hulu, Amazon Prime, happy hour budget, dating budget)
→ Household goods (toilet paper and cleaning supplies)
→ Beauty products (or stuff like beard oil, if that's your thing)
→ Pets (or kids if you #adulted real fast)
→ Don't forget to write down any expenses you may pay annually as well.

You get the point.

Subtract your outflow from your monthly take-home pay, and you've got yourself a basic understanding of your cash flow.

→ *Get a positive number?* Lucky you, because you actually don't have every penny accounted for yet! This means there's some money available to put into savings. But you need to pay yourself first so it doesn't get spent. No more "Siiiiiigh, I just never have anything left over at the end of the month to save" mentality.
→ *Seeing that aggressive negative sign in front of your total?* It's time to move on to the next step.

Find Places to Slash Your Spending

They may be cliché tactics, but things like cooking at home, cutting the cord on your cable, making your own coffee, and brown-bagging your lunch are easy places to start saving, and they really add up over time—as long as you don't spend that money on something else. Other ways to save include canceling gym memberships, online subscriptions, and other paid installment services or luxuries you don't use. Walking/biking/carpooling or taking public transportation wherever possible also conserves cash, as does shopping around for better deals on something you want or need or going in on an expensive item that can be shared with a friend or roommate. Even bigger savings can come from looking into refinancing your debt to a lower interest rate (which could save you hundreds to thousands of dollars), selling to other people valuable items you never use that are in good condition, or calling to negotiate your current rates with utility companies and service providers.

Just doing one of these smaller habits (like brown-bagging your lunch at least once or twice a week) can put an easy $15 minimum into your savings account each month. I know it sounds absolutely insane to only save $15 a month, but just start. Soon you'll find that the habit motivates you to not only keep going, but increase your efforts.

Look into an Income-Driven Repayment Plan for Student Loans

Student loan payments may be crushing your ability to tuck anything away in a savings fund. If those loans are federal, you should seriously consider placing them on an income-driven repayment plan. This will ensure your payment is affordable relative to your income. Granted, this affordable payment is dictated by your state's version of discretionary income, but it does tend to reduce the burden. The Repayment Estimator from Federal Student Aid (find it at studentloans.gov) can provide you with a basic idea of your new monthly payment. The lower student loan payment will free up some cash to put into savings until you get to at least $1,000. It should be noted that going on income-driven repayment will increase the interest that accumulates over the life of your loan. If this appeals to you, be sure to read all the details in chapter 9.

Do a Cash Diet for Two Weeks

Run your budget to see how much you can spend per week. Then hide your cards and take out cash. Hopefully the tactile experience of handing over an Andrew Jackson and sensing his judgmental stare glaring at you will make you think twice about whether or not you *need* to make this purchase.

Once the cash is gone, it's gone.* You might want to invest in some rice, beans, and hot sauce to keep in the cupboard before you get started. This can help you reset your spending habits and find where unexpected budget leaks are occurring. Stick with it for a month, and you may find an extra $30 to $50 to reroute toward savings.

Get a Side Hustle

Our generation is becoming well-known for being part of the "gig economy" and holding down more than one job. In fact, your millennial status risks being revoked if you aren't holding down a side hustle. It doesn't have to be a regular gig either. Offer up your room occasionally on Airbnb. Get on Rover.com or DogVacay and work as a petsitter or dog walker. Use Care .com or Sittercity to find babysitting, nannying, or tutoring jobs. Just one or two gigs a month can easily net you an extra $100 or so (before taxes) to put in savings.

Negotiate a Higher Salary

Wouldn't it be just perfect if you're were struggling financially and magically started getting paid more? Well, if review season is coming up at work, then it's time to get your negotiation skills on.† You could also start interviewing for other jobs to increase your salary, or at the bare minimum use another offer as leverage in a salary negotiation.

SAVING MAY NOT HAPPEN AS QUICKLY AS YOU WANT, BUT IT WILL HAPPEN

Building a healthy savings account doesn't happen in a few weeks or months, and in some cases it may take years. Just remember: it's always important to have savings, even if you're currently struggling with debt. It's okay if you feel demoralized at first if you can barely afford to contribute more than the cost of a latte into your savings account, but it's building the habit that matters. As you begin to pay down debt and also earn more, then you can start to contribute larger sums to your savings.

---

* The extended version of how to properly do a Cash Diet can be found in chapter 4.
† Get tips on how to do this in chapter 14.

ACTION LIST FOR GOING FROM SPENDER TO SAVER

❑ Don't wait to just save anything left over at the end of the month; instead, be proactive and pay yourself first.

❑ Start small, and don't be discouraged if you can afford to save only $5 a month.

❑ Automate so you aren't tempted to spend the money before you save.

❑ Put the money into an account you don't check daily or even weekly.

❑ Slash excess spending or pick up a side hustle to find money to pad your savings account.

❑ Gradually increase how much you save every few months, and be sure to increase it when you get a raise so as to avoid completely succumbing to lifestyle inflation.

❑ Use part of your holiday bonus or tax return or any unexpected sum of money to help beef up your savings.

❑ Emergency fund, Fuck-Off Fund, whatever you want to call it, it's important you begin working toward having at least $1,000 saved and ultimately up to six or nine months of expenses.

Chapter 11

I Can't Afford to Split This Dinner Bill Evenly!
(Navigating Finances and Friendship)

THE SCENE STARTED in a typical overpriced Mexican joint in Manhattan. The kind of place that charges $16 for a chicken and cheese quesadilla, without the guacamole included. I entered knowing only the birthday girl and thus already felt knots in my stomach about the awkward end-of-the-meal-paying-the-check dance I knew was coming.

It was my second year in New York City, and my salary had recently increased from $25,000 to $37,500. This still didn't leave much leeway for nights of pricey guac and margs. But it felt uncomfortable to turn down a birthday dinner invite from a longtime friend out of fear of the projected price point.

Determined to be proactive and avoid a budget buster, I thoroughly researched the menu beforehand and went to dinner prepared to order the cheapest meal on the menu. I factored my meal + $12 for tax and tip + an extra $5 to $7 to help cover the birthday girl's meal to = $40.

Then people kept ordering pitchers of sangria and margaritas. Appetizers appeared from nowhere and were hoarded by five people at one end of the table. My palms started to sweat—but I figured those five would be kicking in extra for their appetizers and third pitcher of sangria.

By the time the dinner wrapped and the check got to my end of the table, with only three of ten people left to pay, the balance showed a $240 deficit. "$80 each?!" my mental financial planner screamed. "You can't afford that! Plus, you had a mediocre quesadilla and didn't even drink. You shouldn't have to pay for margs you didn't get to down with the rest!"

Hold on—clearly the first seven people had not anted up to cover their portion. Splitting the full bill evenly would've meant $50 each—only about $10 over my prepared budget. That my bank account could stomach, but not having to pay twice as much because a few people shortchanged the rest of us.

Before I could go full Lady Hulk on those sangria-swilling bastards, the birthday girl's boyfriend plucked the bill from my hand and marched down to confront the cheapos. They coughed up the extra money, and my bank account was saved.

If you're feeling some sort of social etiquette PTSD from this anecdote, I'm sorry. I probably should've provided a warning before launching into it. Also, you're not remotely alone in your terror over this: most of us have experienced some form of this dilemma when navigating friendship and finances. Money is already a taboo subject to discuss in our culture, so speaking up about not having enough or not finding value in the same things as your friends, and especially pointing out that someone is shorting the bill, feels socially repugnant. After all, it's not fun to get a reputation as a penny-pincher. It's one reason we often default to splitting a bill evenly, but you may not be able to afford that luxury early on in your financial life.

Before you start turning down every social invitation, or just accumulate credit card debt because you're too nice to say no, try to implement the following tactics to successfully balance your budget with having a life.*

PREDICTING YOUR FUTURE MONEY DRAMA WITH SCARY, BUT HELPFUL, ACCURACY

→ *Dining out with friends:* Is it a split-this-evenly or cover-your-portion situation? And who is going to be the person who "forgets" about tax and tip and shorts the bill, leaving the rest of you to play an obnoxious game of Clue to pinpoint the Scrooge? Take the anxiety out of the situation and just ask early. As you get older and grow into your career, it will probably become natural to just start splitting the check most of the time, but it's understandable if your early-career salary doesn't provide the funds for you to routinely attend $50 brunches or dinners.

→ *Travel plans for reunions:* Your friends all scatter after college, so of course you want to take time each year to meet up. It's easy to keep

---

* Already made the blunder of accumulating credit card debt? See chapter 8 for an action plan for paying down your debt.

it cheap in the early years when most people aren't making a ton of money, but as you age and some friends take life steps like marriage or baby making and others progress quickly in careers, it can become harder for everyone to agree on destinations for reunions. Do you go to an exotic locale? (Not everyone can afford that.) Do you just visit someone's home? (Not everyone wants to do that.) Once you find a location, what kind of activities do you indulge in when not everyone has the same amount of discretionary income? You get the picture.

→ *Weddings:* One of the biggest budget busters of all time. Whether you're in the wedding, invited to the bachelor party or bridal shower, or just attending as a guest, wedding season in your twenties to early thirties can leave your bank account a barren wasteland. Dropping $1,000 or more to be part of someone's special day can quickly lead to financial resentment if you're not careful. Don't be part of a wedding unless you are prepared to spend the money (and won't get ticked off about it). You should also start putting aside a little money each month around the time you hit 25 to begin preparations for Weddingeddon. It comes for us all.

No matter which version of a friends-and-finances conflict you experience, there's really only one way to deal . . .

BE HONEST

You don't have to disclose your salary or student loan debt or general lack of budgeting skills to your friends, nor do you need to justify your caution even if you're not having financial problems but rather simply don't value spending your money on [insert event here]. You do, however, need to be honest that you don't want to participate or that you do but have a financial limit on how much you can spend, and then not bitch about the result. Here are some ways you can stay on budget and still have fun with your friends as long as you're open and honest:

Set a Budget Ahead of Time

Express that you'd rather not spend more than a certain amount to go out to eat or on a trip, or to be part of a wedding. Do it politely, but firmly, and you'll likely be surprised at how willing your friends will be to work with you. After all, if they're true friends, they'll care more about being able to hang with you than getting you to burn your limited cash on something they want. And, of course, you should work with your friends when they express financial concerns or set budgets as well.

Offer a Cheaper Alternative

One way to still participate with friends in something fun but without breaking the bank is to offer other alternatives that are more affordable to you. You can use the old compliment sandwich technique to offer a solution instead of just stating that your friend's spending habits are an issue for you:

> *"I love spending time with you, and it's really important to me.*
>
> *But I can't [or don't want to] spend $50 on a bottomless mimosa brunch.*
>
> *How about getting bagels and going to the park instead? That way we still get to hang out!"*

(Can you tell I live in New York?)

Don't fret too much about how your friend will take your counterproposal. After years of experience in this realm, I can report that it rarely goes badly, because people generally like to be accommodating, especially if you are honest with them. On the off chance that someone doesn't want to change from their original plan, you can politely decline (without sounding annoyed or resentful, of course) and reschedule a more frugal plan later. And you never know, your friend might also be looking to pinch some pennies but didn't want to lose face or look cheap by diverting from the original plan.

Learn When to Say No

You have to respect your budget and financial bottom line, but you can't begrudge your friends for wanting to still take part in an expensive activity. Sometimes you're just going to have to bow out and say no. Yes, this means the $3,000 bachelor trip to Vegas when you already have five other weddings to go to this year.

KNOW YOUR FINANCIAL FRIENDSHIP DYNAMICS

As you mature into a money-earning adult, you'll start to notice a variation in financial dynamics with friends.

My friend Hannah and I earn similar salaries and have similar financial situations, but from the beginning of our friendship we developed a script for how to deal with money: we always cover our share. There's no rhyme or reason to why we do this, we just do. Could we afford to split a bill evenly? Sure. But if one of us gets an extra drink or has a more expensive entrée, then big spender covers the difference. There's zero animosity in what others may perceive as a penny-pinching arrangement; it's just what we do, and it's never once caused a problem.

When I get drinks with my friend Sam, though, we usually take turns covering the bill. There's a general give and take, but no calculating that we're paying the same amount each time. This method just developed at some point and stuck with us.

You should suss out the financial terms of each of your friendships and abide by your established script, even if that means being brutally honest about your financial hang-ups. If you drastically outearn your friends, you might think it's nice to keep picking up the tab, but eventually that could start to make your friends uncomfortable and you a little resentful or in control of all plans since you're paying.

DEALING WITH A FRIEND WHEN YOUR FINANCIAL LIVES DON'T SYNC

There's often chatter about money driving a wedge in romantic relationships and being a leading cause of divorce, but few people talk about how it can happen in completely platonic relationships too.

Case #1: Stingy Stella

Stella is a pain. Each time you invite her someplace she wants to just pay for her portion of the meal and demands to see calculations on tax and tip. Then there was also that time you went over to her apartment for a wine and movie night—per her suggestion—and she sent you a $6 Venmo charge after you left for your share of the bottle of wine she'd bought.

Being that level of stingy felt sort of okay when you were both fresh out of college and not making much, but it's several years later, and you both make decent livings. You also know that Stella's financial situation isn't dire, so you're getting sick of the constant penny-pinching.

Case #2: Spendy Stinson

Spendy Stinson loves to have a good time, but that always equates to expensive. He plans elaborate outings in which you explore your city in a way you've never seen it, but, damn, it costs you $100 every Sunday to join in the fun. Not to mention, Stinson (your coworker) always wants to go out to lunch with you during the workweek. You really can't keep up and need to learn how to keep Stinson (or at least your outings with Stinson) in check.

You may yourself be a stingy or a spendy, but the issue is that your values are out of sync with the Stellas and Stinsons in your life. When Stella gets stingy about going out to eat, but that's one of your favorite ways to spend money, it's frustrating. And when Stinson wants to travel and you prefer to do a staycation, Stinson gets annoyed.

Express your values. The only way to deal with your Stellas and Stinsons is to be forthright about what you value and why you'd prefer to spend or not spend in certain areas. Your money should work as a tool to get what *you* want, so don't let your friends spend your money for you.

STANDING UP FOR YOURSELF IN AWKWARD MONEY SITUATIONS

Should you ever find yourself in a Mexican restaurant wondering why you would possibly need to pay $80 for a mediocre quesadilla and you don't have your friend's boyfriend to come to your rescue—well, you have to learn how to embrace the moniker of *cheapskate*. Sometimes you just have to Sheryl Sandberg the situation and #LeanIn, but in this case, it's leaning into the fact people may (nay, will) judge you for wanting to only pay your share of a bill.

There is a possible solution: you be the one to carve up the bill.

Many a dinner since my fateful birthday experience has ended with me offering to handle calculating the bill. Often, you'll find people are happy to off-load the task to a designated accountant, and this way you as said accountant get to ensure that you, and everyone else, are only paying for the amount you truly owe.

USE YOUR MILLENNIAL RESOURCES (YES, THAT MEANS APPS)

Gone are the days when a friend "just kept forgetting" to bring cash to group outings and you all had to cover them but never seemed to get paid back. This allergy to carrying cash is no longer a problem because, of course, there's an app for that. Using services like Venmo or Popmoney or

Square Cash helps reduce the awkwardness of hounding friends for their share. You can pester them digitally and eliminate the face-to-face interaction and open communication entirely—a millennial's dream.

As a word of caution: be sure to stick with your already established financial friendship scripts. If you've always taken turns covering rounds and it's worked and never caused issues, don't start sending your friend a bill for the round of drinks you offered to buy. That's just tacky.

 ACTION LIST FOR KEEPING IT REAL WITH FRIENDS AND FINANCES

❏ *Budget for looming expenses:* There are certain financial obligations for which you can prepare. Christmas comes the same time every year, and wedding season will eventually wallop you over the head. So start a savings account specifically for these kinds of pop-up but pricey moments in life so they don't blow your regular budget.

❏ *Be honest:* Try the compliment sandwich to segue your friend's expensive suggestion to one that's within your own budget.

❏ *Stand up for yourself, politely:* Let your friends in on your expectations and/or budget restrictions, but you can't be resentful if they still choose to partake.

❏ *Don't be a financial foe:* Pay what you owe and/or be willing to negotiate if your buddy needs a cheaper alternative when hanging out.

❏ *There's an app for that:* Stop feeling frustrated about tracking down your friends for cash, and just use apps to get paid back.

Chapter 12

Getting Financially Naked with Your Partner

HE CAST HIS EYES DOWN and exhaled slowly. His leg twitched as he drummed his fingers on the table. I could feel the nerves emanating from him. My foot kept tapping the ground to release the tension from my own body or perhaps just to make a distracting noise to break the silence.

We'd talked about taking this step before, but it would be the first time for both of us, so we were understandably anxious. How would it feel? I'd heard it could be painful, and once it happened there was no going back.

Then Peach steadied himself, looked me square in the eyes, and told me his number.*

FINDING OUT YOUR PARTNER'S NUMBER

For other generations, "the number" might refer to former bedfellows, but you as a millennial have another number to be concerned about: the debt burden.

Forty-two percent of our generation carries some student loan debt, according to the Harvard Institute of Politics (IOP) at the Kennedy School.[1] And that number does not include those who have other forms of long-term debt, such as an auto or personal loan or credit card overspending. This makes the likelihood high that those of us fortunate enough to escape the clutches of carrying a financial burden like debt will eventually be yoked to it in marriage.

I made my college decision based on the desire to graduate debt free,

---

* Peach is the sickeningly sweet nickname I am using for my boyfriend and what I actually call him in real life. (No joke. And yes, he agreed to let me share that nice little detail about us in this book.)

but I'd fallen in love with someone without the privilege to do the same.* This is why the time had come to get financially naked.

The timing of getting financially naked is a delicate thing. I don't recommend asking your partner about his or her relationship with money while you're getting handsy in a dorm room or sending steamy messages after you both swiped right. It *really* doesn't make for sensual foreplay, unless you're both massive finance geeks who get funny feelings downstairs when you discuss maxing out your IRA in addition to your 401(k) contributions. Man, I'm getting flushed just thinking about it!

Peach and I casually chatted about money early on in our relationship. We'd routinely talk about vague topics like how much we felt comfortable spending on Christmas presents or what sounded like a good budget for a special date night or when we'd go dutch versus when one of us would just pick up the tab. These smaller conversations eventually progressed to the bigger-picture discussions, which is how I discovered Peach had student loans. But it wasn't until we realized marriage could be a serious possibility (around year three of our thus far six-year relationship) that I asked him to share his number.

Chalk it up to my type-A personality, but I wasn't willing to discuss an engagement, let alone a marriage, without knowing the financial situation in which I'd find myself after the "I do's." And neither should you.

WHAT NEEDS TO BE SHARED

The first step in getting "financially naked" with your partner is to create a list of what needs to be shared about your individual financial situations. No, this doesn't mean writing down a list of demands about what your partner needs to share as though you're holding a hostage. Think of it more as a mental checklist that doesn't need to be discussed all at once. Not all partners are going to be up front or willing to remove more than one piece of financial clothing at a time, so it could take weeks or months and multiple conversations before you arrive at full-frontal financial nudity.

You may dismiss the notion of baring your deepest financial secrets and decisions to your partner, because it's *your* money and *your* problem, but that baggage will follow you into a marriage. Trying to keep those secrets (like hiding credit card debt or student loans) can create a breeding

---

* You can read all about it in chapter 9 if you've taken the à la carte approach to this book.

ground for fights and ultimately fracture the trust you two share. Discussing your financial failures, successes, and goals bonds you two as a team, so even when you disagree, you have the proper foundation to handle the problem. Not to mention that deciding not to be transparent before saying "I do" could mean that the officiant at your wedding pronounces you two in debt, without you or your spouse even knowing.

You two should be willing to share:

→ What type of debt you have. Common types of debt include:
  ♦ Student loans
  ♦ Credit card debt (as in carrying a balance month to month)
  ♦ Auto loan
  ♦ Personal loan
  ♦ Medical debt
  ♦ Past-due bills in collections
  ♦ Mortgage (this would be impressive)
→ How much debt. Be warned that this number may get downplayed the first time you have this conversation, so follow up at some point in the future, in a completely non-accusatory way, of course.

   Discussing money is not unlike doing a juice cleanse or hitting the gym extra hard the first time you're about to get naked with someone. That version of your body may not be the most accurate a few months after you've gone through cuffing season and gained a little relationship gut.

   How exactly do you check in without seeming like you're assuming your partner lied? Revisit the idea of how you two plan to pay down your debts, and then ask your partner to confirm that you remember how much debt he or she is carrying correctly. If you fudged the numbers on the first attempt at this conversation, then it's important to fess up; otherwise you're already planting seeds for an argument early in a marriage or long-term partnership.

→ Your credit reports and scores. A lackluster credit report and score isn't exactly a reason to ditch a new love, but it is your STD panel for the financial world. Sharing your credit scores and reports provides some insight into how each of you have handled your existing lines of credit by seeing if one of you has ever been (or is consistently) delinquent or in default on loans, or missing enough payments to have items sent to collections.

A poor credit past doesn't always mean a future of risky financial decisions. However, a credit report can tell you whether your partner is making an effort to correct youthful money mishaps or if the tendency to miss payments and skip out on bills is a persistent issue. This step means exposing your financial vulnerability to your partner if you've had a history of bad money moves.

Again, I'm not advocating for you to ditch a relationship just because of bad credit, but sharing information does help illuminate potential pain points in your financial future together and give you an opportunity to work through them together.

→ How you're currently handling the debt. Ultimately, you want to enter a discussion about how you're both handling your debt currently and paying it off and your visions for how a couple should deal with money together. We'll cover some in-depth strategies for doing this later on in the chapter.

WHO NEEDS TO SHARE

With money often cited as a reason for tension in a marriage that can lead to divorce (and divorce is expensive), it seems logical to start getting financially naked early on in order to minimize your risk of a life of squabbling over spending choices or even falling victim to financial infidelity.

It isn't just the indebted person who needs to strip down to their financial skivvies. You *both* need to undress, even if one of you has that unicorn of millennial money: a positive net worth.

Of course, this doesn't mean you have to pull up all your bank statements, credit card bills, student loan payments, and investments during the first talk, but it's imperative that you both disclose approximate numbers, positive or negative, when the time is right. It's hard to actually feel intimate and connected if one partner gets naked while the other one just sits there and stares.

When Peach disclosed his debt burden, I in turn shared my net worth. It would be unfair to ask him to financially strip down in front of me while I got to stay bundled up in the comfort of being debt free. This is why both partners need to share their financial details.

Sharing our numbers didn't mean we suddenly swapped ATM PINs and ran to get a joint bank account. Instead, it provided a foundation with which we could create hypotheticals about how we would handle money if we decided to get married.

Contrary to what you may think, given my bluntness, the conversation didn't just arise from me simply turning to him one night and saying, "Hey, how much debt do you have?" Starting any taboo conversation requires a bit more tact.

HOW TO HAVE "THE TALK" (OR, RATHER, THE MANY TALKS)

It's unlikely you're going to have a financially naked one-night stand. Who wants to share financial details with an absolute stranger? So before you hit full-frontal nudity, it's likely you're going to traverse other common financial conversations.

Financially Naked 101: To Go Dutch or to Be Traditional?

Factoring in financial considerations with dating can be complicated. Not in a "what app do I use" kind of way, but marry the tension of sexual expectations with the taboo of money and you've created a cocktail for lots of awkwardness.

The end-of-the-date check dance can actually be a make-or-break moment for some people. Those in heteronormative relationships may feel strongly that the man should always pay on the first date, and same-sex couples may find protocol to be the asker pays. Or you could be on a date with someone who always wants to "go dutch" (split the bill evenly) regardless of who asked or gender norms. Like I said, it's complicated.

Given that money plays a role in most relationships from date number one (unless you just Netflix and chill), new couples actually have to discuss money, at least to some degree, early on.

Common scenarios include:

→ *End-of-the-date check dance:* Personally, I think it never hurts to offer to go dutch on a check, especially early on. However, you can't get annoyed if your date takes you up on the offer, so actually be ready to shell out the cash. It also seems quite fair that the *asker* pay for the *askee*. However, continuing to date probably means you eventually need to start going dutch or just switch paying on and off. It seems unfair to constantly expect one person in the relationship to foot the bill.

→ *How fancy are we?* One way to determine early on if you're financially compatible is to see what type of dates the two of you go on. If your partner wants to keep spending lavishly and you're more of a one big date night a month with more low-key events in between person, then that can help determine if you two are a good fit. You also can usually tell from the type of dates someone plans what their relationship is to spending versus saving. That's not to say all savers refuse to splurge or that all spenders never save, but it does give you an inkling as to how your date is handling his or her personal finances.

→ *How much to spend on gifts:* Birthdays, holidays, Valentine's Day, anniversaries—how much are the two of you going to spend on each other? The best way to handle this is just to be forthright and honest about your budgets. You don't have to tell details of what you make or your debt (depending where you are in the relationship), but you could mention if you'd prefer to keep a $50 or $100 cap on any gift giving. You could also consider combining your purchasing power to partake in an activity together instead of buying material goods.

→ *Splitting finances when you move in together:* If things are serious enough for the two of you to be moving in together, then you should be moving on to 201-level financial nakedness. However, if you're uncomfortable with disclosing numbers quite yet, then you at least need to have an open dialogue about how bills will be paid. Are you splitting everything evenly, or is one partner picking up more of the tab? Who is actually paying the bills? Does there need to be a checks-and-balances mechanism to ensure the bills did get paid? (Woof—that can cause some serious drama.)

Once you've reached a point in the relationship where you believe this could be your lifetime (or, at least, long-term) partner, then it's time to strip it all off.

Financially Naked 201: Full Frontal

The hardest part about getting financially naked is starting the conversation. As with other intimate acts, it makes sense to start with some smaller stuff first. Granted, financial foreplay isn't quite as exciting unless you're both going to whip out well-endowed bank accounts and investment portfolios.

Begin with asking some vague topics about money. Ask each other things like:

→ "How much do you think it's important to have saved in an emergency fund?"
→ "What are your feelings about credit card debt?"
→ "What's your biggest financial fear?"
→ "Do you believe in leasing a car, getting a loan, or buying it outright?"
→ "Would you consider debts brought into a marriage the couple's problem or each person's issue?"

Answers to these questions may not give you specifics about your partner's financial situation, but they will certainly illuminate his or her general relationship with money.

Later talks can cover more specifics. And, no, this conversation shouldn't happen the next day.

→ "Do you have student loan debt?"
→ "Have you ever carried a balance on your credit card?"
→ "Do you know your credit score?"

After laying the groundwork of financial foreplay, you can finally reach the climax of the conversation and get direct (sorry, it's just not going to be as much fun as having sex).

→ "How much debt do you have?"
→ "What's your credit score?"
→ "Do you have items in collections?"

If you're on the marriage track, you should eventually take some time to discuss your joint financial futures, even though it's less sexy than discussing names of hypothetical children and your plans to globe-trot for a year before starting a family.

→ "Do you want kids, and if so, how much do you think it will cost to raise them?"

→ "Have you started saving for retirement?"

→ "What's your vision of retirement?"

→ "What are your financial expectations for the future?"

Keep Judgment Out of It

As a woman who struggles with a face that shows her every thought and feeling (a friend of mine used to constantly whisper to me, "Fix your face!" during work meetings), I understand why it can be difficult to keep judgment out of a financial conversation. But it's essential to do so. Work on your poker face, and don't judge your partner—and don't let your partner judge you! Money is already a sensitive topic and one you or your partner may feel self-conscious discussing.

You wouldn't laugh at your partner the first time he or she got physically naked in front of you. Judging about money is no different. One wrong facial expression or snarky remark, and your partner may never feel comfortable chatting about finances with you again. That certainly wouldn't bode well for a future together. We've all made missteps with our money (and life in general), so learn how to be supportive, and figure out how to tackle any remnants of poor financial decisions as a team.

Should you find yourself getting too frustrated during the initial run at getting financially naked, that's okay. Take a break from talking about finances and revisit the discussion in a few days or weeks once you've had a chance to collect your thoughts and calm down. The most important thing is to try not to let your feelings or judgment get in the way of being honest with your partner (and vice versa).

DECODING THE POTENTIAL FOR A JOINT DEBT

Honestly, it's probably easier for most people to get physically naked in front of someone for the first time than to expose their bank accounts, outstanding debts, and credit reports to them. But becoming legally tied to another individual without getting financially naked first is the money equivalent of unprotected sex. And much like the bumps, burning pee, and other icky stuff that can be contracted through negligent sexual acts, getting into a contractual, financial relationship with your partner without being open with each other about the state of your financial health could be painful.

A contractual financial relationship can involve many different things: your budget for cohabitating with your partner, buying property together, co-signing on a loan, sharing a credit card, having a joint bank account, loaning him or her money, or having children together. It can feel good to face these financial milestones together, like moving in or buying a home, but that can be a temporary euphoria should you eventually discover that your partner isn't handling his or her money well and is therefore impacting your wallet.

You may find that your partner is acting cagey about discussing money. These warning signs could predict future money woes:

→ Always dismisses your request to talk about finances.
→ Isn't interested in having joint bank accounts (granted, some couples prefer never to comingle without it being a bad sign).
→ Refuses to share a credit score or credit report.
→ Gets calls from collection agencies.
→ Uses payday loans or title loans for short-term money needs.
→ Uses cash advances on a credit card.
→ Has lots of department store credit cards.
→ Currently pays a wage garnishment or tax liens.

These warning signs don't mean you need to dump your partner immediately, without an attempt at financial rehab. However, it does mean you need to have a serious conversation before you allow someone else's financial situation to impact your own.

Should your partner exhibit any of the behaviors listed above, you shouldn't use it as an excuse to be shady and pull some junior private investigator shenanigans like searching their mail, trying to hack your way into their bank accounts, or looking at their e-mail for bills you may not know about. Instead, suggest that the two of you go to a neutral third party to discuss your finances—preferably someone who doesn't have a relationship with the two of you to begin with and is coming to the situation with a completely fresh set of eyes and no preference for one person or the other.

This person could be a professional like a Certified Financial Planner (learn more in chapter 17).

If your partner continues to refuse to talk about money, and you've expressed that such a conversation is important to you and for the two of you to thrive as a couple, then you have some tough decisions ahead of you. After all, you might be facing financial abuse or financial infidelity, even if you don't know it yet.

$ *Married couples should be wary of having only one partner handle all the financial matters. This can set up one person to be a victim of financial abuse or make it incredibly difficult if the keeper of the money dies unexpectedly.*

WHEN TO GET OUT: FINANCIAL ABUSE AND FINANCIAL INFIDELITY

There may be a time when you *should* cut a partner loose because of money, particularly if financial abuse or infidelity has become a problem.

Financial abuse includes but isn't limited to:

→ Using your money without permission.
→ Using your identity to gain access to credit and loans.
→ Refusing to allow you access to money without first going through him or her.
→ Hiding assets.
→ Not allowing you to work in order to bring in your own income.
→ Marginalizing your feelings or opinions because your partner earns more than you.

Financial abuse is often used as a means of control in what may also be a physically and/or emotionally abusive relationship, which makes it particularly difficult for victims to leave. Being financially dependent on an abuser and possibly having ruined credit makes it a struggle for victims to walk away without an outside support system in place, such as family members or a local domestic abuse organization.

Financial infidelity can be closely linked to financial abuse but focuses more on the duplicitous nature of a partner hiding something from you about his or her finances or how your joint money is being spent. Warning signs of financial infidelity include:

→ Your partner doesn't share household bills with you and is evasive when you ask.

→ Your partner seems to be getting calls from collectors but dismisses your concerns.

→ Collection agencies call the house or your cell phone.

→ Your partner isn't willing to share his or her credit report.

→ Your partner won't encourage you to attend meetings with a financial planner or accountant and dismisses your interest in participating as unnecessary.

→ Bills come in the mail for financial products that you didn't realize your partner had or that were taken out in your name.

→ Items show up on your credit report for which you didn't apply.

Financial infidelity can be relatively easy to uncover by pulling credit reports, reviewing bank account statements, and checking investment portfolios.

Should you believe you're a victim of financial infidelity, you may want to seek help through financial therapy (a growing field) and find a financial planner with whom you feel your voice is being heard. A nonabusive relationship may be able to recover from financial infidelity.

Those experiencing financial abuse as part of a relationship involving domestic abuse should consider reaching out for help. The following Web sites provide information and resources that can help:

→ Safe Horizon—http://safehorizon.org

→ The National Domestic Violence Hotline—http://www.thehotline.org/

→ National Coalition Against Domestic Violence—http://www.ncadv .org/need-help/get-help

→ Domestic Shelters—https://www.domesticshelters.org/

The potential for finding yourself in such a relationship is another reason for you to always have an emergency savings fund (read more in chapter 10). Depending on your trust levels and prior experiences, you may prefer this fund to be your own stash of cash that your partner cannot access. However, be aware that if you hide the fact that you have this money from your partner, then you are committing financial infidelity. If you want your relationship to be a healthy one, then he or she should know you have a personal savings account and approximately how much you have saved.

Knowing how much each of you have saved, have invested, and are in debt takes you to the final step in getting financially naked.

CREATING A FINANCIAL PLAN TOGETHER

Do you have a team mentality about money or an individualistic approach? This question is the first one to answer before building a financial plan together, even a hypothetical one for the future.

When Peach and I had our big financial talk, he immediately became defensive about his debt, announcing that he would be taking care of the payments. It was a gesture I appreciated, but I didn't feel it would be fair to our hypothetical marital ledger. Why should he exclusively carry the burden of debt repayment when our financial decisions before and after marriage would impact each other? We could combine forces and get rid of his debt relatively quickly.

This isn't to say that all married couples should have joint banking accounts. There are arguments for and against it, and each couple must figure out the best way for them to merge their money. But handling debt should absolutely be a team effort. Otherwise, it can quickly become a breeding ground for resentment and counting each other's purchases down to the pennies.

\$ *Decide on an amount each of you can spend per month without checking in with the other person. This money can be used to purchase whatever you want, no matter how trivial the other person finds it (like comic books, daily coffees, or weekly manicures).*

Any plan you create with your partner needs to take three things into consideration:

→ Is it good for your mental health?
→ Is it good for your wallets?
→ Is it true to your values?

Peach and I ran several hypothetical strategies. Peach wants to feel ownership over his debt, while I want to get back in the black as quickly as possible. After analyzing those two values, we determined a plan of attack.

The Plan: The two of us would live off of my salary, while Peach's salary would be used almost exclusively to pay down his debt (except for making contributions to an emergency fund and retirement account). This way, Peach retains ownership over his debt by making all the payments with money he earns, but I also feel like part of the team by financially supporting our day-to-day expenses. Not to mention, it means the debt is gone sooner than it might be otherwise.

EARLY DISCUSSIONS DETERMINE FINANCIAL COMPATIBILITY IN RELATIONSHIPS

My debt conversation with Peach made it easy for the two of us to be transparent in other money talks. It also helped us develop a team mind-set about finances before being legally tied to each other.

These conversations should also help you determine if a partner is actually a good fit for you. Finances are a leading cause of contention in relationships. So why enter a marriage or a long-term relationship if you can't have honest discussions with your partner or see major red flags like credit card abuse, routinely missing payments, or refusing to deal with existing debt? Love might make us blind, but that isn't a passable excuse for lenders, bankers, and credit bureaus.

THE GETTING-FINANCIALLY-NAKED ACTION LIST

❑ *Prepare yourselves to have the talk:* This talk shouldn't be happening in a bar while yelling over the sounds of woo girls and trying not to stare at that couple just really going at it in the corner. Plan to get financially naked in the comfort of someone's home (as long as a roommate isn't going to burst in while you're dishing the dirt), and maybe bring a six-pack or bottle of wine. You should also both know you're going to get financially naked and not blindside your partner by just asking a ton of questions out of nowhere.

❑ *Determine what you're each going to share:* You don't have to share all the details in the first sit-down, but be open about what you're both interested in knowing and currently feel comfortable sharing. Eventually, you should both know each other's debt loads, the type of debt, your credit scores, why the credit scores are what they are, and your net worths.

❑ *Be open and honest:* Keep judgment at the door and be honest with your partner. If you think he or she may not have stripped it all off, then be sure to return to the conversation in a few weeks or months.

❑ *Discuss your visions of the future:* You know the debt loads and the saving account details. Now, what are your thoughts for the future and how realistic do those feel? If you thought buying a house in three years seemed feasible, but it turns out your honey has $120,000 in student loan debt, then maybe you reprioritize.

❑ *Create a game plan for the future together:* Now that you know the details, what's the plan to work toward your financial goals as a team?

❑ *Implement the strategy:* The plan can be hypothetical at first, but once you're legally bound to each other or you've decided to combine your finances without the contract of marriage, then it's time to get your game plan going.

❑ *Have routine check-ins:* Once all the information is out there, the strategy is set and in motion. Then you need to set routine meetings. They could be weekly, monthly, quarterly, or whatever works best for the two of you. Just be sure you're checking your progress against your goals and then readjusting when necessary.

Chapter 13

Paying Rent to Your 'Rents: Overcoming the Emotional and Financial Battles of Living at Home After College

"HOW IS IT POSSIBLE I'm getting two of these awards and can't find a job?" I thought to myself on the eve of my college graduation. Sitting in a squeaky fold-up chair on my university's beloved basketball court, I waited for my name to be called so I could go up and receive two plaques and a commemorative clock acknowledging that I'd been the runner-up for our journalism department's highest accolade and selected as the top student in the theater department (out of about seven, so it wasn't that impressive). A 3.87 GPA—that 0.03 away from summa cum laude still haunts the teacher's pet in me—and a strong résumé, including a summer spent interning for CNN's Atlanta bureau, had gotten me nowhere.

Instead of relishing those last days of living in a collegiate bubble, I'd started to panic and applied for any job in decent driving distance from my parents' house now that they were stateside again. By any, I mean being a salesclerk at Books-A-Million in Charlotte, North Carolina, was currently my one and only job lead. I'd gotten a phone call requesting I come in for an interview a few hours prior to the awards ceremony.

You may think that my panic was premature. Droves of millennial graduates before me had walked the stage to get their diplomas with no job waiting on the other side. It was 2011, after all, and the workforce still seemed to be in its slow crawl out of the Great Recession. Certainly the naïveté of youth combined with that powerful millennial feeling of self-importance should've kept me sane, at least for a few months.

Except an offhand comment from my dad kept playing on a loop in my head:

"Well, you'll have to pay rent if you return to living at home after graduating."

That bomb had been dropped about five months earlier during a trip home over winter break. At the time, I didn't press the subject. As I would *obviously* have multiple job offers before I graduated from college, duh, it was a nonissue.

But here I was, another overeducated, underemployed millennial stereotype.

My dad put my overanxious mind slightly at ease with an offer to give me a three-month runway (the time of a regular summer break) before beginning to charge me rent in September, when I normally would've been returning to school. He also assured me that rent would not be market price, but a small stipend based on an affordable ratio of whatever salary I started earning. I began hoping Books-A-Million paid more than minimum wage.

Fast-forward a mere three weeks, and my sojourn at my parents' home came to an end. I packed two suitcases and got on a flight to New York City, ready to start my first post-college job. So I never wound up having to pay rent, but you can bet it highly motivated me to get myself employed fast. Not to mention, I genuinely believe that your parents don't owe you a place to crash, especially after you turn 18 and are legally an adult. A shared bloodline does not obligate them to let you return to the nest, but their love and compassion will likely allow you to do so.

But plenty of other millennials, like the ones featured in this chapter, have experienced life back under Mom and Dad's roof for more than a few weeks. If this is (or is about to be) your reality, let's discuss how to handle it without too much emotional or financial calamity.

By the way, the Books-A-Million job never came to fruition.

WHY MILLENNIALS ARE LIVING AT HOME FOR SO LONG AFTER GRADUATION

It feels like a smear campaign from older generations: "Just another lazy, entitled millennial living in their parents' basement." "How are millennials supposed to succeed if they're living in their childhood bedrooms?" "Do they know what they're doing to their parents' ability to retire?"

We get it. Boomerang kids are looked down upon as a symbol of all that's wrong with our narcissistic, selfie-taking generation. But moving back home isn't exactly the future our participation-trophy-winning selves were envisioning when we went off to college with dreams of grandeur in our heads. (Listen, *we* didn't give ourselves those participation trophies and gold stars!)

It's easy to point fingers at the Great Recession, wage stagnation, the burden of student loan debt, underemployment, and the intense chasm that is the wealth divide in the United States today. All of these factors certainly play a role in the boomerang kid trend, but there is also one major, eerily simple explanation. We're just not getting married as young as previous generations.

Regardless of your reason for living at home, it can take an emotional and even financial toll. Let's dig into some of the ways in which you can alleviate the burden of your roommates being the same people who wiped your poopy butt.

THE EMOTIONAL COST OF LIVING AT HOME

While moving back home is a prudent financial move, it can be demoralizing, particularly when stereotype after asinine stereotype is lobbed in your direction.

$ *I always tell people I meet that they should feel zero shame about living at home, especially if they have any debt. I tell them that they should live at home as long as their parents will let them, assuming it's a safe and friendly living environment. In addition, you're hopefully sharing a home with people that you know how to share a living space with and get along with. Living with Craigslist randoms is always a gamble.*

—TJ, now 31, lived at home in California for ten months after graduating from college at 24

The Self-Imposed Conflict

"In many ways, it feels that my life has been on pause since returning home," 25-year-old Bryan Clark explained. "In the time since I graduated, multiple friends have landed entry-level jobs, received promotions, gotten married, and started families. I'm happy for the friends and college acquaintances who achieve these life milestones, but it feels strange that I'm still at home trying to figure out a career path. At times, it feels like I'm doing things wrong."

Clark graduated from college in 2013 without a job offer in hand, so he returned home to Wellsville, New York. He resumed a summer internship doing public relations for a nearby university that he'd held throughout college, but he continued applying aggressively for other jobs. Nearly three years later, Clark has had a string of short-term gigs, but nothing that has led to a career position. He's keen to move out on his own but is waiting for a job that provides the means to cover living and housing expenses.

Twenty-three-year-old Emelia Patterson boomeranged back home as well, but for a slightly different purpose.

"About a month before I graduated from college, I was offered a job at a small marketing agency in my hometown, a suburb north of Chicago," Patterson said. Like many recent graduates, she felt so excited to have something lined up after graduation that she accepted almost immediately, despite the low salary.

Patterson knew immediately she wouldn't be able to cover the cost of living alone in the expensive suburb, even with roommates, so she needed to adjust to life back at home, which happened to be a seven-minute drive from her new job.

Similar to Clark, Patterson also felt her return home put her in a state of arrested development compared to her friends.

"The hardest aspects were lack of privacy and feeling like I was behind all of my friends who had moved out," Patterson told me. "I was so used to living on my own with my best college friend at our apartment at school for three years that it was a big adjustment." She even watched her younger sister leave for college just as she returned.

"It felt as though we were switching places; she was off on a great big adventure, and I was stuck at home."

A bulk of the emotional trauma about moving back home with the 'rents may be self-imposed, but parents don't always make the experience drama free either.

The Parent-Imposed Conflict

"My parents are champions of what I like to call the 'family guilt trip,'" said Patterson, who dealt with her parents making her and her siblings feel guilty if they wanted to see friends or go out. (We've all been there when home between semesters!) "I wanted to shout 'I LIVE HERE, YOU SEE

ME EVERY DAY' all the time, but in retrospect, I know they were just trying to make the most of their time with me before I eventually moved out for good."

$ *I feel pressure to validate the confidence and expectations my parents, family, friends, and mentors have expressed for me in the past. I want to be making a living and living a life that allows them to be proud of me. At times, I feel that I'm letting those people down as I've gone through the employment successes and setbacks of my post-college career.*

—Bryan Clark

Parents often don't mean to put undue pressure on their children, and some of the time we may be overdramatizing our parents' actions.

However, there are moments when the conflict with your parents isn't because they love you so much that they're trying to squeeze in every ounce of time with you they possibly can. In some households, there may be instances of emotional and physical abuse. There are times when parents may even be taking advantage of a child financially.

If you feel you're unable to move out because of your financial situation or because you want to be at home to protect siblings or a parent, then please consider reaching out to one of these resources:

→ Safe Horizon—http://safehorizon.org
→ The National Domestic Violence Hotline—http://www.thehotline.org/
→ National Coalition Against Domestic Violence—http://www.ncadv .org/need-help/get-help
→ Domestic Shelters—https://www.domesticshelters.org/

"YES, I DO THINK YOU SHOULD PAY RENT"

If a blind rage of millennial indignation shot through your system when I shared my story about my parents asking for rent, I'm sorry for what's about to happen to our relationship.

I understand this is breaking millennial code, but I encourage parents to charge boomerang millennials rent, and I urge my fellow Gen-Yers to pay up without complaint. Now, I'm not advocating that your parents' charge you what you'd be forking over to live solo. I'm thinking a reasonable $100 a month, maybe less if you're working part-time at Books-A-

Million, or more for those working a regular salaried job but still crashing at home. Obviously, the advantage of living at home is saving money, and you should still be able to do so. However, the paying rent rationale is two-fold:

1. *Not all parents can afford to have a child move back home.* You might not even know that's your parents' situation. Our parents notoriously want to shield us from the unpleasantnesses of life, which may include their own financial issues. Adding another body back into the house means an increase in the bills (you want to eat and have electricity and take showers, right?). Perhaps your parents' own living situation has changed since you went off to college, and it would be difficult for them to accommodate your return.

2. *Why wait to figure out how to manage your bills?* A cliché argument, to be sure, but seriously, do you really think balancing your books is going to get easier when rent takes up 40 percent of your take-home pay, your student loans are due, and you still need to feed yourself? Paying a paltry sum to the Bank of Mom and Dad each month helps you learn some budgeting basics or teaches you a harsh lesson on overdraft fees. Either way, get it out of your system while you're still in the protective bosom of your parents' home.

The Parental 401(k) Program

To the parents and fellow millennials who are simply appalled at my mere suggestion of charging loved ones rent: the fainting couch is to your right. Jokes aside, there is another option: the parental 401(k) program.

Parents charging their kids rent when the money isn't needed to help with the family finances do have the option of setting these contributions aside as a form of forced savings. Better yet, don't tell the child this is what's happening. What a delightful move-out surprise! The most generous of parents may even be willing to provide a parental match on the amount saved during the child's tenure at home. You may even mention this option to your parents if you know for certain they're charging you rent as a life lesson and not in order to have help paying the bills. A contract might also be helpful in reducing any emotional tension about paying rent; it can even outline your responsibilities as a tenant, because money does change the dynamic.

When you, the child, pay rent, your living situation shifts into landlord-tenant mode, which could make a child less keen on helping with chores or odds and ends around the house because, hey, you pay to live there.

OPTIONS OTHER THAN PAYING RENT

Your parents may be generous and financially stable enough to have you back at home without it causing any strain to the family budget. Or perhaps the idea of charging a child rent is just culturally or socially abhorrent. Whatever the reason, don't take advantage of their kindness.

"I offered to help in any way I could, whether it be shuttling my youngest sister around, running errands, or performing other miscellaneous tasks," Emelia Patterson, who wasn't asked to pay rent, emphasized. She also assumed financial responsibility for her cell phone, insurance, and pet cat while living at home.

Bryan Clark too looks for options in which he can contribute to the household in non-financial ways. He does chores, never asks for spending money, and gets up at a reasonable hour each day so as to be a productive member of the household.

Not paying rent either? Here's your checklist of ways to be a productive tenant:

❏ Do every favor that's asked of you, because you're the freeloader!
❏ Proactively handle errands your parents would be more than happy to off-load.
  → Walking the dogs
  → Cooking family meals a few times a week
  → Doing the laundry
  → Cleaning the house
  → Driving your siblings to activities
❏ Keep your room clean if that's your parents' preference.
❏ Respect your parents' schedules (don't make a crap ton of noise when they're trying to sleep).
❏ Don't ask for entertainment money.

❏ Pay for the bills you can afford to cover.
   → Your own groceries
   → Cell phone
   → Netflix subscription
   → Car payment
   → Insurance
❏ Be nice! Don't revert back to being a sullen teenager (you're a twentysomething now).

FOLLOWING THEIR RULES

Their house, their rules. It's an obnoxious expression that feels like something a preacher in an '80s rom-com should be yelling at his daughter who just wants to dance. Yeah, that may be the plot of *Footloose*, but the sentiment is valid. If you're living back at home, then you're subject to the laws your parents see fit to dictate.

However, you should have an open dialogue with your parents about treating you as an adult instead of a high school kid. That is, of course, if you're acting like one. Should you have a curfew? Hopefully not. But perhaps you negotiate no curfew if you check in at certain times to prevent your mom from lying awake at night wondering if you've flipped your car into a ditch.

TOTAL SAVINGS

Even though the emotional toll of living at home, whether that's flak from family or the self-imposed frustrations, can be taxing at times. It certainly can provide a quick windfall for your finances. Both Clark and Patterson were able to save significant sums in less than a year.

"I was able to save a bit over $9,000 in the nine to ten months I lived at home," said Patterson, who admits she could've saved even more if she'd focused in her early months of living at home instead of indulging in some mindless spending.

"While working for Rivalries Unlimited from August 2015 to April 2016, I put aside around $10,000 in savings," Clark told me. "I would say that I typically placed two-thirds of my bi-weekly paychecks toward my savings account during that period."

Both Clark and Patterson are using their savings to set themselves up for life after living with Mom and Dad. The money provides fully funded emergency savings, plus enough for a security deposit and first and last months' rent.

Creating a healthy savings account and/or paying down debt is certainly one of the biggest—if not *the* biggest—advantage of living at home, especially in those early years after college. You just have to ensure you're actually taking advantage of the situation instead of validating your spending habits.

 ACTION LIST FOR MAKING THE MOST OF LIVING AT HOME

❏ *This isn't an excuse for mindless spending:* "At first, it was really easy to get caught in the trap of 'I have barely any expenses—I'll spend everything!' and I spent a lot, during my first couple months working, on clothes and other miscellaneous things I didn't need, because I'd never seen that much money before," explained Patterson. "Eventually, I had my direct deposit automatically route 50 percent of every paycheck directly into savings, and used the other 50 percent to pay my bills [cell phone and insurance] and have fun."

❏ *Finding a job is your job:* "I'm usually awake, dressed, and working on job applications and work-search activities no later than 9 a.m.," said Clark, who also likes that this routine keeps his body accustomed to traditional working hours.

❏ *Say yes to every favor:* It could be picking up your sibling from soccer practice or helping to paint the house—just do it. If you have more of a tenant situation worked out, well, that might change the relationship to a landlord-renter dynamic. You could just decide to not be a dick about it, though, and help your parents anyway.

❏ *You can still date:* But it takes a lot of the awkwardness out if you understand and respect your parents' rules. Don't try to be sneaking people in and out of your childhood bedroom if that's not cool with your roommates—aka your parents. You should probably also mention to your dates relatively early on in a relationship that you live at home.

❏ *Have a plan and talk it over with your parents*: Walk your parents through your career strategy, your anticipated timeline for leaving, and the proactive steps you're taking to strike out on your own. Keeping them in the loop from the beginning will help keep the nagging during family dinners at bay, especially if you have a younger sibling who's showing you up in the career success department.

Chapter 14

How to Negotiate Salary (or Anything Else) by Learning to Ask for What You Want

THERE'S NO BIGGER ENEMY in a negotiation than your self-doubt. I learned this lesson in the most embarrassing way: mid-negotiation.

No longer a rookie in the workforce, I'd spent three years of my post-collegiate life in jobs that weren't long-term fits. The first had been working as a page for the *Late Show with David Letterman*. It was the best possible way to delay the true experience of entering the real world out of college, but it was a one-year gig and paid terribly. We're talking about $1,000 a month with no benefits kind of terribly. This being my reference point for income, the $37,500 plus benefits at my next job in public relations made me feel rich.

Two years later, I knew public relations wasn't where I saw myself in one year, let alone five or ten, and I wanted out. A kismet series of events led me to the door of a brand-new start-up with no employees looking to hire a content manager for its blog.

"Okay, draft up a job proposal, and we'll take a look," I was told.

I drafted out the details of the job and stopped on the point of compensation. Rather, I agonized over this topic for several days before submitting the proposal. Desperate to leave my current job and worried about pricing myself too high for a start-up, I decided to ask for $50,000 (because it felt like a big bump but should still be affordable for a New York City–based start-up company), plus it included a benefits plan that mirrored the one at my current job: employer-paid health-care coverage, four weeks of paid vacation, and a 4 percent employer-matched 401(k).

I hit the send button on my e-mail and anxiously awaited their response.

A few days later, I met with the cofounders in their Manhattan office.

"We've looked over your proposal, and everything looks good," one co-founder said. "When would you like to start?"

That's when it hit me: I'd undervalued myself. They hadn't made even the slightest attempt to counter my proposal, especially my salary. I should've gone higher.

THE BIGGEST NEGOTIATION MISTAKE THAT YOU PROBABLY ALREADY MADE

"I didn't negotiate my first job out of college," 33-year-old freelancer and personal finance writer Kristin Wong told me. "It didn't seem like negotiating was an option, and at the time, I didn't understand the whole process of negotiating. I felt grateful just to have a job, and I think that's a problem for a lot of people."

Like Wong, and probably you, I didn't negotiate on my first job out of college, or on my second job when I switched fields from entertainment to public relations.

Unfortunately, this move could be costly in the long run.

"A study from George Mason University and Temple University found that an employee who neglects to negotiate their first-ever salary could lose out on $600,000 over the course of their career," Wong said.[1] "Yes, there are other variables to consider with this figure, but it shows just how much not asking for more money can add up over time. You lose out on hundreds of thousands of dollars."

This study determined that those who negotiate on starting salaries usually end up with $5,000 more than their non-negotiating counterparts (Wong, me, probably you). That amount might seem like chump change at first, until you factor that into the entirety of your career, which is where that freakish extra $600,000 over the span of a 40-year career comes from.

You may have tried and failed to negotiate your starting salary at your first job because some companies draw a hard line on entry-level compensation and that's it. If you find this to be the case, make an effort to negotiate for something small just to get the experience. Perhaps request two days a month to work remotely, or ask the company to cover a continuing education course that's related to your job. At the very least, this will give you some practice in negotiation, and you may even find that the company is willing to meet your demands.

KNOW, BUT DON'T SHARE, YOUR BOTTOM LINE

Whether you're negotiating for a job or trying to buy a house, it's important to know your bottom line—the bare minimum you're willing to accept or pay. This number needs to be kept a secret in your head. Your opponent—yeah, we're going to call the person across the table your opponent—is going to try to get you to reveal this number. Don't do it.

Okay, *opponent* may be the wrong word, because Wong raises a good point.

"It's not about confrontation or trying to squeeze the other party," she said. "It's about coming to a mutually beneficial agreement. After all, you're providing value. They're getting something out of the process too."

A mutually beneficial agreement is important; however, letting someone know how much you expect to be paid makes it pretty easy for you to get low-balled. Even when you offer a range—like stating $62,000 to $70,000—you've made it clear that you'll accept $62,000. You need to know your bottom line—and stick to it. Don't negotiate against yourself.

This becomes a bit challenging for freelancers since you set your own rates, but there are a few ways around this that will be discussed later on in the chapter.

LEARN HOW TO VALUE YOURSELF

This obnoxious abstract phrase provides the foundation for your entire negotiation strategy: you have to know your worth. "I have a bad habit of undervaluing myself, so I always force myself ask for 15 percent more," Wong told me. "There was a report from Clarke University that said employers can typically afford to offer 15 percent to 20 percent more than their initial rate, so I think it's a safe rule of thumb.[2] When I have to toss out the first number, I typically tack on 15 percent more than my knee-jerk rate, because I know my knee-jerk rate is usually low."

Tips for the traditionally employed (employees at companies)

→ *What are other people making?* Know what people in your position at other companies are making by using Web sites like Salary.com and GlassDoor.com and by just asking real-life people. Be sure you're asking people who work in the same or a similar city in order to get the most accurate information.

→ *What's the cost of living?* Don't forget to account for the cost of living in your area when searching the median salaries for your job. You can often filter online search results for your local market.

→ *Don't get mad—get paid!* Don't get mad if you determine you're underpaid relative to the market average for your position or just within your own company. Instead, get ready to negotiate!

Tips for freelancers (the self-employed)

→ *Research means talking, not using Web sites.* Unlike the traditionally employed, it's a bit harder for freelancers to search for median salaries on Web sites, so it's imperative to talk, talk, talk to other freelancers about rates. One of the biggest reasons companies can get away with underpaying freelancers is our lack of communication with one another.

→ *Awkward chats help raise the collective price point.* It may feel incredibly vulnerable to share with a fellow freelancer how much you're making on a project. She could judge your ability to negotiate, or you might feel awkward that it's a high number, or you may not want to risk a client getting snaked. All valid points, but the only way to keep raising the collective price point is if more people in your field start to demand more money.

→ *Ditch the scarcity mind-set.* Some clients may very well look for someone at a lower price point, but that's their loss. You want to work with clients who are willing to pay you what you are worth. And those clients do exist. It can be scary to cut lower-paying clients off your roster as you grow, but it's an important part of getting paid what you deserve.

Whether you are negotiating on a starting salary or meeting with a boss for an annual review or communicating to a client that you're raising your rates as a freelancer, it's important to learn the delicate act of making your demands, but with tact and, more importantly, proof to back up your claim that you deserve more.

GO INTO A MEETING WITH PROOF OF YOUR WORTH

Your parents may tell you how successful you're going to be, and your dog may look at you with nothing but adoration, but neither of these things are going to make an employer want to pay you more money. You need proof.

The common time to begin a conversation about a raise or other change in compensation comes during your annual review. You're usually going to get some advance notice of this meeting, but two days before isn't the time to scramble for metrics. You should be tracking those all year.

→ *Have a success folder:* Keep a folder on your desktop and fill it with proof of your awesomeness as it manifests. Take screenshots of metrics (like that time your tweet chat trended), save copies of e-mails from clients praising your work, and chronicle moments a higher-up complimented your input on a project. This way you don't need to try to think back over your successful moments from the last year because you've got them all ready to go and with evidence.

→ *Track improvement:* Getting negative feedback from a boss or colleague sucks—a lot—but you can use it as an opportunity to prove growth later on, especially if it's chronicled in previous reviews or sent to you via e-mail. In your next review, you should pull out the old feedback and address specifically how you changed your behaviors and improved. And I mean specifically. Don't say, "It was previously reported that I had issues with time management, but I'm doing better now." No, no—you need to go in with something like "Last year, it was mentioned that I had issues with time management, so this year I've ensured all reports were delivered before due dates, and I alerted my team to any potential issues for delays on projects, such as the time . . ."

→ *Know who can speak to your worth:* Learn how to cultivate strong relationships with colleagues, managers, and superiors so you're able to have people who will advocate for you during your company's compensation discussions. Start building these relationships by taking actions like the following: requesting bi-weekly or monthly one-on-ones with them; requesting to take on new and challenging tasks; cc-ing your direct superior on positive feedback from a client or coworker; taking the initiative to understand the job level above your own and beginning to do some of the work in the position above your own, and requesting some of those responsibilities to prove you're ready for a promotion; doing your best to be viewed as a team player; and anticipating the potential needs of your superiors.

→ *Provide proof you're being underpaid:* That sounds a bit aggressive, and it's certainly a moment that needs to be handled with diplomacy, but you should let your boss know that you know you're underpaid. It's helpful to base this assessment on the median salary in your market by using Web sites like Salary.com and GlassDoor.com, but it's easy for your boss to counter with something like "We don't have the budget for a raise that big this year" or "We're not as big as XYZ company." Instead, it's more valuable if you know your coworkers' salaries, as long as they're in the same or very similar positions. Just be prepared: it's possible your boss may be able to tell you exactly why your coworker is outearning you.

These tactics translate to salary negotiations during job interviews. Proving what you accomplished at a previous position and having references can go a long way with an employer and help you understand how to set your value.

For Freelancers

This advice all applies to you too. Long-term contracts or relationships with clients mean you'll eventually need to have a conversation about increasing your compensation. You're going to want to have proof that you've done a swell job for the last year. Metrics are particularly important, such as increased page views on work you've done, or the "open and click through" rate of an e-mail marketing campaign, or the increase in social media followers on a profile you're handling. You should also gather testimonials from clients as you go that may be helpful in sharing with other clients when you explain that you're raising your rate for the year.

ASK FOR IT!

You know your worth and have your proof. Now it's time to actually "ask for the order," to borrow a piece of wisdom handed down to me from my mother during my childhood to show me how to get what I want in life: you can't just expect things to be handed to you—you need to ask for them. If you want to earn a certain amount, then go into that room, make your case, and state why you deserve a $10,000 raise. Do it politely and diplomatically, but ask nonetheless.

This advice applies far beyond the context of personal finance; it should be used in your regular day-to-day life.

$ *When I asked for the order: After a year of employment with the afore-mentioned start-up, I took my annual review as an opportunity to do some big-time negotiating. By analyzing what other people doing my job earned and by proving my worth with success metrics, I negotiated a 40 percent raise—from $50,000 to $70,000. It makes you wonder how much I could've been earning in year one if I'd just known how to value myself better. It makes me wonder, at least!*

LEVERAGE IS HELPFUL, IF YOU'RE WILLING TO WALK

A common negotiation tactic, whether it's for a salary or when you're making a big purchase, is to have a competing offer and to threaten to walk away from the deal. It can be incredibly effective—if you're actually willing to walk.

> Maria didn't care for her job anymore. She'd outgrown the position, but there were no open jobs within the company for moving her up the ladder. Maria felt overworked and was by all accounts definitely underpaid, so she started shopping around for another job. After a few interviews, she finally got an offer, but it would require a 45-minute commute for a job that paid only slightly better and took her a little bit off the career trajectory she saw for herself. Maria contemplated using the offer as leverage in her current position, but realized she really didn't want to have to walk if her employer failed to match her salary demands. So she elected to decline the offer and not take the risk.

Using another offer as leverage does create a double-edged sword situation (it's a cliché, but an appropriate one). Maria will never know if her employer would've increased her salary to keep her, but had her employer said no and she'd stayed, it could have lessened her leverage in the future as her employer would know she'd already tried this tactic once before and failed to follow through.

FREELANCERS: YOU'RE PROBABLY UNDERCUTTING YOURSELVES—BY A LOT

You enter the negotiation dance the moment someone reaches out to hire you.

As a freelancer, you're potentially saving clients oodles of money. They're not paying for your health care or retirement accounts, or withholding money from your paycheck for taxes. You have to factor all those things into the cost of your service, and honestly, you're probably undervaluing yourself. Here's one way to shift power back in your favor.

The Counterstrategy

When a client asks you, "How much would you charge for [insert scope of work here]?" try countering with this: "Actually, I'd really be curious how much your budget is for this project. Then I could tell you what I could offer based on your total available budget."

On more than one occasion I've netted myself thousands of dollars by answering a question with a question. I'm not kidding, thousands.

A major financial company asked me how much it would cost for three articles. Given that it was a well-known organization (you'd know the commercials), I mentally hoped for $1 a word, which would mean around $800 per article. But I tried the counterstrategy described above and was told, "Well, we have a budget of $4,000 for three articles. Would that work for you?" Yes—yes it would!

Offering an à la carte approach to your services can be beneficial to negotiating with your client as well. You can try saying, "Let me know your budget range, and I'll get back to you on the services I can offer for each tier."

$ *"It sounds crazy, but I felt truly successful the first time I negotiated and got rejected," Kristin Wong admitted. "I forced myself to ask the client for a higher rate, and, unfortunately, they said their budget was limited. You would think I'd be disappointed and maybe somewhat embarrassed. But I actually felt confident. People always say, 'The worst that happens is they say no.' Well, the 'worst' happened, and it wasn't bad. You still get work. Life goes on. Plus, I knew I had done everything in my control to maximize my rate, and that made me feel powerful."*
You can learn more about Kristin Wong on her site TheWildWong.com

YOU CAN NEGOTIATE ANYTHING

Mastering the art of negotiation isn't imperative just for increasing your salary and getting paid your worth. You should be taking this skill into just about every area of your financial life, especially if you're about to make a large purchase like a car or a home.

You could even start practicing in low-risk situations to begin preparing yourself for big-sticker costs like a car or a home. Going to a yard sale or trying to buy something from Craigslist or eBay provides a great opportunity to ask for a price and try a counter—"That's more than I was prepared to spend. I was thinking more along the lines of . . ." You can then progress to negotiating with a landlord who's trying to increase your rent or with your cell phone provider. Always be sure to counter with an amount that's slightly below what you actually are willing to pay so you can come up a little bit and actually reach the amount you're happy to fork over.

This mentality, of course, works the reverse in a job negotiation, in which you should go in higher to provide room for a counter. Let's say you would do the job for $70,000. The company offers $67,500. Go in a little higher than what you're actually willing to accept; for example, counter with $72,500. Then when the company comes back with $70,000, you can feel comfortable agreeing to the terms since you're actually getting what you were prepared to take.

🔧 5 STEPS TO PREPARE FOR YOUR NEGOTIATION

1. *Practice:* Doing a mock negotiation with a friend or parent is a good step, but try negotiating with some stakes at risk. Call your Internet provider and try to get a better deal, or see if your credit card company will lower the APR on your account (there's more about that in chapter 8). Any and all experience with negotiating, even if the stakes are saving only $10 a month on Internet, is helpful.
2. *Know your worth:* Do the research to go into the meeting prepared. Know the average wage of someone doing your

job in your city and at other companies and your own. Provide detail if you are aware of other employees in the company doing the same work and earning more than you. And you should be getting a salary that more than keeps pace with inflation each year.

3. *Have your metrics ready:* Have physical proof of the improvements you've made and the successes you've had since your last review; use them to prove that you're ready for a promotion and/or raise.

4. *Ask for the order:* Tell your employer (or client) what you want. State plainly how much you expect to see in a raise or that you want the promotion to Junior Executive Head of Something or Other and the associated pay raise.

5. *Understand how your company's compensation works, and find someone willing to vouch for you:* Some companies determine raises by getting managers together in a room and hashing it out. You need to know how your company doles out money and have someone in there ready to advocate for you. If you're a freelancer, it's important to have a strong backlist of current and former clients who are willing to act as references on your behalf.

Chapter 15

Investing: No, It Isn't Gambling!

I'LL NEVER FORGET THE DAY I stopped being intimidated by the stock market. It occurred in the summer of 2009, and like many of my formative money lessons, it came as the result of two sentences from my dad.

We were in the car, and I nonchalantly asked him if I should think about investing in the stock market. A saver by nature, I'd managed to squirrel away a decent amount of money during college by working as a resident assistant (hey, it was an easy job for good pay).

Instead of just giving me a basic overview of how the stock market worked and ways I could start to dabble without having to do eons of time-intensive research, my dad took this moment to tell me exactly how much money my parents' portfolio dropped during the Great Recession.

A significant sum of money.

"But we didn't panic," my dad said. "The stock market is cyclical, so if you just leave a well-balanced portfolio alone, it will come back around."

It did.

That sentiment took this typically risk-adverse, natural saver of a young woman and made her an aggressive investor who isn't afraid when her net worth fluctuates a bit during downturns in the market.

Now let's get you there too.

BEFORE WE BEGIN, A LESSON ABOUT THE GLORIES OF COMPOUND INTEREST

Compound interest is the eighth wonder of the world. He who understands it, earns it. He who doesn't, pays it.

—Albert Einstein (probably)

The basic way to explain compound interest is that it's your interest earning interest.

For example, if you invest $100 and get an 8 percent return after year one, you have $108. You decide not to invest anything else and to just leave the $108 alone. In year two, you would be earning interest not only on your initial $100 investment, but on the additional $8. If you get another 8 percent return, you've earned $8.64 and now have $116.64.

When you dabble enough in personal finance content, you'll hear over and over that investing is well-suited for the young investor. The reason is compound interest. Compound interest favors the young because you have a longer time to get a return and to weather the ups and downs of the market.

At age 25, I put $3,000 into an S&P 500 index fund. Using a conservative estimate that I'll receive an average 8 percent interest rate each year (some years will be higher and some lower), I can expect the investment to have grown to around $6,476.77 by the time I'm 30.* Let's say I leave it alone until I'm 60. That initial $3,000 investment would be worth $44,356.03 without me continuing to contribute a single penny. If I waited until I was 35 to invest $3,000 and received the same 8 percent return, I'd have $20,545.43 by age 60. Ten years of waiting to invest $3,000 would cost me nearly $24,000.

Compound interest notoriously works against you when you have debt. It's the reason it feels like the principal balance on your credit card just never seems to go down.

Okay, so if the math of why it's important to start investing doesn't get you hot under the collar like it does for me, then maybe explaining why investing isn't actually guesswork and is 100 percent accessible to you will help.

WHY SHOULD I PUT MONEY IN THE STOCK MARKET?
INVESTING FEELS LIKE GAMBLING!

Ah, the common question: isn't investing just a crapshoot? In short, yes and no. There is always risk associated with investing, but there's also risk in just letting your money sit in a savings account losing purchasing power

---

* This doesn't account for any fees I may have to pay. Play with calculations yourself using the U.S. Securities and Exchange Commission's Compound Interest Calculator: https://www.investor.gov/tools/calculators/compound-interest-calculator.

for decades thanks to an old foe known as inflation. Investing gives you the opportunity to examine asset allocation and rebalance from an aggressive to moderate to conservative portfolio over the course of your life.

Too much technical talk for the start of this chapter? Let me rephrase: investing equals fat stacks in retirement, while putting money in a traditional savings account means you'll be eating cat food, if you're lucky.

"There are a lot of people who feel this way, especially with what we've seen during the 2008 financial crisis," 26-year-old licensed financial advisor Kevin L. Matthews II told me. "Even though those memories of the Great Recession are real, there are several big differences between gambling and investing. Those differences can be explained in one word: ownership."

Matthews, who founded the site Building Bread and authored the book *Starting Point: How to Create Wealth That Lasts*, explained that when you're gambling, you don't own a slot machine, nor do you own the casino. But an investor does own a piece of a company when purchasing stock. While your returns aren't guaranteed, you still own a small portion of the company, which means you can receive dividends and vote on whether the CEO should receive a bonus.

Kristin Wong, a 33-year-old freelancer and personal finance writer based in Los Angeles, also dismisses the notion of investing being gambling.

"If investing feels like gambling, you're doing it wrong. Yes, day trading can very much be a gamble, and some people enjoy that. However, 'buy and hold' investing is a whole different animal. It's based on long-term returns, not day-to-day fluctuations," Wong said.

Spending less and saving more are two key pillars on the path to wealth, but they're pretty pointless without investing. Unless you've somehow made millions upon millions already and plan to not give into lifestyle inflation at all. If that's your situation, then go do whatever you want. Everyone else, I have a secret to tell you.

WAIT A SECOND, I'M ALREADY INVESTING?

One of my favorite conversations to have with friends about investing goes a little something like this:

Friend: "I don't know, Erin. The idea of investing just really stresses me out."

Me: "Do you have a 401(k) at work?"

Friend: "Yeah."

Me: "And are you contributing money out of each paycheck to that
   401(k)?"

Friend, sensing a trap: "Yes . . ."

Me: "Then you're already investing."

It's a common misconception among millennials that investing is only individual stock picking or suited-up white guys with slicked-back hair screaming at one another over something called futures. Or you may think investing is just completely cost-prohibitive because you need a lot of money to get started.

You don't have to be bringing home a six-figure salary to start investing, nor do you need a lot of technical knowledge. If you set up a retirement plan at work or contribute to a Roth IRA because you heard that's a good idea, then you've already started investing.* Now, was that really so hard? Saving for retirement is a good first step, but you also need to learn how to invest outside of your 401(k) and IRA. You know, just in case you want money you can touch before you're nearly dead—I mean 59 and a half.

$ *I started investing with my first job. They offered an employer-sponsored 401(k), and I was lucky to have that encouragement. I was young; it was the first time in my life I had made more than $10 an hour, so I was hesitant to sock away that cash in a boring old retirement account. Thankfully, my coworkers convinced me to set up an automatic savings from my paycheck. They said I'd never miss it. Oddly enough, even though my salary wasn't huge, they were right: I didn't miss it. And after a few years, I had saved up nearly $10,000. That was hugely encouraging.*

—Kristin Wong, personal finance writer and founder of TheWildWong.com

Investing Terms You Need to Know

→ *Actively managed:* A professional is managing the investment directly and trying to beat passively managed funds. You pay a premium to have an actively managed fund. Some managers can beat

---

* Want to pause and understand IRAs? Flip to chapter 16.

the indexes on long stretches, but passively is usually the way to go for rookie investors looking to get the most value.

→ *Stock:* On the most basic level, you own a piece of a corporation and therefore have a claim on the assets and earnings of a company.

→ *Shares:* For the sake of simplicity, you can think of it the same way you should stock. Shares are technically what a company's stock is divided into. But if you own stock, then you own shares. (It sounds more complicated than it is.) If the stock of a company is pizza, then the individual slices are shares. If you bought a whole pizza, then you obviously have some slices.

→ *Shareholder:* What you're called when you own stock in a corporation—aka you're technically part-owner of a company.

→ *Equity:* Technically, equity is assets minus liabilities, but for the sake of investing, we'll say that owning equity is the same as owning stock because you have a share of ownership in a corporation.

→ *Bond:* You're a lender when you own a bond. A bond is a purchase of an organization's debt. There is a maturity rate on a bond, which means that in a predetermined period of time, the organization will pay you back the amount you lent (the principal) plus interest. The interest rate is also determined when the bond is issued.

→ *Dividend:* Dividends are one of the ways you can make money when investing in stocks, the other being selling the stock. However, not all companies offer the option to receive payout via dividends. Dividends are cash payments a company will make to its shareholders, typically every quarter (every three months). Dividends are determined by the company's board of directors, so what you get from investing in Company A will be different than dividends from Company B.

→ *Mutual fund:* You combine your purchasing power with other investors to buy into a specific portfolio—aka a group of stocks or bonds, or stocks and bonds all bundled together. No, you don't know these other people. This way, you can use a small amount of money to buy into the market and diversify your exposure. You're diversified by not buying one single type of stock in a solitary sector. For example, your mutual fund may have both international and domestic stocks and bonds instead of just some shares in a single tech stock or shares in multiple tech companies. Mutual funds are actively managed by professionals who make decisions about the investments to try to make the most profit for investors. High profits aren't always achieved, and there will be down years. Because these funds are actively managed, there are higher expense ratios.

→ *Index fund:* A type of mutual fund that allows you to buy shares to match a specific stock market index. The Standard & Poor's 500—commonly referred to as the S&P 500—and the Total Stock Market Index Fund are two common examples of index funds. These are passively managed, so you avoid some of the fees associated with actively managed mutual funds. If you buy $100 worth of an S&P 500 index fund and Apple stock makes up 3 percent of that index, $3 of your $100 goes toward Apple stock.

→ *Exchange-traded fund (ETF):* This type of fund gives you a bit of two worlds. It's built like a mutual fund/index fund, but operates like buying individual stocks. You can usually buy in for the cost of a single share of an ETF instead of needing to save up $3,000 to open an index fund or mutual fund. It makes sense to purchase this type of fund if you want to trade instantly during any time of the day, the way you would a stock.

→ *Target date fund:* This is a type of fund found within retirement accounts, like IRAs or 401(k)s. It's a set-it-and-forget-it-type fund because you pick one associated with your anticipated retirement year, such as Target Date Fund 2055, and then the fund rebalances your investments from aggressive to moderate to conservative the closer you get to retirement.

→ *IRA:* Individual Retirement Arrangement (you'll also sometimes hear people say "Individual Retirement Account"). It allows you to tuck money away for retirement by investing in stocks or bonds or even leaving money in cash reserves. There are tax advantages of contributing to an IRA, but as a general rule, you can't withdraw funds without paying a penalty until you're 59½ years old. The IRS also imposes limits on who can contribute (high earners get phased out) and how much. In 2016, you can contribute up to $5,500 if you're under age 50.

→ *Roth IRA:* This is a form of IRA or 401(k) in which you contribute after-tax dollars so you don't get the tax advantage today, but you won't have to pay taxes when you take money out in retirement.

→ *401(k) and 403(b):* Two similar types of retirement accounts often offered by an employer. A 401(k) is through a for-profit employer, while non-profit employers provide a 403(b). When you hear the expression "Get your employer match," it's usually referring to the amount your employer will put into your 401(k) or 403(b). There will be options for mutual funds, index funds, bonds, and other forms of investments within your 401(k) or 403(b).

→ *Asset allocation:* Your asset allocation should be based on your risk tolerance, when you'll need to use the invested funds, and your age. The asset allocation determines how much of your money goes toward riskier investments (such as stocks) and how much is held conservatively in bonds or even cash reserves.

→ *Risk tolerance:* This one is pretty self-explanatory, but how much risk are you willing to take in your investing? Be careful about letting your risk tolerance be the sole dictator of your investing plans, because being high-risk close to retirement could mean too much is in stocks, and having a low risk tolerance in your twenties means you are not investing aggressively enough.

→ *Expense ratio:* How much you, the shareholder, have to pay in order to help cover the operational costs of a fund. Brokerages have to make money too!

→ *Brokerage account:* This is how you'll be able to buy and sell investments. You'll need to go through a brokerage firm, but that doesn't mean you have to have a specific broker you call, like you see in the movies. You can facilitate this yourself online with companies like Vanguard and Fidelity.

→ *Bear market:* A downturn in the market when prices start dropping is known as a bear market. It often means people start to sell their investments because they anticipate losses.

→ *Bull market:* When the market is in an upswing and prices start to rise, which often makes people buy.

Now that you're familiar with some of the lingo, let's debunk a few deep-rooted myths about investing.

COMMON MISCONCEPTIONS ABOUT INVESTING

Investing isn't only for the wealthy. You, with your average income and your basic understanding of how money works, can start investing as soon as you put this book down (and get on a password-protected Wi-Fi network because ain't nobody got time for getting hacked).

Before you get started, Kevin Matthews and Kristin Wong encourage you to try to erase these common misconceptions from your mind:

1. Don't believe that investing is a short-term deal—that you buy a stock on Monday, watch it closely, and sell it by Wednesday or Thursday. While some people certainly do that, successful investors usually hold their investments for years before deciding to sell. It is a lot like planting a seed and waiting for a tree to grow. It's about time in the market, not timing the market.
2. You don't need to be a stock picker in order to invest.
3. It doesn't take some sort of secret skill to invest, and you don't need a finance degree. Most "Wall Street experts" would be lucky if they were right 50 percent of the time. All you need is patience, consistency, and time.
4. You don't have to understand everything about investing before you start.
5. Don't panic and sell when the market takes a tumble. That's actually a decent time to put some more money into your index funds because it's like everything just went on sale.
6. Perhaps the most harmful misconception, however, is that you should watch investment news and stock tips on TV. The problem here is that the person you're watching does not know you or me; we have different time horizons (when we want to access our money), and we might react to risk differently. You have to invest based on your own goals, not what someone you've never met tells you those goals should be.

$ *If you have a good asset allocation and you're rebalancing, then all of that market fluctuation is kind of a moot point. If you have an allocation that's aligned with your risk tolerance and your time horizon for when you need access to that money, then you'll be weathered from market fluctuations.*

—Anjali Jariwala, CFP®, CPA, and founder of FIT Advisors LLC

SHOULD I WORRY ABOUT INVESTING WHEN I HAVE STUDENT LOANS AND OTHER BILLS?

You may assume that investing in the stock market is a laughable concept if you're struggling to cover your monthly bills right now. Should you seriously be thinking about investing if you have debt? Well, yes, in a way.

Save for retirement: You need to at least be contributing toward a retirement account, even if you have student loans. The only real exception to this rule is if you will start missing monthly minimum payments on credit cards or student loans by putting 3 percent to 5 percent of your paycheck toward a 401(k).

The next decision about continuing to invest beyond retirement contributions while in debt depends on your tolerance for being in the red and the interest rate you're currently paying.

If you have low-interest-rate debt (5 percent or less) and can stomach having debt: If you're making a surplus of cash and you'd rather invest some instead of just paying down your debt, then this isn't a terrible decision.

If you have low-interest-rate debt (5 percent or less) and can't stomach debt: Then just contribute to get your employer match on a 401(k), or maybe just a little bit above the match, and aggressively pay down that debt! As Sophia Bera, CFP® and founder of Gen Y Planning, told me, "I've never had a client say, 'You know what I regret? Paying off my student loans. That was dumb.'"

If you have high-interest-rate debt (like credit cards): It doesn't matter if you can stomach having debt or not, you should focus your extra funds on knocking out that dead weight. If we assume you'll get a conservative return of about 8 percent in the stock market—or even if you believe the slightly outlandish claim that you can assume 12 percent—you're still losing money by carrying that 18 percent APR credit card. Just pay it off and then redirect your focus.

KNOW YOUR RISK TOLERANCE BEFORE YOU START INVESTING

The first step to successful investing is understanding your risk tolerance and how it will impact your strategy. Let's say you're the type of person who is going to panic when a major event causes the stock market to go into a free fall. You'll be compelled to start selling everything possible to mitigate your losses, when you really should sit tight and wait it out. You probably should just avoid logging into your portfolio entirely on days the market is taking a tumble.

Those with a low appetite for risk may not get aggressive when they're young and have the glories of compound interest and time on their sides. Those with an appetite for risk taking could wait too long to rebalance for a more conservative portfolio and risk the market dropping around the time they planned to start making consistent withdrawals, like around retirement age.

Having to battle with your own gut instinct is one reason handing your investments over to a financial planner can be a good idea, if it makes sense for your budget. But for the average, rookie millennial investor, technology makes it pretty simple to get started on your own.

ARE YOU FINANCIALLY READY TO START INVESTING?

(In addition to retirement savings, that is.) Here's how to tell if you're ready:

- ❏ You contribute to a company 401(k) or 403(b).
- ❏ You have three to six months of living expenses saved.
- ❏ You have no high-interest debt.
- ❏ You'll actually read this entire chapter.
- ❏ You're willing to do some research to ensure you don't pay too much in fees or get swindled into an expensive investment product.

Check yes to everything? Okay, let's get started.

HOW DO I EVEN GO ABOUT INVESTING IN THE FIRST PLACE?

I should've been more analytical about my first investment outside of a retirement savings. I'd read a motivational article about why it's important to start investing when you're in your twenties, because compound interest, duh, and I decided to just get 'er going. I phoned up my bank, did absolutely zero due diligence about fees, and dumped $3,000 into a mutual fund geared toward young investors. At least that's what the nice lady on the phone told me was the best fund for my overzealous self.

This isn't the best method for picking a brokerage or investment platform.

How to Pick an Investment Company:

→ *Is there a minimum investment requirement?* The gamification of investing with apps makes it seem like you can easily buy into the stock market with just a few cents. That's not always how it works. Some investment companies do set investment minimums to start a fund, but you don't have to keep dumping in that much each time you plan to buy. In June 2016, Vanguard requires a $3,000 minimum and Fidelity asks for $2,500 to invest in the companies' S&P 500 Index Funds. But you can contribute smaller sums like $25 a month after that initial investment.

→ *What are the expense ratios?* An expense ratio tells you how much it costs the company to operate your investment, such as the operational costs of providing an index fund. Your returns are going to be reduced by this amount, which is why you should know how much you're paying the company to operate the investment. It's pretty simple to find this information either directly on a company's Web site or through third-party sites like Morningstar or Yahoo! Finance. Even passively managed funds have an expense ratio because the investment companies do need to make money, but the fees are usually quite low.

→ *What are the transaction fees?* Check to see if you're being charged each time you buy or sell a mutual fund or stock. It's not an uncommon practice, but you want to go with a low-fee option.

→ *Can I have passively managed accounts?* Unless you feel strongly about paying for an actively managed account, be sure you have the option to invest in a no-frills index fund that doesn't charge investment management or advisory fees.

→ *Do the investments align with my values?* Be aware that buying into index funds can mean you're purchasing shares in companies that may not align with your sensibilities (think mega corporations that do things college students stage sit-in protests about). However, socially responsible investing is incredibly difficult if you want to maximize profits. #JustSayin'

Investment Companies for Your Consideration

There are ample options to choose from, but my top recommendations for you to research are:

- → *Vanguard:* Founded by Jack Bogle, the father of the no-load mutual fund and ultimately the one to create and introduce the world to the first index fund. The site could use a face-lift, but the customer service is friendly, as are the fees.
- → *Fidelity:* A traditional name that's working on becoming more accessible to millennials. The fees are competitive with Vanguard, and the cost to start a fund is often lower than Vanguard's.
- → *Betterment:* A robo-advisor that actually uses some Vanguard funds in their portfolios. It's geared toward millennials, is simple to use, and provides a well-designed user experience.
- → *Wealthfront:* Also a robo-advisor that angles to help even those without much in assets enter the stock market with a $500 account minimum and low fees.

This isn't to say other investment companies aren't valid options, but these are the four I'm most comfortable recommending to fellow millennials based on personal experience and extensive conversations with financial advisors.

HOW MUCH DO I NEED TO START INVESTING?

With some investment companies, you don't need any minimums to open certain retirement funds, like an IRA or your company 401(k). So yes, you can just get started now. But if you want to start investing in addition to preparing for retirement, then you probably need some savings. However, you should follow these steps first:

- → Continue contributing to your company retirement plan.
- → Have three to six months of emergency savings set aside.
- → Pay off any high-interest debt, like credit cards.

You next need to decide which investing platform you want to use. You may need to save $2,500 to $3,000 in order to open an index fund or mutual fund, but once it's open you don't need to wait for your next $3,000 to keep investing. Instead, you could just contribute $25 a month. Mutual funds, exchange-traded funds (ETFs), and individual stocks may also have a relatively low buy-in depending on what specifically you're looking to purchase. For example, a single share of Apple may cost $108, while a technology ETF may provide exposure to multiple types of technology stock, with a buy-in of $120 for a share. However, one share in a company doesn't really get you much.

WHAT DO I INVEST IN IF I'M NOT PICKING STOCKS?

If you've read this chapter and still consider investing just the action of stock picking, we need to have a deeper conversation. Investing does not have to equal stock picking. In fact, index funds are my personal favorite way to invest in the market. And despite my repeated pleas to focus on index fund investing, my friend Lillian loves individual stock picking. She texted me one morning about purchasing Netflix stock, to which I typed back, in obnoxious all caps: INDEX FUNDS. Lillian's feeling is that index funds are boring, and it's fun to put money into individual stock picking (which is a lot more like gambling). Putting a little bit of fun money— money you're totally comfortable losing—into stock picking is fine but shouldn't be your only investing strategy. So for all those fans of stock picking over index funds, here's what I say: *Index funds are boring and effective because building wealth isn't about gambling.*

Even Warren Buffett advocates for index funds! In one of his annual letters to Berkshire Hathaway shareholders, Buffett wrote:

> My advice to the trustee could not be more simple: put 10 percent of the cash in short-term government bonds and 90 percent in a very low-cost S&P 500 index fund. (I suggest Vanguard's.) I believe the trust's long-term results from this policy will be superior to those attained by most investors—whether pension funds, institutions, or individuals—who employ high-fee managers.[1]

No person alive has made the stock market his bitch quite like Buffett. So if Buffett says to keep it simple and invest in index funds, then you can bet this is solid advice for you to follow.

Not convinced? It's been reported that Buffett gave LeBron James the same advice. So if it's good enough for the Oracle of Omaha and King James, then it's good enough for you and me.

Index funds are a good place to start, but you may eventually want to speak with a financial advisor about your asset allocation in order to make sure you're diversified and not being too aggressive when you should be moderate or too conservative when you should be aggressive.

Should you feel compelled to do some stock picking, then keep this advice from Anjali Jariwala in mind:

> I would look at how much excess money [you] have that offers [you] a little play bucket. After maxing out on a 401(k) and having a good emergency fund of three to six months plus a healthy savings rate— then maybe [you] have a little play money to do stock picking.

$ *I don't pick individual stocks, but I've tried it in the past. I wanted to see what it was all about. I write about money, so I figured I should know how it works. I spent $2,000 picking individual, volatile stocks and actively trading them. In the first few months, I earned a $1,000 return, then I lost $500 in the next few months. In two years, I ended up walking away with $2,500. Not bad, right? But I also spent hours upon hours researching and mulling over those stocks. In the time I spent doing that, I could have taken on another client or picked up a side gig and earned considerably more money. Some people have more luck with it. For most of us, though, buy and hold investing is a better strategy.*

—Kristin Wong

WHERE SHOULD I GET INVESTMENT ADVICE?

Probably not from the person trying to sell you on an investment product. If a broker is getting a commission, then you could be led into an investment that's suitable, but not the best option for you.* You should also ignore people screaming at you on TV about when to buy and sell, because as Kevin Matthews told me, that person doesn't know you, your individual investment needs, nor your time horizon.

Instead, I recommend consulting a Certified Financial Planner. A CFP

---

* Don't forget about the difference between suitability and fiduciary standards; see chapter 17.

can help you rebalance portfolios and invest in accordance with both your risk tolerance and your time horizon for when you plan to use the funds. You should also consume as much content about investing as possible in order to start to make intelligent investing decisions on your own.

Not ready to commit to paying a professional, but hoping to learn even more? Try out some of these free resources:

→ Investor.gov
→ Investopedia.com
→ ObliviousInvestor.com
→ Radical Personal Finance podcast

Depending on how entrenched in the investing world you want to get, you can start by picking up these books:

→ *The Intelligent Investor* by Benjamin Graham
→ *The Little Book of Common Sense Investing* by John C. Bogle
→ *A Random Walk Down Wall Street* by Burton G. Malkiel

DO I REALLY NEED TO INVEST? CAN'T I JUST SAVE THE MONEY?

We've talked about this—no, you can't just save the money under your mattress, in a candy tin buried in the backyard, or tucked away into a savings account. Yes, you do really need to invest, even if that's contributing to a company 401(k). The longer your money just sits around in that pitiful savings account—even if you did already switch it over to one that earns at least 1.00 percent APY—then you're not doing much to help yourself accumulate wealth.

Due to inflation and the natural erosion of your purchasing power by leaving your money at 1.00 percent APY, you aren't doing yourself any favors by saving alone. That means your money is losing value if it's just sitting around in savings. You know how you hear older people at work grumble about this year's raises not even keeping up with inflation? They're grumbling because their income, even if it stays the same or increases a tiny bit, still won't buy as much this year as it did last year due to inflation. It's the compound interest received from investing that helps your saved money mature and grow to beat inflation and make you a millionaire with minimal effort. It's hard to save your way to a million without investing or creating something Google wants to buy.

🔧 ROOKIE INVESTOR ACTION LIST

❑ Know yourself—what's your risk tolerance? Will you be able to handle it when the market dips down, or is that going to send you into a sell, sell, sell–induced panic? If you're likely to get trigger-happy when the market takes a downturn, then you should probably avoid checking in on your investments more than once a quarter.

❑ In fact, market drops are completely normal, so stay calm and carry on.

❑ Understand expense ratios before making the investment so you know just how much you're paying for the pleasure of investing.

❑ Start investing early and consistently to properly take advantage of compound interest.

❑ Investing is a gradual process, and you'll learn with time.

❑ Evaluate your investments by the progress over time, not overnight.

❑ Investing *should* be boring—stick with the buy and hold mentality.

Chapter 16

Retirement: Can It Ever Happen for Me?

"Guess who has two thumbs and a 401k!" Aiden, a former coworker, wrote on my Facebook wall.

"SOOOO proud," I commented. I was, but I estimated he'd lost $5,400 before market returns in employer matches by waiting more than three years to set up his 401(k). The company matched at 4 percent, and he'd been working there for three years and earned around $45,000. That meant he'd failed to collect $1,800 a year for three years just by not contributing 4 percent of his paycheck into the 401(k).

That's $5,400 of free money. That's right, it's *free*.

Aiden is a great example of so many millennials experiencing apathy when it comes to setting up a 401(k). He knew it was the right thing to do. He knew how to do it. He knew that he'd get matched 100 percent up to 4 percent and be immediately vested—which will all be explained later in this chapter—but he still didn't take the 30 minutes to set it up.

I found out about Aiden's lack of saving through a hilarious interaction with his dad. Aiden must've mentioned to his dad that a coworker blogged about personal finance, because I received a Facebook comment on my Broke Millennial page from a man asking me to encourage his son to set up a 401(k).

The notification popped on my phone, and I burst out laughing when I saw the man's last name matched Aiden's.

"Hey," I called to Aiden in our typical-open-floor-plan office, "is your dad's name Roger?"

"Yeah," he responded. "Why?"

Walking over to keep the conversation between the two of us, I said, "He just told me to tell you to set up your 401(k)."

"Seriously? How?" Aiden said, a slow flush creeping into his cheeks.

"It was cute. He commented on my Broke Millennial Facebook page," I responded, trying to take any sting of embarrassment out of the situation. Aiden's lack of a 401(k) became a running gag.

Every few months, I'd ask if Aiden had set up his 401(k). I even once ran a calculation of how much he was losing in the employer match and offered to help him crunch his budget to free up some money to contribute. No dice. Aiden was going to do it on his own time—nearly two years after his dad's Facebook comment.

DO YOU REALLY WANT TO WAIT UNTIL YOU'RE 72 TO RETIRE?

Recent surveys have speculated that the traditional retirement age of 65 isn't going to be possible for our generation. The new number is looking more like 72 to 75 years old. It comes as no surprise when you see these stats:

→ The average balance in a 401(k) in March 2016 is only $87,300.
→ The average IRA balance is $89,300.[1]

Those numbers include averages of accounts across a wide variety of ages, so even with the millennial generation lowering the average, it is unsettling to see averages this low.

Before you say it—yes, it's understandable why the burden of student loans is forefront in your mind and retiring seems far too abstract a concept. The student loan excuse is one of the reasons millennials consistently say they can't save for retirement. However, I think you have more ability to save than you're giving yourself credit for.

Because I know that you're already thinking it—yes, it is possible to get started, and yes, saving just a little is better than saving nothing at all.

COMPOUND INTEREST: REAL-LIFE MAGIC

If you skipped the investing chapter, let's do a quick refresher on compound interest and all its glories. (I encourage you to read chapter 15, "Investing: No, It Isn't Gambling!" before reading this one).

Compound interest occurs when your interest earns interest.

$ *Putting money into a retirement account does mean you're investing. You have lots of options like stocks, bonds, money markets, and certificates of deposits.*

Let's say you put $1,000 into a savings account that earns 1.00 percent APY. At the end of the year, you'll have $1,010 in savings. In year two, the 1.00 percent APY is being applied to your $1,010 in savings and not just your original $1,000. Even though you didn't add any money to your savings account, your interest is earning interest. By the end of year two, you'll have $1020.10.

Compound interest favors the young because the longer you have to get a return and to weather the ups and downs of the market, the more you'll add to your net worth. This is why I'm going to sound like every other financial expert ever and say *yes*, it's really important that you start saving for retirement now!

LET'S PLAY A GAME: WHAT HAPPENS WHEN YOU WAIT TO SAVE

Marshall, 25, earns $50,000 a year and receives a 3 percent match from his employer. He puts $250 per month into his 401(k), and his employer contributes $125. Marshall's annual contribution is $3,000, and his employer's is $1,500 for a total of $4,500 per year.

Marshall never gets a raise and magically stays with this employer for 40 years. His average return over those 40 years is 8 percent.

When he retires at 65, Marshall has $1,165,754.33 in his 401(k)—thanks, compound interest![2]

Had Marshall tucked $4,500 into a savings account earning 0.01 percent for 40 years, it would be worth $180,351.45.

But wait, what happens if Marshall doesn't start saving until he's 35? The same $4,500 for 30 years only nets him $509,774.45.

If he waits until 40, woof, Marshall only has $205,928.84.

$ *You can't guarantee that you will be making more money at a later age (it may be likely, but not certain). Secondly, if you haven't built good savings habits for the past 20 years, you will have a really hard time starting then.*

— *Eric Roberge, CFP®, founder of Beyond Your Hammock*

I get that this sounds silly because Marshall would most likely have increased his earnings from 25 to 40. He could totally start contributing way more than $250 a month toward his 401(k). So, let's see what happens in that case.

Marshall is 40 and now earns $80,000 a year and still wants to retire at 65. He has kids and a house now, but he can still afford to put $700 a month toward retirement, and his employer matches at 3 percent, which means an extra $200 per month. New Marshall now has $900 a month going into his 401(k), $525 more than Original Marshall.

At 65, Marshall will have $789,544.15.

Consistently saving $250 and getting an employer match starting at 25 would have earned Marshall an extra $376,210.18.

The Basic Math for You

Here's what would happen if you started saving $150 a year from your first job at age 22 and never increased your contributions until retirement at 65. This table accounts for an average 8 percent return.

Total Contribution per Month (You + Match)	Age You Start Saving	Years until Retirement (65)	401(k) Balance
$150	22	43	$593,249.41
$400	35	30	$543,759.41
$700	45	20	$384,400.50
$1,100	50	15	$358,407.90

If you put $150 a month into savings for 43 years, it would net you only $77,400. Saving $1,100 a month for 15 years would get you $198,000. And yet investing $150 a month for 43 years gets you $234,841.51 more than investing $1,110 a month for 15 years.

This is why you shouldn't wait to invest and try to play catch up.

WHY BOTHER SAVING WHEN YOU HAVE DEBT?

Because trying to play catch-up later is a pain! Did that compound interest example show you nothing?!

Well, that and the potential to get free money.

"There's no question about it. It's challenging to pay off loans, save for retirement, and still live your life on an early career salary," Eric Roberge, CFP® and founder of Beyond Your Hammock, told me. "That's why it's imperative that you take advantage of free money when it's available. I am referring to your employer's matching contribution."

$ *Except for a few exceptions, you can't access your retirement funds until you're 59½. If you tap them early, you'll have to pay a penalty fee.*

Roberge pointed out that on a $40,000 salary, it would take only $100 of your contributions per month to get the full employer match of 3 percent. That means you're ultimately saving $200 a month, but you're only feeling $100 of that come out of your paycheck.

If $100 still sounds like too much, get started by contributing just 1 percent of your paycheck, and then bump it up to 2 percent and then 3 percent and so on every few months. You'll start to realize that you don't actually notice the difference when it's a slow creep.

Sophia Bera, CFP® and founder of Gen Y Planning, will give you only one out for ditching your retirement savings in your early twenties. If you have no employer match *and* have high-interest credit card debt or payday loans *and* are severely behind on monthly payments for your bills, then take a few months to direct potential retirement savings toward getting your debt handled and your financial life back on track. Otherwise, you'd better be contributing to an employer-matched retirement plan or tucking your money away into an IRA.

TAX BENEFITS OF SAVING FOR RETIREMENT

Putting money away for the 40 years from now isn't just about making life easier for the future you. You can also use retirement accounts as a tax advantage for today's you.

Traditional 401(k)s, 403(b)s, and IRAs are funded with pre-tax dollars and so will lower your taxable income today, but you will have to pay taxes in the future when you withdraw money. A Roth 401(k) or IRA is funded with post-tax dollars, meaning you don't get any tax advantage today, but you do get to make your withdrawals without paying taxes in the future.

Lily earns $50,000 a year from her job as a kindergarten teacher. She contributes $300 a month to her 403(b). This will reduce her salary by $3,600—meaning she only gets taxed on $46,400 this year. When Lily decides to withdraw these savings in retirement, she will have to pay taxes—and at the tax bracket she's in at that time.

There are phase-out limits for being eligible for a tax break based on your income and whether or not you're covered by an employer-sponsored retirement plan. The IRS makes these guidelines easily accessible on its Web site.[3]

Don't get too freaked out about the tax play, though. Just saving, regardless of Roth or traditional, is a great place to start. If you want advice on how to legally minimize your tax burden, then a CFP or a CPA can help you develop a tax strategy that's most beneficial for you.

CONVINCED TO START? HERE'S WHERE TO SAVE.

It's really easy to start the process of planning for retirement, even if it isn't accessible through your employer. All you need are taxable wages (so, a job) and access to a computer (so you can set up your account). I guess you could kick it old-school via the phone—but let's be real, you're not going to do that.

For the Traditionally Employed: Employer-Matched Retirement Accounts

Start your retirement savings with an employer-matched 401(k) or 403(b). A 401(k) is the type of account you're likely going to see at a for-profit company. A 403(b) is the retirement vehicle you're probably offered at a non-profit company or in a government position.

This is an oversimplification, as there are slightly different tax breaks and nuances to each account, but for now you really just need to know the terms: 401(k) applies to the great majority of people, so you'll usually see that term more frequently than 403(b). However, if you have a 403(b), you should be heeding the typical 401(k) advice to get your employer match.

You don't have to just stick with your 401(k). You can also contribute to an IRA.

Sophia Bera recommends you contribute enough to get an employer match, then max out a Roth IRA, and then proceed to bump up your employer contributions if you still have money left to put toward retirement. There is one caveat: you need to know yourself. If you're pretty sure you won't actually contribute to an IRA, then just stick with putting as much as makes sense for your budget toward your 401(k).

For the Self-Employed and Traditionally Employed Looking to Double-Down: Individual Retirement Arrangements

There are quite a few types of IRAs, but we're going to focus on four main ones that you should know.

"The best strategy for the self-employed is to open an IRA to get started," Eric Roberge said. "Once you've opened one, you can contribute a small amount every month—as little as $25 in some cases—just to get the ball rolling. Then, when you have larger income months, put in a little extra. Repeat this until you find that you can max out an IRA each year. You can then find another retirement account with higher annual limits."

→ *Traditional IRA:* Investing with pre-tax dollars up to the annual limit ($5,500 in 2016).

→ *Roth IRA:* Investing with post-tax dollars up to the annual limit ($5,500 in 2016).

→ *Simplified Employee Pension (SEP-IRA):* As a freelancer, even with just an employee roster of one (you), you're eligible to contribute to a SEP-IRA. Also, as a full-time employee with side-hustle income you may also be eligible to contribute to a SEP-IRA. This type of account comes with much higher limits than both traditional and Roth IRAs. You can contribute up to the lesser of either 25 percent of your total compensation or $53,000 for the 2016 tax year.

→ *Solo (or individual) 401(k):* This isn't an IRA, but it is another option for the self-employed or traditionally employed person claiming freelance income on your taxes. You can't have any full-time employees, other than you and your spouse, to be eligible for this plan. In 2016, you can contribute $18,000 of your self-employment income as an employee contribution, and you can potentially add another chunk by contributing 25 percent of your total self-employment income (net or total compensation depends on your legal entity, such as being an LLC or S-Corp) as an employer contribution. Yes, this does sound a bit wonky, but it's an accepted practice that the IRS won't audit you for.

$ *I encourage you to talk to a professional about your tax strategy if you're self-employed. Taking advantage of every possible deduction, credit, and cor-*

rect retirement vehicle can add a lot to your bottom line. You also really don't want to mess up when it comes to dealing with the IRS.

Where to Open an IRA

Just like investing in index funds (outlined in chapter 15), you can open an IRA with investment companies like Vanguard, Fidelity, and Betterment.

WHAT TO LOOK OUT FOR IN A RETIREMENT ACCOUNT

When planning to open a retirement account, especially one through your employer, it's important to understand at least a majority of the fine print. Given that you're probably getting slammed with a ton of other welcome-day materials and have to watch inane videos about harassment in the workplace and how taking a pen home is considered stealing from the office, it's understandable why you barely glance at your retirement plan details.

Just be sure you at least get the following questions answered, and then actually get started.

When Are You Eligible to Contribute?

I've harped on for pages now about the importance of saving for retirement, but your company could ice you out when you first start. You might have to work there for a year or so before you can even start contributing. Keep an eye on your eligibility, and be sure to set it up to start as soon as it's available. In the meantime, you should make the same contributions you would've made to a 401(k) to an IRA instead.

Do You Even Get a Match?

What happens if you check and your company has a 401(k) but doesn't even offer to match? At this point, you should be brutally honest with yourself. Are you going to be diligent about setting up a contribution to an IRA on a regular basis, or do you really need that money to be routed out of your paycheck and into a 401(k) by the HR department? You can probably find lower fees with an IRA and tuck your money away there since a match isn't on the table, but do this only if you're actually going to save. Putting money in the company 401(k) is a better deal if that's the method that gets you to save in the first place.

Fees, Fees, Fees: What Will This Cost Me?

"The truth is that retirement plan fees can be hidden," Roberge admitted. "That doesn't mean all retirement plans are bad, and you really need to ask your retirement plan sponsor and your employer about the specific fees involved. Remember, though, even if fees are high, getting a matching contribution that can double your own contribution more than makes up for high fees, at least early on. Where else can you make a 100 percent return on your money?"

Here are some common fees you're likely to see:

Expense ratios: The expense ratio is the price you're paying to hold the investments (probably mutual funds or index funds) in your 401(k). These should be available on your 401(k) statement.

Plan administration and investment costs: Your employer could be sticking you with some of the costs of offering the 401(k) benefit in the first place. It's probably a cost divided out as a fee across your fellow employees' plans. This is pretty common, especially for smaller companies, but it's still good for you to know.

Account maintenance (aka investment advisory, aka management) fee: This depends on the type of investments in your plan. Holding actively managed funds is going to cost more than being in passively managed funds. If you do hold actively managed funds, then you should run the numbers to ensure that the fee is not eating away at your returns too much.

Roberge also recommends that you find an account that offers low-cost investments because you don't need to be paying commissions. A platform with commission-free index funds is a good place to get started.

When Do Employer Contributions Vest?

You should know exactly when you'll get your hands on your employer contributions. The fact that your employer is contributing to your 401(k) plan doesn't mean you get to take all the money when you inevitably leave the company in two or three years, you little job hopper, you. Vesting refers to the time at which you get your employer-contributed money. An account that's 100 percent or fully vested means you can take all your employer contributions right now.

There are three main types of vesting schedules:

→ *Immediate:* This is what you want to see from an employer. Any contributions from that first paycheck onward are available to you when you leave. You could stay for one month and you'd still get that contribution, assuming your 401(k) got set up that quickly.

→ *Cliff:* You get it all at once, but you have to wait. This could mean you need to be at a company for three years before you get your hands on any of the accumulated employer contributions. Naturally, this is a pretty crappy deal for many millennials, considering how often we change jobs.[4]

→ *Graded:* You'll get a percentage of available employer contributions each year until you're fully vested, usually around year six. For example, you get 0 percent the first year, then 20 percent the second year, 40 percent in the third year, and so on. If you had $7,000 worth of employer contributions by your fourth year, then you'd get to walk with 60 percent, or $4,200.

Make Sure You Actually Get the Full Match from Your Employer

"We match 50 percent on up to 6 percent of your opt-out 401(k)," or "We match you 100 percent up to 6 percent."

Wait, what?

This kind of lingo is common and could confuse you into not actually contributing enough to get your full employer match.

In the first example, an "opt-out 401(k)" means your company auto-enrolls you from the get-go. You might assume that your company is ensuring you are contributing enough to get the full match—but guess again. The auto-enrollment may only be for a 2 percent contribution, which leaves a whole lot of free money up for grabs.

Matching 100 percent up to a determined percentage is the clearest way to know how much to set aside. So in the second scenario, you need to put 6 percent of your paycheck into a 401(k) to get your full employer match. On a $40,000 salary, that requires you to put aside $2,400, or $200 per month, which is probably $100 per paycheck since many folks get paid biweekly. If you choose to put in only 4 percent ($1,600 annually), then you're going to get only a 4 percent ($1,600) match from your employer, not the potential $2,400.

You can always contribute more than the allotted match. I encourage you to do so, especially when you get promotions and raises.

Contributing to the Limit—aka Maxing Out

The IRS does stipulate how much you and your employer can contribute to your 401(k). Contributing to this threshold is referred to as maxing out. These limits are evaluated and subject to change each year, so be sure to check them on IRS.gov regularly. In 2016, the max you can contribute is $18,000.

HOW TO PICK THE INVESTMENTS IN YOUR RETIREMENT ACCOUNT

"The truth is that getting started saving is much more important than choosing the right investments," Roberge assured me. "Saving money is going to increase your retirement savings much more than investment returns for the first several years."

(Again, if you didn't read the investment chapter, I encourage you to flip back to it first and then keep reading here. You'll get a lot more out of this section!)

Large cap, small cap, Dodge & Cox—all these terms associated with my first 401(k) had me quite confused. A 23-year-old with no investing experience, I sat there paralyzed for a bit about what to do. I knew I should be contributing to a 401(k)—but what the heck? Where do I put my money? So I did exactly what you're probably going to do—or did do; I called my dad. (Not to be sexist, maybe you called your mom.)

Phoning Mom and Dad isn't a terrible place to start, but despite me weaving many tales about my parents' financial guidance, I often caution people against taking advice from them. Your parents may not have made the best money decisions, so it's possible you'll be led astray. And even if they did make smart choices regarding their finances, that doesn't mean they're particularly well-versed in the world of investing or that what worked for them is best for you.

However, as Roberge said, it's better to at least get started. You can worry about rebalancing your portfolio later.

What to Consider When Opening Your First Retirement Account

→ Don't feel stupid when you don't know the lingo. This is incredibly common early on.

→ You should try to avoid paying commissions, if possible, in your plan.

→ Check the expense ratio on funds available in your 401(k) by using sites like Morningstar.

→ Index funds are probably the way to go, and you'll want to focus on holding mostly stocks for a more aggressive portfolio early on in your career.

→ Diversification is important, but so is keeping it simple. You can easily diversify by investing in index funds (like S&P 500 or Total Stock Market) instead of dumping all your money into company stock or sticking to one sector (e.g., all tech companies).

→ You can stand to take a risk and make aggressive investments when you're young: that means investing in stocks.

→ Know your asset allocation: how much is invested in more high-risk funds versus moderate versus conservative?

→ Stay consistent about your contributions.

→ Don't check your portfolio on days you hear about the stock market performing poorly lest you freak out and start to sell, sell, sell.

Worst-case scenario: just invest in the available passively managed target date fund that's associated with the year you think you'll retire, aka when you turn 65 to 70. As mentioned in chapter 15, this fund will auto-rebalance you from aggressive to moderate to conservative the closer you get to retirement. Once you decide to take the leap and hire a financial professional or get really interested in understanding everything yourself, then you may want to look at transitioning out of target date investing and into a portfolio of your own choosing for your risk tolerance and time horizon.

It's wise to check in on your retirement portfolio at least once a year. See how your investments are performing, double-check fees and expense ratios, and determine if you should be making any tweaks to adjust for risk or your time horizon for retirement.

WHAT HAPPENS WHEN YOU LEAVE THE COMPANY?

"A lot of millennials don't sign up because they don't think they'll be there long," Sophia Bera told me. "But you can take the 401(k) and roll it over to another one."

Whatever you decide to do when you leave a company, do *not* cash out your 401(k)! The following box explains why this is a terrible idea. So please, please, please don't cash out.

WHAT HAPPENS WHEN YOU CASH OUT YOUR 401(k) EARLY

The odds of your leaving your current company before retirement are about as likely as someone sending a sexy pic on Snapchat— high. Electing to cash out your 401(k) when you leave instead of rolling it over to your new company's plan or into an IRA will result in paying tax on the sum plus an additional 10 percent penalty. This could mean paying a withdrawal penalty of close to 50 percent if you're near the top income bracket.

Option 1: You Can Leave the Money There

Being a millennial, I've naturally job-hopped a few times. The first job didn't offer a retirement plan, but the second had a Roth 401(k) option with a 4 percent match. By the time I left there two years later (right on schedule to fit the millennial stereotype), I'd saved up around $9,000 in my 401(k) on a $37,500 salary. This made me eligible to leave the funds with my former employer if I wanted. There was a $5,000 minimum requirement to have the funds remain in the current plan.

When you leave a job, be sure to see if a minimum determines if your money can even stay in the existing 401(k).

Despite having to deal with some paperwork, the idea of leaving $9,000 behind seemed like a future annoyance. Plus, I liked the idea of rolling it into an IRA and continuing to contribute myself.

Option 2: You Can Roll It Over

What you need know about doing a rollover:

→ *Keep it simple by having funds go into the same type of account: Roth to Roth and traditional to traditional.* Rolling a traditional 401(k) into a Roth IRA is technically possible, but it would be considered a

Roth conversion, and you would owe some taxes. It may be financially beneficial for you to do this, but you should speak with a professional first to make sure everything is done correctly. You can't convert a Roth 401(k) into a traditional IRA.

→ *There's a time limit:* You need to move your funds within 60 days of receiving them from your original plan or you'll default into cashing out and have to pay that hefty tax penalty.

Roll into the New Company 401(k)

You can probably roll your old 401(k) into the 401(k) with your new company. This keeps everything in one tidy package for you.

I opted to roll my first 401(k) into an IRA because I contribute to IRAs in addition to my 401(k), similar to what Bera recommended earlier in this chapter.

How to Roll into an IRA

You decided to keep the money in your own hands and to roll your first 401(k) into IRAs by using investment companies like Vanguard and Fidelity. These are common occurrences for both companies, and they're set up to make the transition simple for you. You may even be lucky and have your current 401(k) handled by Vanguard or Fidelity, so the rollover process can stay in house.

Googling the terms "Vanguard rollover" or "Fidelity rollover" takes you to landing pages that can help you initiate the rollover process. Or just go straight to the company's Web site and search for IRA information.

When you have a Roth 401(k) with an employer match, you may have to do two rollovers—one into a Roth 401(k) for the contributions you made, and one into a traditional IRA for the contributions your employer made. I didn't realize until I rolled over my first Roth 401(k) that my employer contributions were being added pre-tax; this got flagged while I was filling out paperwork to roll over my 401(k) into Vanguard IRAs. It really wasn't too difficult to handle; I just needed to ensure that the funds got sent separately and to the appropriate accounts.

THE CONSEQUENCES OF TAKING OUT MONEY EARLY

$ *If you take out a 401(k) loan and leave the company or get fired before repaying the loan, then you may be required to pay it back immediately.*

Just about every piece of financial advice comes with exceptions to the rule, so I'm going to start this section by saying, yes, there are times when you can withdraw from retirement accounts without a penalty. Those times are very limited, and you should really avoid robbing your future self by taking out a 401(k) loan or raiding your IRA. Please consult a financial professional before you make that move, and understand any and all possible fees, penalties, and restrictions of your actions.

The Retirement Account Rule: No Touching Until You're 59 1/2

In general, you cannot begin to take distributions from your retirement accounts without penalty until you turn 59½ years old. Unless you plan to retire at 59½, you should avoid withdrawing any money until you're actually done earning an income.

What Happens When You Take Out a Loan from a Retirement Account?

You need to read the fine print before taking out a loan from your 401(k), and determine if your employer even allows you to take a loan from your retirement contributions. The IRS also limits how much you can borrow. In 2016, it's 50 percent of your vested account balance or $50,000, whichever is less.[5] Your employer will also charge you interest, albeit usually a reasonable rate. Once you borrow the money, you will have to pay it back within a predetermined period of time, typically five years. The danger is, of course, that you're robbing from your future self and paying interest on a sum that would otherwise be compounding and accruing money for you. You could also end up having to pay back the entire sum all at once if you quit or get fired from your job.

Again, Don't Cash Out

And, in case it didn't sink in before: cashing out means paying tax on the sum plus an additional 10 percent penalty.

DON'T COUNT ON SOCIAL SECURITY COVERING YOU

Lest you read (or skim) this entire chapter and still think to yourself, "Meh—I'll have my Social Security paycheck," think again. The average Social Security check paid to retirees will be $1,341 in 2016.[6] We're talking just barely over $16,000 a year. Even if you paid off your mortgage, that's not a whole lot for most people to live on until the end of their days. This also doesn't account for the likelihood that Social Security will go through major changes before you get to retirement age and potentially may not exist anymore. So who knows if you'll have access to even $1,300 per month?

No matter how abstract retirement feels to you right now, especially as you deal with starting a career and paying off student loans, it's important that this chapter at least leave you with the impression that it's important—nay, imperative—that you start saving now.

🔧 SAVING FOR RETIREMENT ACTION LIST

❏ Save enough to at least get your employer match.
❏ No employer-sponsored retirement account? Then open and regularly contribute to an IRA.
❏ Save consistently, preferably with automatic contributions from your paycheck.
❏ Check the fee structure of your retirement plan, and make sure you aren't bleeding money.
❏ Understand when your employer contributions vest (meaning you get to take the money when you leave).
❏ Be sure your portfolio is being rebalanced every few years to be aligned with when you plan to retire and your risk tolerance. You should be shifting to a more conservative portfolio the closer you get to retirement.
❏ Don't leave your 401(k) behind when you switch jobs—roll it over!
❏ Start now—like, put this book down and get started kind of right now.

Chapter 17

I'm Not Rich Enough to Hire
a Financial Planner

STOP! I know you're planning to skip right over this chapter. After all, you're a broke (or just barely above broke) millennial. The notion of paying someone to help you with your finances sounds about as ludicrous as asking someone on a date over the phone. Except, maybe it isn't. Maybe it's exactly what you need right now and more affordable than you think. Gone are the days of financial planning being accessible only to silver-haired multimillionaires. At least skim this section before completely dismissing the notion. You might even need some of the knowledge for later—you know, after you develop an app Google acquires or become a media darling thanks to starring on the newest hit reality TV show or your blog turns into a book deal. Hey, it could happen.

WHAT EXACTLY DOES A FINANCIAL PLANNER DO?

A financial planner helps you get your financial house in order (aka makes sure you have your shit together). In many cases, you may be able to do yourself what a financial planner handles if you just buckle down enough to learn the ins and outs of how money works. But lots of folks would rather just off-load that task to a professional. I mean, we're in a world that now allows us to hire people to stand in line to buy the new iPhone for us or have groceries delivered right to our door; why would we want to handle our money plans solo—right?

The other big perk of hiring a financial planner is having an objective third party evaluate your finances and help you develop a practical plan. This can be key during major life transitions like buying a home, getting married, having a baby, inheriting money, or getting divorced.

In some cases, you can even hand over the reins and have someone else inform you on investing, retirement planning, and how to best (legally) keep money in your bank account instead of Uncle Sam's.

Is It Planner or Advisor? Why Do I Keep Seeing Both Words?

Frankly, it is just a little confusing. These terms can have different meanings and can also be used interchangeably.

The simple way to differentiate is that a financial planner often has an area of expertise—e.g., investing or retirement planning—and may hold certain certifications. A financial advisor is more of an all-inclusive term. You could say that a financial advisor is social media while a financial planner is Facebook, Twitter, Instagram, Snapchat . . . you get the point.

When you read "advisor" in this chapter, it's just a catch-all phrase for a financial professional who helps you with your money. If you elect to speak with a financial advisor, then you need to ensure he or she is certified and meets certain standards, which are discussed below.

FINANCIAL PLANNER OR FINANCIAL SCAMMER? THE ISSUE WITH AN UNREGULATED INDUSTRY

The government has never stepped in and set standards for financial advisors in the same way it does in other industries like medicine or law, as Alan Moore, MS, CFP®, and the cofounder of XY Planning Network, points out. You can't just call yourself a doctor or lawyer without some level of education and credentials.

It's been a buyer-beware-type marketplace, unfortunately.

—Alan Moore, MS, CFP®

The titles *financial planner* and *financial advisor* are used by so many unfit individuals that they're nearly useless terms signifying no true credentials. You could call an insurance agency or a brokerage and speak with a "financial advisor" or "investment advisor" whose real job is to get you to purchase a product, whether or not it's the best fit for you. The only requirement for calling yourself an investment advisor is to pass the Series 65 exam administered by the Financial Industry Regulatory Authority (FINRA), which Moore says is more about understanding how to avoid getting sued than indicating any true competency.

Once you buy a product from one of these financial or investment advisors, he or she gets a commission. It's hard to assume you're getting quality, unbiased advice in such a scenario, but it's perfectly legal because these financial advisors only need to meet the suitability standard and not the fiduciary standard.

FIDUCIARY VS. SUITABILITY: WHO IS REALLY LOOKING OUT FOR YOUR BEST INTERESTS?

> *Suitability is a salesman who sells you a suit that fits. Fiduciary is selling you a suit that actually looks good on you.*
> —Alan Moore, quoting his XY Planning Network cofounder, Michael Kitces

Fiduciary standard: Recommending a product that's in your best interest and not in the best interest of a financial advisor. *Suitability standard:* Recommending (or selling) you a product that's—as the name implies—suitable. Or, as Moore explains it, "suitable enough to not get the advisor sued."

A TALE OF SUITABILITY AT PLAY

Peach decided to get a basic life insurance policy because his parents were cosigners on some of his student loans.* He called up one of the major insurance providers (yes, you'd recognize the name) and explained his situation. The insurance agent emphasized why whole life insurance would be the superior option for him, citing the fact that it would accumulate cash value, unlike term life insurance, which is a use it (you die during the policy's coverage) or lose it (you live) policy. When worded this way, yeah, whole life for sure makes sense. But that's not really the whole story, nor is whole life at all the best product for a healthy, 25-year-old man with no dependents. The whole life policy cost him $50 a month for $50,000 of coverage. When Peach decided to switch from whole to term after learning more about the differ-

---

* Read why this is important in chapter 9.

ences, he got the hard sell from the agent to stay with whole. He finally changed policies to term and ended up with $150,000 worth of coverage for 70 years to the tune of $24 a month.

There is no legal obligation for any financial planner to be held to the fiduciary standard, unless you have a signed oath that he or she will do so. The fiduciary oath is one you can personally print off and take into a potential financial planner's office and ask him or her to sign. Certain firms or financial planner networks may require all of their members to be held to the fiduciary standard—XY Planning is one such network—but you should still be proactive and get the dotted line signed yourself.

HOW DOES YOUR FINANCIAL PLANNER GET PAID?

A fiduciary standard versus a suitability standard is relevant because of how the payment structures work within the financial planning industry. There are three main ways your financial planner (or advisor) gets paid:

1. Commission
2. Fee-only
3. Fee and commission (sometimes called fee-based)

→ *Commission:* Obviously, if a person is working based on earning that sweet, sweet commish, then he's probably more likely to slot you into whatever product puts the most dough in his pocket, just as long as it's remotely suitable for you. Now, if held to the fiduciary standard, it would need to be the best possible product for you, regardless of commission rates. Luckily, it is possible to remove the temptation of commission entirely in order to get the most unbiased advice: thus the fee-only payment plan.

$ *There are bonus programs or competitions to sell a certain amount of policy A or policy B. Whether it's right for the client or not doesn't really matter. They're incentivized to sell a product, but you just don't know how they're getting incentivized. And they're not required to tell you, so it's very challenging to find out what commission folks are being paid.*

—Alan Moore

→ *Fee-only:* This works exactly as it sounds; the fee-only advisors, as defined by the CFP Board, never take a commission for any advice they give. There's even an additional level of strictness that dictates that advisors cannot even put themselves in a position to possibly accept a commission at some point. You pay fee-only advisors a flat-rate fee for their services.

→ *Fee-based:* This does blur the lines between strict fee-only and suitability-focused commission advisors. These advisors sound legit up front because the planning is fee-based, but they can earn a commission on recommended products (e.g., an insurance policy). To add in another layer of confusion, their financial advice can be fiduciary, while their product recommendations could be suitability. Does your brain hurt yet?

Fee-only just simplifies your relationship with a financial advisor.

WHY A CERTIFIED FINANCIAL PLANNER IS IMPORTANT

To fill the vacuum left behind by the government's lack of regulation, the CFP Board developed a rigorous program with strict regulations in order to create a credible gold standard within the industry. This standard is the Certified Financial Planner.

$ *CFPs are not all-knowledgeable, but what we're really good at is spotting BS and knowing where to find the real answer.* —Alan Moore

What is required to be a CFP:[1]

→ Bachelor's degree (or higher)

→ Completion of CFP Board education requirements covering the major personal finance planning areas:

♦ General principles

♦ Insurance planning

♦ Investment planning

♦ Income tax planning

♦ Retirement planning

♦ Estate planning

- ◆ Interpersonal communication
- ◆ Professional conduct and fiduciary responsibility
- ◆ Capstone course: Financial plan development
→ Passing the CFP exam
→ Three years of relevant, full-time professional experience or two years of apprenticeship experience
- ◆ In addition, CFPs must also fulfill continuing education requirements.
→ A background check and adherence to the CFP Board's ethics and standards

You don't *have* to use a CFP as your financial advisor, but doing so should help you get the best value for your money.

WHAT YOU SHOULD LOOK FOR IN A FINANCIAL PLANNER

Despite the unregulated nature of the financial planning industry, it's actually not too difficult to vet a potential financial planner. Moore recommends checking off the following boxes before agreeing to an ongoing relationship with an advisor.

- ❏ *Check for a CFP designation.* Double-check the validity of the advisor's CFP title on the CFP Board Web site: http://www.CFP.net /utility/verify-an-individual-s-CFP-certification-and-background. You'll only need to know first and last name, company name, city, and state to confirm that your potential advisor is legit.
- ❏ *Have your advisor sign the fiduciary oath.*[2] Not just say, "Yes, I'm a fiduciary," but actually be willing to sign a fresh oath just for you if that makes you more comfortable.
- ❏ *Be sure the advisor has worked with clients in your situation.* Your advisor needs to be an expert in your particular area of need. If you're struggling with student loans and the advisor has never had a client with student loans, then this person probably isn't the best pick for you.
- ❏ *Insist on fee-only.* There are reputable advisors who aren't fee-only, but why deal with the potential ambiguity? Working with a fee-only advisor just simplifies life.

It should be noted that you usually can't get client referrals because of compliance rules precluding a CFP from giving you a client's information. This is a reason you also won't see client testimonials on an advisor's Web site.

FINANCIAL PLANNER RED FLAGS

Doing a gut check may not always be the best way to determine if a financial planner is right for you. That's the same gut that made you think a date went great right before you got totally ghosted.

So if your intuition has proven fallible in the past, then check if your potential financial planner hits any of these red flags:

→ Commission-only or fee-based.
→ Won't sign a fiduciary oath (especially if she claims to be a fiduciary advisor).
→ Offers primarily free services: he's getting paid somehow, so it probably means you're getting slotted into some lackluster products because he gets a kickback. However, a one-time free consultation as an intro isn't unusual.
→ Claims to be a CFP but is not registered or is not in good standing.
→ Never worked with someone who has your particular set of financial concerns.

A CFP'S RESPONSE TO YOU SAYING "I CAN'T AFFORD A FINANCIAL PLANNER"

"I usually ask another question: 'Why do you think that?' and it's often something to do with 'I don't have a million dollars, so no one will work with me,' or 'I hear financial planning is really expensive,'" Sophia Bera, CFP® and founder of Gen Y Planning, explained. "A lot of times I just start asking a lot of about their current situation, and I can find a few ways financial planning could be really valuable."

But Bera also acknowledges that not everyone is ready to speak to a financial advisor quite yet and that other professionals, like a non-profit credit counselor from the National Foundation for Credit Counseling (https://www.nfcc.org/), may be a better fit at first.

If you can't find an affordable financial planner, Moore has one quick retort: "Then you're not looking in the right place."

Moore concedes that plenty of financial advisors are too expensive and cater to the traditional notion of wealth management with asset minimums; basically, you'd best be in double-comma land ($1,000,000) in order to walk through the front doors. However, other networks do exist that serve the non–white hairs and tech moguls of the world. Here are a few of them:

→ *XY Planning Network:* Cofounded by Alan Moore, MS, CFP˚, and Michael E. Kitces, MSFS, MTAX, CFP˚, CLU, ChFC, RHU, REBC, CASL (yeah, it's a lot of designations), XYPN is an organization of fee-only financial advisors specifically focused on Generation X and Generation Y clients. Advisors are required to be both CFPs and fiduciary advisors and to have a signed copy of the oath available on their profiles. There are no asset minimum requirements, and each advisor offers a monthly retainer service. You can also reach your advisor virtually. You can learn more at XYPlanningNetwork.com.

→ *Garrett Planning Network:* Founded by Sheryl Garrett, CFP®, AIF, Garrett offers clients access to a network of fee-only, fiduciary CFP professionals. Members of the network do not accept commissions or any other compensation directly from clients. Clients can hire advisors by the hour, which means you can have one-off meetings to address a specific issue, if you'd like. There are no income or net worth minimums in order to be a client. You can learn more at garrett planningnetwork.com.

→ *The National Association of Personal Financial Advisors (NAPFA):* NAPFA was founded in 1983 by a group of advisors interested in creating an organization of highly trained financial professionals who only accepted fee-only compensation. NAPFA is still fee-only financial planners who are also CFPs and fiduciary advisors. However, you may find that NAPFA advisors have asset minimums for clients as the organization has no rule dictating otherwise. You can learn more at www.napfa.org.

CAN I JUST FOCUS ON ONE ISSUE FOR ONE MEETING?

It's quite possible you'll hit a wall while doing research for yourself or you (dramatic sigh) "can't even" with all your financial problems at the moment. Wanting to off-load the drama on a knowledgeable person who can then help you come up with solutions makes sense, but the price points for a long-term relationship can be intimidating at first.

There are financial planners who do offer one-time consultations and who dig in a little deeper than a free, 30-minute session. You will probably need to pay upward of $500 for such a session, but depending on your money issues, this could pay for itself if it gives you actionable items to get debt free, or start investing, or understand how to handle your cash flow.

Ultimately, it is recommended you establish a long-term relationship with a financial planner just as you would with a dentist, doctor, yoga instructor, or anyone else who helps keep you healthy.

BUT SERIOUSLY, HOW MUCH DOES ONE COST?

The real answer to this question is slightly infuriating: it depends.

$ *Moore's Rule of Thumb: If your advisor costs more than 2 percent of your income, he/she probably isn't a good deal for you anymore.*

Traditionally, the financial planning world focused on a "percentage of your assets" fee structure, according to Moore. For example, an advisor might earn 1 percent of the assets under management, which is why so many advisors enforced asset minimums. This structure is starting to change, which is why it's possible for you, with your less than $1,000,000 in assets, to now access a financial planner.

While the answer really depends on your needs and the specific financial planner, Moore provided some broad stroke estimates:

→ Comprehensive financial plan development: $1,000–$1,500
→ Monthly, ongoing relationship: $100–$200 per month
→ One-time consultation: $400–$500

Bera, for example, offers a one-time consultation that ranges from $499 to $799.

The session includes:[3]

→ A 90-minute video call (either Skype or Google Hangout)
→ An in-depth discussion of your *two or three* most pressing financial topics. Popular questions include:
  ◆ Which payment plan should I choose for my student loans, and how can I pay them off faster?

- How do I sign up for my 401(k) and choose the investments?
- Can you help me with a budget or spending plan?
- How much should I set aside for emergency savings versus savings for other goals?
- What steps can I take to improve my credit, and which credit card is best for me?
- How do I start a Roth IRA, and where should I set up the account?
- Can you help me read my company benefits package and choose my benefits?
- How much and which kind of life insurance should we have if we just had a baby?

→ A follow up e-mail with recommendations and an action checklist within 24 hours so that you can take action right away.

Clients with in-depth, specific questions requiring Bera to perform time-intensive tasks such as an insurance analysis for how much life insurance a client should purchase would fall on the high end of the price range.

After receiving a lot of the same questions in her one-time consultations, Bera developed a suite of courses; one is "Smart & Easy Retirement Planning for Millennials." Her clients can still opt to have a one-time consultation, or they can elect to use courses for more foundational learning and then progress to a longer-term financial planning relationship.

These prices may sound steep, and truthfully, they can be, depending on your phase of life. If you're just trying to figure out how to do some basic budgeting or need some 101-level knowledge, then being a DIY-er by reading this book, consulting a money coach (who isn't a certified professional, just a niche expert), or reading blogs is perfectly fine. As you hit life milestones (marriage, home buying, baby making) or find yourself increasing your overall wealth, then it may be time, and worth the money, to turn to a professional.

WHEN SHOULD I DECIDE TO HIRE A FINANCIAL PLANNER?

A key reason to bring in a financial planner is when you're starting a transitional period in your life. Common reasons include:

→ Balancing money goals with debt like student loans
→ Buying a home
→ Getting married
→ Having a baby
→ Inheriting wealth
→ Getting divorced

Moore highly recommends bringing in a third party when you're financial planning with someone else, like a spouse, because we all have such different approaches to money. Moore himself says if he were married he'd bring in a financial advisor to bridge the communication gaps, even though he is one himself.

HOW TO FIND A FINANCIAL PLANNER

Advisor networks like XY Planning, Garrett Planning, and The National Association of Personal Finance Advisors (NAPFA) are good places to start in your search for a quality financial planner. Be sure to use the checklist we went over earlier to vet your potential advisor:

❑ Has a CFP designation.
❑ Will sign fiduciary oath.
❑ Has worked with clients in your situation.
❑ Payment is fee-only.

Advisors are often more than happy to refer you to other advisors who may be a better fit for your particular needs. Say the first advisor you speak with really specializes more in retirement planning; she can probably connect you with someone who knows a lot about student loans. Never be embarrassed about asking an advisor for a referral to someone else if it's just not a good fit.

You should also feel comfortable, and never embarrassed or ashamed, when speaking with your financial advisor. Talking about money can make you feel vulnerable, so your financial advisor needs to be someone with whom you can be open and honest, because lying about your finances completely defeats the purpose of asking for help. And asking for help is one of the smartest moves you can make with and for your money.

Chapter 18

But My Broker Said I *Can* Afford This Much House

LAUREN BOWLING WANTED TO stop throwing her money away. Cutting her landlord a rent check month after month after month felt like a bad investment, especially in her city of Atlanta, where home costs were fairly reasonable.

Bowling had returned to Atlanta after living in New York City for a few years and working as an executive assistant at a hedge fund with a large profit-sharing plan. Her $9,000 bonus was going to serve as her down payment on a home, until her mortgage broker made a suggestion.

"I applied for and received $15,000 in down payment assistance from the City of Atlanta, which was used for the down payment, closing costs, and to reduce a small portion of my principal," 29-year-old Bowling said.

The payment assistance came with stipulations about where and what type of home Bowling could purchase.

"In order to get the money, I had to buy a foreclosed home in a specific zip code that had been hit hard by foreclosures during the recession, and I had to make less than $50,000 a year as a single person," Bowling explained.

She moved forward with the process and ended up purchasing a $65,000 home, which she felt would be affordable on her marketing job salary. After a couple of years, and many renovations later, the security of being a homeowner enabled Bowling to make a drastic career move.

"Owning a home with a lower mortgage than I'd get renting anywhere in Atlanta allowed me to leave my full-time job and not have to worry about paying my bills and keeping a roof over my head," Bowling told me. "If I'd been renting, I doubt I would've felt financially comfortable enough to take that leap."

Bowling works as a freelance writer and blogger for her site Financial Best Life, where she chronicles her experiences of being a young, single homeowner, aggressively paying off credit card debt and all things money.

IS RENTING JUST THROWING AWAY YOUR MONEY?

Bowling and plenty of others feel like renting is basically throwing your money into the void. But is it? Well, that depends. I don't consider renting as throwing away my hard-earned money, even though it costs me $1,150 for my half of a two-bedroom apartment in Astoria, Queens. My rent is double what some of my home-owning friends pay for their mortgages, and they're building equity in a property. Yet I still don't consider rent just tossing my money down the tubes, for a few reasons. Renting can be a smart financial move in the following circumstances:

→ *You can't afford the price point to buy into your local housing market:* I simply can't afford to buy in New York City. Well, I can't afford to buy in areas in which I want to live or apartments that afford me more than 200 square feet. Plus, dealing with a co-op board seems like the worst, and that's pretty much unavoidable in NYC.

→ *You don't plan to live there long:* Don't buy unless you plan to live there for five to seven years. This general rule of thumb is largely based on the logic that it takes you a while to actually build equity in your home. Those early mortgage payments are primarily going toward interest.

→ *You have better career opportunities in your high-price market:* There's an argument to be made for living in the country's more expensive cities if that translates to a hefty paycheck. And I'm not just talking a paycheck that's slightly adjusted for cost of living. I mean, your job doesn't exist in cities with a lower cost of living, or your salary would drop drastically. This argument, however, does get made by plenty of folks who really can move but just choose not to, so do your research before assuming this is your situation.

→ *Being transient is advantageous for your career:* Some jobs require you to be transient, and you never quite know when you'll be asked to move. Then it really makes sense to rent instead of own, unless you want to start purchasing rental properties.

You may be both ready to buy a home and living in an affordable housing market. Before you meet with a mortgage broker, take the time to give yourself a reality check about just how much you can really afford. I'll bet you $5 the mortgage broker says it's more than you're comfortable spending.

CALCULATING HOW MUCH HOME YOU CAN AFFORD

The mortgage for which you get approved and the amount of house you can afford probably don't line up. It's possible to get access to high mortgages relative to your income because you don't *have* to put 20 percent down on the home. Even though you can get these high mortgages, be realistic about how much you can, and really want, to put toward housing costs each month.

$ *Financial planners typically advise you to not put more than 28 percent of your gross income toward housing expenses. This includes your principal, interest, taxes, and insurance payments.*

Erlich earns $75,000, has $10,000 left to pay in student loans, and has $13,000 set aside for purchasing a home. He won't have enough to cover a 20 percent down payment, but he's still keen on getting into the housing market and willing to pay private mortgage insurance (PMI). PMI is an added cost for those who purchase a home by putting down less than 20 percent. Your mortgage lender will require you to pay for such an insurance policy on your mortgage until you reach 20 percent in equity. PMI often does come with a hefty price tag and may even be almost as much as your mortgage payment. Based on the rule of 28 percent, Erlich should be spending no more than $21,000 a year on a home. That means his mortgage payment, PMI, property taxes, home owner's insurance, HOA fees (homeowner association fees, generally used to cover communal upkeep and services, may be required in certain neighborhoods), and any other related expenses need to be less than $1,750 a month total.

$ *Millennials have a fear of commitment about buying a home. They're uninterested in committing to one location for a period of time.*

—Scott Trench, licensed real estate broker

But, like many rules of thumb, this number may seem absolutely ridiculous for you and your budget. The bigger factor to keep in mind is that you need to avoid pushing yourself to your financial limits when purchasing a home.

Scott Trench, a 25-year-old Denver-based licensed real estate broker and VP of operations for BiggerPockets, has one goal when it comes to housing: spend as little as possible and eliminate the expense entirely ASAP.

"If you make a pie chart of your expenses, your home is always going to be a huge chunk of that pie," Trench told me. "A lot of people say 'Oh, I'm going to cut out my latte,' but if that's 3 percent or 5 percent of your budget and housing is 50 percent or 30 percent, then where should you focus your time over the next year and be disciplined? Is it drinking that latte, or is it finding a place to spend zero on your housing?"

This set Trench on a mission to stop paying rent in the pursuit of financial freedom.

Trench started aggressively saving money after only a few months into his first job as a financial analyst. He saved $20,000 within a year and decided to purchase a fixer-upper duplex in Denver. He purchased the property in November 2014, fixed it up himself, and started renting it out by March 2015. Less than a year later, Trench purchased a second duplex in a more desirable area of town. He now rents out his original duplex and lives in one side of the new home and rents out the other.

Finance experts will debate for hours about investing versus real estate as a means to wealth, and like everything else with personal finance, it's personal. Trench's goal puts a significant focus on building a real estate portfolio, while others may be inclined to hold onto a mortgage with a 3 percent interest rate and invest the difference in the stock market.

THERE'S NO WAY I CAN PUT 20 PERCENT DOWN

Both Trench and Bowling purchased homes without putting 20 percent of their own money down. However, each had a specific plan in mind for how to speed up the equity-building process to make the properties stronger investments.

Trench, who saved aggressively to tuck away $20,000 in a year, decided to put 5 percent down because he didn't want to wait another couple of years until he could put down $60,000 to $80,000. He considered his potential purchase a windfall because he had an actionable plan to turn it into an investment property, plus an emergency savings buffer in case anything went awry in those early months. He lived in the duplex and soon enough rented out the other side to create some cash flow. After crunching the numbers, Trench told me he created $100,000 of equity in about 15 months by purchasing a fixer-upper and doing most of the work himself. It was work he didn't know how to perform prior to being a homeowner, but YouTube can teach you how to do anything these days.

Bowling got creative with the down payment assistance program in order to finance her home in Atlanta. The $15,000 Bowling received was more than a 20 percent down payment and even reduced a small portion of the principal on her $65,000 home. The catch: she had to live in the home for five years in order for the loan to be forgiven. A percentage of the loan gets paid off each year she stays, so moving early would mean paying back a portion of the $15,000.

$ *Sure, 20 percent down is always nice, but given the competing financial priorities for millennials (student loan debt and low wages), I'm not sure it makes sense for millennials to forgo homeownership until they can save up that amount.*

—Lauren Bowling

In addition to the down payment assistance program, Bowling put about $58,000 of a FHA 203(k) loan into the renovations of her property, as well as $14,000 of her own money when some shady contractors failed to do a job properly.

Needless to say, fixing up a home isn't cheap, but Bowling still pays less on her mortgage than she would renting a home anywhere in Atlanta. Plus, she rented out some of the rooms in her house for additional cash flow.

"Even though three years ago my home was in a bit of a sketchy neighborhood, it's now extremely up and coming, and my home value increases year over year," Bowling said. "The longer I wait to sell, the more money I will make."

Can You Put Less Than 20 Percent Down?

Putting down less than 20 percent can put you in a weak financial position if you're not committed to making aggressive payments or if you end up pushing yourself to your financial limits when purchasing the home. Here are some of the things that can happen when you put down less than 20 percent:

→ *Your mortgage rate may be higher:* Even with your pristine credit score and stable job, a lender may still deem you a higher risk if you put less than 20 percent down.

→ *You have to pay PMI:* Private mortgage insurance (PMI) helps mitigate any risk for your lender, to a degree. PMI in no way is a benefit to you, the borrower, and it's not to be confused with homeowner's insurance. Well, there is one benefit: its existence makes you able to purchase a home without putting 20 percent down. Keep in mind that PMI can be pricy, even close to the cost of your mortgage, in some cases.

→ *Your equity in the house is low:* This could become a problem if property values in your neighborhood decline, if you lose your job and struggle to make the monthly payment and can't refinance, or if you need to sell the house and you owe more than the home is worth.

→ *Your mortgage origination fee will be higher:* It's just simple math here. You're going to pay a 1 percent origination fee and your home costs $220,000. You put down 5 percent ($11,000) instead of 20 percent ($44,000). That means you have to pay 1 percent of a $209,000 mortgage instead of 1 percent of a $176,000 mortgage. While a difference of $330 in your origination fee really shouldn't keep you from buying a house, it is another added expense when you put less than 20 percent down.

UNIQUE PROGRAMS THAT MIGHT HELP YOU OUT

Programs like the one Bowling used to finance her home aren't unique to Atlanta. There are national and local programs in place that may help you move from renter to homeowner.

→ *Federal Housing Administration (FHA):* The FHA, which is part of the U.S. Department of Housing and Urban Development (HUD), is willing to insure your loan, so your lender can give you a better deal.[1] These loans are often geared toward first-time homeowners. You can search for local offers in your state by going to HUD.gov and looking for FHA loans. You may also be able to use an FHA loan to make your home more energy efficient as well as purchase a mobile home or factory-built home.

→ *Veterans Affairs (VA):* The VA provides assistance to service members, veterans, and eligible surviving spouses. These loans will be provided by a private bank or mortgage company, not the federal government, but like FHA loans, the VA will guarantee a portion of the loan to help you get better terms. Learn how to apply at http://www.benefits.va.gov/homeloans/.

Be sure to also investigate any options specific to your city. A mortgage broker should be able to help with this process.

IT COSTS MORE THAN JUST THE DOWN PAYMENT AND MONTHLY MORTGAGE

The first time I daydreamed about buying a home, because it seems delightfully affordable in most places outside of New York City, I fiddled with some numbers and determined I could buy a house in Nashville, Tennessee. For weeks, I dreamed of owning a home that I'd rent out for a while and then eventually move into. I crunched the numbers a whole bunch of times and thought that even though it was a little bit tight, I could make it work. I went so far as to get into talks with a realtor. Then I learned a little bit more about the true cost of owning a home.

$ *Don't forget about an emergency fund just for your house! The amount you put down to purchase your home should not wipe out your savings. You need a stash of cash set aside in case a pipe bursts or a tree falls through the roof in those early months (the tree thing happened to my parents).*

Sure, I could've put 20 percent down on a house that needed a little sprucing up and have enough saved to temporarily cover the mortgage when renters didn't live there. I didn't, however, account for all the other costs associated with buying a home. It seems like fees on top of fees on top of fees get piled on when you're working toward becoming a homeowner. My dream of purchasing an investment home outside of New York slowly faded away.

Here are some of the costs other than your down payment and monthly mortgage that you need to consider before deciding to buy a home:

→ *Closing costs:* A slew of crazy fees you have to pay to do things like prove the current owner of the house is actually the owner, do a survey, have the home appraised and inspected, and in some cases, determine if the home is in a flood zone. Be sure to talk to your mortgage broker about the estimated cost of all these fees and have him walk you through exactly what you are paying for.

→ *Homeowner association fee (HOA fee):* It depends on where you move, but it might cost you a monthly fee to live in the neighborhood.

→ *Property taxes:* You get the delight of paying even more taxes when you're a homeowner!

→ *Origination fee on your mortgage:* An origination fee costs you a percentage of your total mortgage. For example, if your mortgage is $300,000 and the origination fee is 1 percent, then you'll pay $3,000.

At least being a homeowner could potentially get you some tax breaks!

RED FLAGS TO WATCH FOR WHEN BUYING A HOME

Sometimes you're just so excited to get into a home and finally finish the house-hunting thing that you leap at the best option you find without doing all your due diligence. A coworker of mine purchased a home on a quick time frame and moved in during the peak of summer, only to find out that the central AC system the seller claimed existed, well, didn't.

You need to be sure to hire a reliable inspector to properly vet a house before you put down tens of thousands of dollars. But there's also some rookie signs your untrained eyes can look out for when considering a house:

→ Make sure the air conditioner/heating system actually exists and works.

→ Flip the electrical switches to ensure they're working and lights aren't flickering.

→ Keep an eye out for mold.

→ Look for cracks along the walls or in the ceilings.

→ Do a smell check—literally. A strange smell could indicate a larger issue like a bad septic system or mold.

→ Check the interior and exterior for signs of rotting wood.
→ Does the current owner try to keep you out of a specific area of the home during a showing? Do not buy!

POTENTIAL FIRST-TIME HOMEOWNER CHECKLIST

Scott Trench is quick to point out that, as with all other goals for financial success, it takes the ability to spend way less or earn more while continuing to spend less in order to save up the funds to buy a home.

Yes, you probably can seriously purchase a home—in an affordable neighborhood. Bowling left New York City and purchased in her native Atlanta. Trench started with a duplex in a neighborhood he wouldn't necessarily have considered an ideal location.

As you start making a plan to become a homeowner, be sure to check these items off the list:

❑ You want to live there for at least five years.
❑ You have a healthy credit report and score; remember, high credit score = lower interest rate on your mortgage.
❑ You have a separate emergency fund saved for your home, in addition to the down payment and closing costs.
❑ The mortgage + PMI = less than average rent in your area.
❑ You can comfortably fit the monthly cost into your budget.
❑ You don't buy out of your price range (no matter what a mortgage broker says you can afford).
❑ You're ready to take on all the maintenance involved with homeownership that your landlord currently handles, like lawn care, gutter cleaning, painting, heating and air-conditioning, and any unexpected expenses.

Epilogue

Now That You're A Financial Badass, Keep It Up!

IN THE TIME since I started Broke Millennial (the blog), I went from PR girl to start-up employee to full-time personal finance writer and speaker. While it could be argued that it was the blog that changed the direction of my life, I'd counter with this: understanding money allowed me to feel empowered and take more risks, which led to me creating the blog and to where I am today. Learning how to get your financial life together keeps you from feeling helpless in many situations: being stuck in a job you're ready to leave, staying trapped in the paycheck-to-paycheck cycle, remaining in a bad relationship because you're unable to support yourself, and even passing on poor financial behaviors to the next generation. And the good news is, you're already on the path to getting your financial life together! (#GYFLT)

No matter how you elected to approach this book, I sincerely hope it's provided you with the groundwork to begin building (or rebuilding) or tweaking or validating your approach to finances. Personal finance is nothing if not personal, so the variety of voices and techniques should help you find the options for budgeting, paying down debt, building and maintaining a strong credit score, investing, negotiating, and saving for retirement that are ideal for you.

The style of this book makes it easy to flip back through the previous chapters when you find yourself in a financial rut or just need a refresher on how to handle a specific money matter. You can even take it a step further and start breaking the taboo of talking about finances by having financial chats with friends or getting financially naked with your partner. Money isn't a dirty, shameful topic; in fact, our whole society would probably be a lot better off if we stopped being so afraid to discuss it. So go on and get talking.

Maybe you'll even be inspired to start chronicling your journey on a blog. Those sure can take you to unexpected places.

Feel free to get in touch! Have a question? Don't hesitate to reach out to me. You can find me on Twitter @BrokeMillennial or Facebook (https://www.facebook.com/BrokeMillennial) or, of course, on my Web site at BrokeMillennial.com.

Acknowledgments

First, a thank-you to *CBS Sunday Morning* and then-producer Ed Forgotson, who featured me in a piece about millennials in the workplace, which was then seen by my masterful literary agent, Eric Myers of Dystel, Goderich, and Bourret Literary Management. Thank you, Eric, for taking a chance on a then-26-year-old blogger who hoped to ink a book. You were unbelievably patient and kind while guiding me first through the proposal process and then navigating the unfamiliar waters of looking for a publisher.

Next, thank you to my editor, Stephanie Bowen, as well as Amanda Shih, Brianna Yamashita, Angela Januzzi, Kelli Daniel-Richards, and the rest of the TarcherPerigee team. You saw my vision and allowed me to be myself in a book about such a serious topic.

Thank you to Nick Clements and Brian Karimzad for helping me develop a great BS meter for banking products, learn how to decode the fine print, and understand the inner workings of the banking world, and for being so supportive during the book writing process.

Thank you to Mary Burke and Sam Saeli for being willing to read chapters of the book and provide feedback; to Kim Nonato, Lillian Madrigal, Erica Schoch, Tony Burke, Sonia Jarrett, Laura Bennett, Toru Momii, Katie Ellis, Jenny Brewer, and Jackie LeBoeuf-Thorn for helping me bounce around title ideas and brainstorm must-cover topics; and to Jake Sonner for taking the time to look over my first literary contract! To Hannah Atkin and Mason Gallo for being there with champagne and ice-cream cake when the first draft got submitted. And to all of you for dealing with my pendulum of emotions while birthing this book.

Thank you to Mindy Jenson, Kali Hawlk, Melanie Lockert, and Kelsey

Audagnotti for helping connect me with sources featured in this book and for all your kind words of encouragement.

To those who joined my launch team and believed in me and Broke Millennial (especially those of you who have no blood relation or "IRL" relationship with me personally).

Thank you to my family (Mom, Dad, and Cailin), without whom most of these stories wouldn't exist. Your support helped me in the many life transitions I've faced since founding Broke Millennial (and obviously, before then too!).

Finally, thank you to Joe (aka Peach) for allowing me to publicly share so much about our lives and for being the person who bore the brunt of the day-to-day emotional roller coaster that accompanied writing this book.

And to anyone else who helped that I may be forgetting in this moment as I use my last few watts of brainpower to pen the final words of my first book.

Financial Resources Guide

Here are a few of my go-to Web sites and resources I use to continually expand and deepen my own knowledge of money matters and issues and to keep up to date on the latest developments in the world of personal finance. This list also includes resources mentioned in the book, so you don't have to struggle to skim full chapters looking for that one Web site or tool I mentioned that you want to check out.

STUDENT LOANS

→ **Federal Student Aid** (http://studentaid.ed.gov): Any additional information you need, plus the links to get to the proper landing pages for repayment plans and forgiveness.

→ **National Student Loan Database** (https://www.nslds.ed.gov): How you can track down all your federal loans.

→ **Consumer Financial Protection Bureau** (http://www.consumer finance.gov/paying-for-college/repay-student-debt): They've got your back if a private lender starts acting shady.

CREDIT REPORTS AND SCORES

→ **AnnualCreditReport.com** (https://www.annualcreditreport.com/ index.action): The best way to gain legitimate, free access to your reports from all three bureaus.

→ **Credit Karma** (https://www.creditkarma.com): Access your free credit score.

→ **CreditWise** (https://creditwise.capitalone.com/#/login): Access your free credit score.

→ **Discover Credit Scorecard** (https://www.creditscorecard.com/registration): Access your free credit score.

INVESTING

→ **Investor.gov:** Home of my favorite compound interest calculator, Investor.gov is a valuable resource for all rookie and seasoned investors looking to do a little more digging.

→ **Investopedia.com** and **ObliviousInvestor.com** also provide ample information in digestible amounts.

TAXES/RETIREMENT

→ **IRS.gov:** The site for all things tax-related, which can also link you to information about how to best use retirement accounts. Any question you have about taxes can probably be answered somewhere on this site. Just beware: there are lots of copycat sites when it comes to tax information. You want the .gov, not .com or .org or anything else!

CONTINUING YOUR PERSONAL FINANCE EDUCATION

→ **Reddit** (https://www.reddit.com/r/personalfinance): Always be a little wary about taking advice from forums like Reddit, but I do encourage you to read true stories from people on Reddit's personal finance subreddit. It can be motivating, educational, a good warning of what not to do, or even provide details on current scams common in the finance world. You may also find more niche threads pertaining to specific areas of interest, like debt repayment or early retirement.

→ **MagnifyMoney.com:** Full disclosure, MagnifyMoney is the start-up I used to work for, but it's also a good place to comparison shop for financial products; you might want to read its blog about financial matters as well.

→ **Personal finance blogs:** I certainly couldn't write a list of favorite resources without recommending that you explore the hundreds (probably thousands) of personal finance blogs on the World Wide Web. No matter your interest, someone is out there writing about it. I hope you'll also continue this conversation by going to BrokeMillennial .com.

→ **Podcasts:** Podcasts are my strange (probably not-so-strange) addiction. Start plugging into podcasts to up your money and entrepreneurship game with shows like Planet Money, Freakonomics, The Tim Ferriss Show, StartUp, and my own, Broke Millennial.

YOUR FINANCIAL PROTECTION

→ **Consumer Financial Protection Bureau (CFPB)** (http://www.consumerfinance.gov): The CFPB provides a wide array of tools and articles for consumers. It also allows you to report shady practices by financial institutions, including banks, private student loan providers, collection agencies, auto lenders, and more.

→ **Federal Trade Commission (FTC)** (https://www.ftc.gov and https://www.identifytheft.gov): The FTC strives to help consumers avoid unethical or deceptive business practices. The FTC also allows you to submit complaints and report identity theft.

Notes

Chapter 2

1   The link between your relationship to time and your financial health was studied by MagnifyMoney.com and Professor Philip Zimbardo in 2014. Find the full survey results here: "Time Personality and Financial Health Study," MagnifyMoney.com, http://www.magnifymoney.com/timeperspective//index.php/HTML/results.

Chapter 3

1   Table taken from Dalton, Michael A., James F. Dalton, Joseph M. Gillice, Thomas P. Langdon, *Fundamentals of Financial Planning*, 4th ed. St. Rose, LA: Money Education, 2015, 94.

2   "Understanding your debt-to-income ratio," Bank of America, https://www.bankofamerica.com/credit-cards/education/what-is-debt-to-income-ratio.go.

3   "What is a debt-to-income ratio? Why is the 43% debt-to-income ratio important?," Consumer Financial Protection Bureau, http://www.consumerfinance.gov/askcfpb/1791/what-debt-income-ratio-why-43-debt-income-ratio-important.html.

Chapter 5

1   The CFPB used these reports from the available 628 banks to calculate the revenue on overdraft and NSF fees. Gary Stein, "New insights on bank overdraft fees and 4 ways to avoid them," Consumer Financial Protection Bureau, http://www.consumerfinance.gov/about-us/blog/new-insights-on-bank-overdraft-fees-and-4-ways-to-avoid-them/ and "Variation in Bank Overdraft Revenues and Contribution," Consumer Financial Protection Bureau, http://files.consumerfinance.gov/f/201602_cfpb_variation-in-bank-overdraft-revenues-and-contribution.pdf.

Chapter 6

1 "When Inquiries Appear on Your Credit Report," Experian, http://www
.experian.com/blogs/ask-experian/2014/10/15/inquiry-will-appear-on-report
-whether-application-is-approved-or-declined.

2 "How Long Late Payments Stay on Credit Report," Experian, http://www
.experian.com/blogs/ask-experian/2012/04/11/how-long-past-due-remains.

3 Nicholas Pell, "A Secret History of Credit Scores: Who Determined What
Matters and Why," Main Street, https://www.mainstreet.com/article/a-secret
-history-of-credit-scores-who-determined-what-matters-and-why.

4 "What's in my FICO Scores," myFICO, http://www.myfico.com/credit
-education/whats-in-your-credit-score.

5 Ibid.

6 "New credit," myFICO, http://www.myfico.com/CreditEducation/New-Credit
.aspx.

7 "What's not in my FICO Scores," myFICO, http://www.myfico.com/credit
-education/whats-not-in-your-credit-score.

8 "Credit Checks & Inquiries," myFICO, http://www.myFICO.com/credit
-education/credit-checks/credit-report-inquiries.

9 "How to Understand Credit Scores," Credit Karma, https://www.creditkarma
.com/credit-scores.

10 "CFPB Spotlights Concerns with Medical Debt Collection and Reporting,"
Consumer Financial Protection Bureau, http://www.consumerfinance.gov/
newsroom/cfpb-spotlights-concerns-with-medical-debt-collection-and
-reporting.

11 "When Is Negative Information Removed from Credit Report," Experian,
http://www.experian.com/blogs/ask-experian/2013/08/28/when-negative
-information-will-be-removed-from-your-credit-report.

12 Diane Moogalian," FAQ: How Long Does Information Stay on My Credit
Report?," Equifax, http://blog.equifax.com/credit/faq-how-long-does
-information-stay-on-my-credit-report.

13 "Chapter 7 & 13: How long will negative information remain on my credit
report?," myFICO, http://www.myFICO.com/crediteducation/questions/
negative-items-on-credit-report-chapter-7-13.aspx.

14 "I've been contacted by a debt collector. How do I reply?," Consumer Financial
Protection Bureau, http://www.consumerfinance.gov/askcfpb/1695/ive-been
-contacted-debt-collector-how-do-i-reply.html.

15 Stephanie Lane, "The statute of limitations ran out on my credit debt. Can the
collection agency still contact me?," NOLO, http://www.nolo.com/legal
-encyclopedia/the-statute-limitations-ran-credit-debt-can-the-collection
-agency-still-contact-me.html.

16 "Debt Collection," Federal Trade Commission, https://www.consumer.ftc.gov/
    articles/0149-debt-collection.

Chapter 8

1 Ethan Wolff-Mann, "The Average American Is in Credit Card Debt No Matter
   the Economy," Money, http://time.com/money/4213757/average-american
   -credit-card-debt.
2 The CFPB Office of Research, "CFPB Data Point: Payday Lending," Consumer
   Financial Protection Bureau, http://files.consumerfinance.gov/f/201403_cfpb
   _report_payday-lending.pdf.
3 "Payday Loans and Cash Advances," Consumer.gov, https://www.consumer
   .gov/articles/1011-payday-loans-and-cash-advances#!what-to-know.

Chapter 9

1 CFPB template letter: Rohit Chopra, "Consumer advisory: Stop getting
   sidetracked by your student loan servicer," The Consumer Financial Protection Bureau, http://www.consumerfinance.gov/about-us/blog/consumer
   -advisory-stop-getting-sidetracked-by-your-student-loan-servicer.

Chapter 12

1 "Student Debt Viewed as Major Problem; Financial Considerations Important
   Factor for Most Millennials When Considering Whether to Pursue College,"
   Harvard IOP @ The Kennedy School, http://iop.harvard.edu/student-debt
   -viewed-major-problem-financial-considerations-important-factor-most
   -millennials-when.

Chapter 14

1 "Study Reveals the Secrets to Negotiating a Higher Salary," George Mason
   University, http://eagle.gmu.edu/newsroom/843.
2 "Negotiating Your Salary," Clarke University, http://www.clarke.edu/page
   .aspx?id=4298.

Chapter 15

1 "Berkshire's Corporate Performance vs. the S&P 500," Berkshire Hathaway,
   http://www.berkshirehathaway.com/letters/2013ltr.pdf.

Chapter 16

1 Analysis done by Fidelity based on 21,800 corporate defined contribution plans and 13.9 million participants, as of March 31, 2016. These figures include the advisor-sold market but exclude the tax-exempt market. Also excluded are non-qualified defined contribution plans and plans for Fidelity's own employees. Fidelity's IRA analysis was based on 6 million IRA customers. "Fidelity First Quarter Retirement Savings Analysis: Account Balances Lower, Long-Term Savers See An Increase," Fidelity, https://www.fidelity.com/about-fidelity/employer-services/fidelity-first-quarter-retirement-savings-analysis.

2 Compound Interest Calculator, Investor.gov, https://www.investor.gov/tools/calculators/compound-interest-calculator.

3 "Retirement Topics—IRA Contribution Limits," IRS, https://www.irs.gov/retirement-plans/plan-participant-employee/retirement-topics-ira-contribution-limits.

4 "Retirement Topics—Vesting," IRS, https://www.irs.gov/retirement-plans/plan-participant-employee/retirement-topics-vesting.

5 "Retirement Topics—Plan Loans," IRS, https://www.irs.gov/retirement-plans/plan-participant-employee/retirement-topics-loans.

6 "2016 Social Security Changes Cost-of-Living Adjustment (COLA)," Social Security, https://www.ssa.gov/news/press/factsheets/colafacts2016.html.

Chapter 17

1 Taken from the CFP Board: CFP® Certification Requirements, CFP Board, http://www.CFP.net/become-a-CFP-professional/CFP-certification-requirements.

2 An example of the fiduciary oath can be found here: http://www.thefiduciarystandard.org/wp-content/uploads/2015/02/fiduciaryoath_individual.pdf.

3 Session description taken from Bera's Web site: http://genyplanning.com/financial-planning.

Chapter 18

1 Learn more at HUD.gov: http://portal.hud.gov/hudportal/HUD?src=/topics/buying_a_home.

References

References used for the writing of this book include:

→ The Consumer Finance Protection Bureau Web site (http://www
.consumerfinance.gov)

→ The Federal Trade Commission (https://www.ftc.gov)

→ myFICO (http://www.myfico.com)

→ The FDIC Web site (https://fdic.gov)

→ The Experian, TransUnion, and Equifax credit bureau blogs

→ The Web sites as well as cardholder and bank account holder terms
and conditions of multiple financial intuitions

→ Interviews with personal finance experts and financial professionals, as well as millennials willing to open up about their financial
concerns

Index

About the Author

© David Rodgers

Erin Lowry is a millennial personal finance expert, writer, and speaker. She founded BrokeMillennial.com as a way to reach her fellow millennials who are struggling to understand basic personal finance concepts. Lowry's writing has appeared in *New York Magazine*, *Forbes*, and *U.S. News and World Report*, and on Business Insider and Thought Catalog. Some of her many opinions have been featured in *USA Today* and *The Wall Street Journal*, and on *CBS Sunday Morning*, *NBC News*, Refinery29, Marketplace Money, and Mashable. Lowry lives in New York City with her spunky rescue dog, Mosby.